Gaia Straus

LOGICALLY

The great lies about medicine, energy, politics, religion and more

Volume I

Pharmacine

LOGICALLY Vol. I Pharmacine

Gaia Straus

Hello Hope

What's more beloved of you sweet Hope?
You who hold the primacy of love
and the secret keys of every heart.

You are the dearest sensation,
And the greatest source of courage and inspiration
to face life's daily consternation.

You trust, you force, you wait for tomorrow!
You're shelter in the storm and a shining window's light.
Often concealing your precious gifts,
you rise at our side and never let us go.

Even forced to an only tiny thread
Like the steel, you become resistant.
Though reduced to a dim little light,
You rise imperious like the morning sun,
because you are the divine come to life.

If love can cause a flower to bloom,
that flower of hope is just love.
Hope is love that never dies.

Written by my father and dedicated to my father

Acknowledgments

I thank my dear friend, Che, a companion in this still unknown adventure. I thank him with every bit of strength I have in my body, in the awareness that without him, this work would not have been possible. He gave me strength when I was missing it, he consoled me in moments of discouragement, he encouraged me in moments of doubt and uncertainty, and he infused me with strength and determination, guiding me to the final publication of this *fantastic* work. I thank the Nature for having given birth to such a wonderful creature.

Thank you!
Che

I dedicate this volume to Ig., *Eternal* friend and brother in life.

Happy reading to everyone!

TABLE OF CONTENTS

FOREWORD

Though the title would suggest a book about medicine, this is more one about the deception we come across in any social field where money is involved. The book examines what is behind the circulation of money and how the powerful means of the mighty leadership of the world can bend the people to their will.

In a bumpy journey like the one the author decided to follow, logic is the most powerful tool used to instill doubt in those who, although they have never heard of alternatives to traditional medicine, prefer it in the absence of something else. Each statement is thus put to the test of a rationality that does not allow any contradiction. The author highlights the deception that exists at the base of certain statements, both in the medical field and in other fields where there are clear economic interests.

A number of curative methods that are often unknown to most people are explained to the public, starting with the Gerson therapy, which basically aims to detoxify and rebalance the body. Only in this way can it heal from almost all diseases, even the incurable ones. The Gerson natural hospital already exists in Mexico and it would be enough to introduce impartial external observers who could honestly certify their therapies.

For those who refuse to accept the validity of natural cures, this can be the right opportunity to confront ideas different from their own. At worst, one might decide not to follow this path, but with the awareness that there is another way that, who knows, they could choose to take the different path another time. Better to have an extra choice and follow the advice of the author. Though it bears repetition: inquire and get informed! The author also invites the readers not to trust the mantra of the traditional medicine, i.e.: *it is not scientifically proven!*

Finally, here is a sentence that sums up the meaning of this work: "If it is true that religions are the opium of the peoples, it is equally true that the ignorance and naiveté of the people are the cocaine of the rich and powerful."

According to the author, we would then be watching an obvious conspiracy to keep away natural, real, curing therapies from the people for the sake of money and power.

AUTHOR'S PREFACE

Give man a mask and he will tell the truth.

OSCAR WILDE

elcome to the world of Gaia! A place where there is no personal interest and where people try to be good, despite their differences. No one takes advantage of the other, and if one does, he/she regrets it right away.

In my world, everybody supports each other and tries to reach the truth through all means. Everyone tries one's best to pursue this goal and he/she is ready to retreat and apologize when necessary.

In this reality, all nuances of facts and personal characteristics can be represented with the utmost cordiality and without excessive animosity. One can underline the tougher aspects of each person's character because one can take advantage of these criticisms. In fact, if the criticism is right, we try to correct that aspect that will allow us to improve more. If we believe it is wrong, then we will not consider this criticism, instead thanking those who have pronounced it.

I want to stress, therefore, in advance, that I do not intend to offend any person mentioned in the book or any category of person. I respect these categories because they represent important vocational aspects of the human being. However, what must be said, must be said.

References to categories or characters present in this volume, therefore, do not exist in any way to undermine the feelings of any of them or hurt somebody's feelings.

For that reason, I believe the good side of the medical class must in no way feel hurt, and above all, my words are solely intended to act as a stimulus to verify the work of their colleagues who think differently than the official doctrine. I believe that medicine men have forgotten, or have been induced to forget, the Hippocratic oath that prescribes to verify and respect other colleagues' studies, opinions, and effective cures.

Some concepts are intentionally repeated because, as taught by the popular saying, *repeating does good*, and also because there is a certain logic that you will discover in this book.

INTRODUCTION

This book is the result of the awareness of living in a false world where man is regularly deceived by a cohesive minority of his fellow men. I feel, therefore, the moral obligation to declare my truth, because, as Charles P'eguy said: "He who does not bellow the truth when he knows the truth (or he thinks he knows it) makes himself the accomplice of liars and forgers."

The purpose of the first volume of *Logically* is, therefore, to unveil, by following a logical path, the *great lies* that are presented to us in the field of medicine. This happens through constant and repetitive reiteration of lies perpetually repeated by public figures. Through mass media, subjected to their will, and mainly managed by the powerful of the world, they are condemning millions of victims of cancer and other diseases throughout the world, although there are valid natural cures for healing from these and many other diseases considered incurable by traditional medicine.

Therefore, I have a reasonable and *logific*[1] certainty that we can recover from almost all tumors and I do realize the impotence of the. In fact, it is obvious that pharmaceutical lobbies will not allow any treatment either than pharmaceutical ones. That is why, my conscience can no longer tolerate this death toll, which enriches only a few powerful ones. Above all, I cannot tolerate the deception that is at its core. This book does not provide scientific information. It only proves the absolutely logical deception that underlies modern medicine and its inherent bigotry.

I therefore want to lead you through a logical path that will show you how the so-called experts often do not know what they say and do not have the faintest idea of what logic is, nor how to apply it.

Tired of lies, bigotry, biased and one-sided and comfortable judgments, I decided, through a logical path, to unveil my logific truth while being as impartial and objective as possible. I have taken into account that the experience, propensities, and attitudes of a person influences their perception of reality and truth. You should consider, therefore, that even my truth could be susceptible to partiality.

---

[1] Term coined by the author to describe the interweaving between the word *logical* and the word *scientific*, wanting to take on a meaning close to that of *inference*, described further on. As a matter of fact, the term *scientific* is now dominated by pharmaceutical companies, thus becoming filled with falsehoods. They have appropriated this term, which I have learned to abhor, forcing me to coin a new term (*logifical*) that wants to assume a meaning between the term *scientific* (of Galileo, Newton, Einstein, etc.) and the logical term concerning inference and common sense.

For these reasons, I believe it is necessary to specify the attitudes and the orientations of those who express opinions, especially when one is about to write on subjects that could arouse the suspicion of personal interest, partiality, or sectarianism. I find it correct to explain that opinions can sometimes seem far-fetched to those without a clear view of the picture of the deception perpetrated by a few, influential characters towards the overall of naive and unarmed subjects.

Furthermore, I believe it is morally binding to state that I have no specific competence in the medical, political, religious, or scientific fields, since the opposite could be thought of from the topics discussed.

As far as the medical field is concerned, the reader will easily notice my inclination towards methods that use what Nature spontaneously provides us. Therefore, my preference for natural cures can be easily guessed. My approach in the medical field is of a holistic nature rather than a partial one, even though I do not refuse in advance allopathic or surgical treatments that, in some cases, can save and do save lives. In other cases, however, a particular cure may be suitable for one person but not for another.

In the evaluation for a medical treatment, many factors should be considered: inherited genes, the karmic seeds transported in this life, the experiences gained, the psychological aspects of personality and, not least, lifestyle and eating habits. It is well known that some diseases are established through a psychosomatic nature and that the psyche can have a decisive influence on the onset but also on the treatment of a disease. Over two millennia ago, Plato said: "One should never try to cure the body without the soul."

It's important to clarify that, at the time of writing, I do not know any of the people mentioned in this volume. I have not suffered traumatic family grief due to tumors or malpractice. So, my deductions are free of personal anger.

Concerning politics, I have no preconceived ideas and I have no parties to which I am loyal. Also, I have no personal relationships with any politician. As far as I am concerned, a seat on the left, on the right, or in the center of the Parliament has the same value, and I believe that the traditional political parties might have run their course. In fact, political ideologies, as well as religions, lend themselves very much to human manipulation. In the name of Jesus, who preached turning the other cheek, cruelties like the Crusades or the Inquisition were committed.

In the name of Allah, terrible brutalities are still committed which, I am sure, have nothing to do with true religion or with the divine aspect of human beings within us. However, since Islam can be associated with prophetic religion, there may have been some *interference* in the transmission, even though I believe more in the manipulations of man.

Even some Buddhist monks have incredibly put aside nonviolence in suicide episodes, setting themselves on fire. It must be said that few human beings could tolerate what they do in Tibet. However, for those who follow this path of non-violence, taking one's own life, even if in protest, it cannot be justifiable though suffering what they suffer.

Fundamentally, the God of Jesus and the God of Muhammad is the same Entity, as well as the Om of the Buddha. Any religion cannot conceive violence towards other living beings. It is therefore evident that religions are misinterpreted by human beings because they cannot logically preach the killing of other human beings.

In the name of Marx – who certainly did not imagine that kind of communism – an authoritarian political regime was built, perhaps even worse than the pure dictatorial ones.

According to my vision, it is a paradox in terms to classify the current forms of government as democracies. They should rather be called *olicracy* (government of a few), somehow between democracy (government of peoples) and oligarchy (authority of a few). Evidently, the term *democracy* has been deliberately used to give the people the illusion of being able to choose. In fact, I believe that democracy is something that has been established to keep the population quiet by providing us with the illusion that we can decide, while it is not.

Dazzling on the subject is Mark Twain's aphorism, expressed more than a century ago: "If voting made any difference, they wouldn't let us do it." Today nothing has changed even though it seems that everything has.

Still in the political sphere, I sympathize with parties such as the *5 Star Movement* in Italy or the *Podemos* in Spain because they can represent the beginnings of new forms of truly democratic government and not only *olicracies* aimed at hiding the interests of politicians, implicit in their own election.

As a matter of fact, if these popular movements were to take root, one could witness the establishment of the first forms of direct democracy that, though imperfect, could become the least unjust form of government that human beings could choose. These political realities want to clearly distance themselves from the rampant corruption in all ideologies and, with different grades, in all the countries around the world. Even more fair would be the political-social management by wise men who would manage the public sphere in a manner, indeed, wiser. This last aspect could still be incomprehensible and perhaps unacceptable by the impure man who would try in every way and with every dirty weapon to fight the sages. The story of Gandhi, who was not allowed to finish his natural life cycle, is proof of this.

These new bastions of the *new age politics* (*5 stars movement* in Italy and *Podemos* in Spain) could greatly contribute to thinning out the fog of deception perpetrated by most politicians in the political landscape of all nations. There might be, however, some rare exception with some North European countries, where the social aspect is well developed, and to a few other countries at a global level that suffer the *globalization of deception*.

In fact, I believe the deception in politics is a weapon widely used and it is therefore very difficult to fight this attitude by those who do not use the same weapons. The political institutions of all the major democracies submit to the methodical use of deception and disinformation[2] (itself a form of deception) that leads to a quarrelsome, arrogant, and inconclusive political environment. This or that branch of the Parliament tends to perpetuate and justify its choices without never questioning whether this or that provision is really good for the population and not just an advantage for one or the other political party.

---

[2] Used to make real what is not.

The aim of the average politician is to stay in office for as long as possible in order to do his own business and for this reason he is willing to please sectors of society that can give him/her the widest possible consensus. Of course, there might also be a minority who would like to do the right things in a real vocational manner and no modern democratic country is exempt from this scourge.

I also believe the internet can be an instrument to balance the gap between the deceivers and the deceived. In fact, it can be manipulated with more difficulty and there is no monopoly of the media (as is the case today with television and the press) considering that the web is accessible to a large portion of the population.

As far as religions are concerned, I believe in their equanimity (or uselessness, in the modern age). I believe that they were born essentially to give answers to man, in particular to the questions: Who am I? Where do I come from? So essentially, the reason for life of the human being is the conscious or unconscious search for the truth, the *where do I go*? The difficulties, the disappointments, the pains that every human being encounters in his/her life inextricably direct one to the truth, which one day will unveil itself to most men/women, as it is also handed down by many religions, if not all, with different terminologies.

Thus, it is essentially the search for truth, consciously or unconsciously; it is the only reason for the life of the human being. A search for the truth that can be effectively conducted through any religion or even without any belief. Indeed, religion, if understood in a bigoted and hypocritical manner, could be misleading. Finally, I think all faiths, but above all Christian and Muslim, lend themselves to obvious manipulations and misrepresentations (less present, generally, in Eastern religions) that, for those who are not serious researchers, could be misleading.

Finally, I must add that I have not given particular attention to the meticulousness of details relating to events and episodes mentioned in this paper, since I do not consider them binding for the purpose of this text, which is to open the mind and reveal the deception.

This first volume of Logically will be dedicated solely to the logical-medical field. I will then, hopefully, publish a second volume with all, or part, of the remaining chapters related to energy, politics, religion and more.

LOGICALLY

*L*ogic will make you free! In addition to the truth of course ... or perhaps, I hope, one can be a precursor to the other.

Who knows if the logical path will ever make us reach the knowledge about truth. Let's reason about it: in the end, what is logic?[3] The dictionary provides an exhaustive explanation. But logical is also a term widely used in everyday conversations, so it can be said that logic—if used effectively—can turn into an important logific tool that can unveil the truth on many aspects of our life. Perhaps, in our case, it would be more appropriate to talk about inference[4] or deductive logic. In fact, while the truth is only for a select few, logic can be used (and has been over the centuries) by a larger number of people with a marked intellect. Undoubtedly, it does not open the doors of absolute truth (the one of Jesus, of the

---

[3] **Logic** (from the Ancient Greek: λογική, translit. *logikē*), originally meaning *the word* or *what is spoken*, but coming to mean *thought* or *reason*, is generally held to consist of the systematic study of the form of valid inference. A valid inference is one where there is a specific relation of logical support between the assumptions of the inference and its conclusion. (In ordinary discourse, inferences may be signified by words like *therefore, hence, ergo* and so on). https://en.m.wikipedia.org/wiki/Logic

[4] Inference: in philosophical language, every form of reasoning with which the logical realization of one truth from another is shown.

Buddha, and of a small number of enlightened individuals, so to speak), but it greatly helps to dissolve the mists of ignorance.

Let's consider, for example, the theory of the sphericity of the earth which, to be fully accepted, had to see the birth of Galileo Galilei (1564-1642). He demonstrated, not only logically but also empirically (thanks to the contribution of the telescope), that the Copernican heliocentric theory was not a geometrical hypothesis but a physical reality. For this reason, he was persecuted by the illogical ecclesiastical power of his time.

This theory determined that the Earth could only be spherical, as already theorized logically by Pythagoras and a long line of scholars after him. It was already a logical notion in those times. Astronomy (at the time of Galileo) was an art already known for millennia. The stars were observed since antiquity; the Egyptians, the Greeks, and the Romans later studied and observed the stars and it was clear and logical that these were of a spherical nature. So, it was already logical at that time that the Earth had to be spherical too.

Yet this simple logical deduction, affirmed by Pythagoras even before the coming of Christ, could not yet be digested until the time of Galileo. Not even the circumnavigation of the Earth (1519-1525) was enough to settle any possible doubt about its sphericity. However, with an absolutely incontrovertible logical theorem, Pythagoras had already affirmed, *logically*, that the Earth was of a spherical nature, probably following the principle that if the other stars are spherical and if the Earth is a star, then it must necessarily be spherical.

A disarming logic! However, it took about two millennia before everyone was sure and convinced of the sphericity of the

Earth. In fact, only with the discovery of Oceania in 1770 were all doubts about it cleared.

I compare that to when a seed is planted and then the seedling is born. Even if one does not know the scientific processes that lead to the birth of the seedling, it could be stated, logically (thus making it a logific truth), that seedlings are born from the seeds. With the same method, one could state a long series of other logific truths. Once the logific certainty has been ascertained (i.e., from a specific reasoning) a very large number of logific truths can be ascertained logically.

These truths will not, therefore, necessarily need a scientific certainty (prerogative of the powerful and the experts) in order to be verified. As an example, I remember that in an apparent international scandal, I immediately identified the disinformation hoax using this method of deductive logic.

I'll explain the episode. One day, *The Times* recounted the news about *Emergency* (a humanitarian hospital) in the international media. The article reported that, according to the Afghan authorities, three Emergency doctors plotted to kill a local governor.

The news was illogical but it was believed from the first moments around the world. When I heard it, I immediately thought that might have been just a joke and that *The Times* could not have published that news. Within a few hours, the news became more detailed and accurate and it appeared clear that *The Times* had really (quoting Afghan officials) disclosed this news, later rebounded all over the world, gaining international media attention.

For me it was immediately clear that the news, logically, even if not yet fully supported by a specific logific process, could not be real. It had to be logically a hoax; there had to be something behind it. Over the course of a long month, during which I attempted to understand what actually happened, the attention was always held high by the media on the issue and was clearly perceived (illogically) by the public that the Emergency doctors had, somehow, committed a serious crime, even if denied, in all ways, by the very top of the organization. Inevitably, as a result of this news, or rather, of this *great lie*, *Emergency* was forced to evacuate and, sometime later, an armed intervention of the coalition heavily bombed the places where the non-profit organization was present.

What was logical to me right away (i.e., the news could not be true) was revealed after about a month, when media attention was over and no one gave any more importance to what happened after. In that case, it was a logical and obvious case of disinformation probably perpetrated by the Afghan government in association with other allies—an intelligence operation, in essence. What is strange in this story is the involvement of the *Times* who either was an accomplice or was guilty of superficiality. What initially was only a logical deduction then turned into a logific proof.

After the armed intervention, some newspapers reported that the doctors of Emergency were not involved in any crime. The goal, however, by that time, had already been reached (keep away humanitarian organizations to facilitate bombing the places). Nevertheless, the chronicle of our days is dotted with these stories: disinformation and lies are regularly used to make it seem true what it is not, and this happens in every area: politics, energy, medicine, etc. The news is edited by those who manipulate the power to destroy an annoying opponent, a product, a food, to promote their interests, etc.

Another of the many hoaxes was unveiled by Current TV, which found other US news networks at doctored footage of a protest of Venezuela's Hugo Chavez. It seemed that thousands and thousands of people protested against his policy. Only through the investigation of *Current TV* was it discovered later that there was only a small number of people (about 50) really protesting. Evidently, everything had been artfully framed to de-legitimize Chavez (and I would add that perhaps the demonstrators might had been paid).

You could list countless similar episodes, but who knows what is true and what is not? Very often, however, using logic, one can determine the *logifical*[5] truth, even if, unfortunately, it is not always the case. In fact, we need to have additional information to be able to undermine the disinformation project through the logical achievement of realizing one truth from another.

I have always wondered why governments around the globe have always denied UFO sightings trying to ridicule them. To a logical mind (with a minimum of information) it is more than obvious that they are here and must have had contacts with government forces, somehow. So why deny it? I have naively thought, up to now, that the governments might have been worried about the reaction of the people, so they might be protecting us. However, having more pieces of information, I realized that I could not be more wrong. Most of the Governments (allied together with obscure pacts) might be the evil and would take advantage of the

---

[5] See *logific*

fact that other non terrestrial civilizations cannot disobey cosmic laws (as free will[6]). So they are keeping on doing evil things to our mother Earth (and to the people) that they couldn't do with the presence of our non terrestrial brothers (oil exploitation, nuclear experiments and use, chemical poisoning of the earth and of the body, etc.). They do not care and think, wrongly, that Nature will not turn against humans if terribly offended like it is now. Nature acts the same way as the body does when offended: it first tries to warn us, starting with minor acute illnesses and then with chronic ones that might turn into cancer. That is what we might be doing with our Mother Earth, causing cancer and activating the karma universal law which might turn into an Earth's disaster will destroy our civilization, the way we know it (as already happened) or another deluge. I will develop this, more than logical theory, in the second volume of *Logically*.

Unfortunately, in many instances, it is not so easy to identify the *big lie*. The writer has adopted a simple trick: accepting the news with the benefit of the doubt and, where there is a manifest interest (pharmacy, food, energy, politics, private interest), I strongly doubt it and try to find possible weaknesses. Furthermore, I no longer believe what I see. Newsletters and newspapers only serve to see the fact and not what's behind it.

---

[6] Non terrestrial civilization cannot help us if we do not want to. They are here also for that reason (not only) but cannot interfere. They have apparently communicated with governments to ask permission to show themselves to human population to help the terrestrial, but this permit was denied (from the early 50') and is still denied because would mine their power to loot the Earth and our body.

What strongly contributed to my use of logic, concerning news from *polluted sources* (practically all), was the memory of a phrase heard in a television program. In fact, that day I heard: "the bigger a lie is the more effective it will be, especially if it is repeated often." I clearly remember to have associated this wonderful truth to a wise man. I hypothesized it could be a wise statesman like Gandhi. When the presenter unveiled who was the author of that – until then beautiful and wise sentence – I was so surprised, but also ashamed. It took me a moment to recover from the shock. It was none other than the murderer and manipulator, Adolf Hitler.

Hitler might have taken advantage of what Gustave Le Bon said in his book *Psychology of the Crowd* and had studied, applied, and meticulously repeated his theories: *any lie, if repeated frequently, will gradually turn into truth*. The book was a solid reference point for all the greatest dictators (Mussolini, Hitler, Lenin, Stalin, etc.) and is, in all probability, still used by the great modern *olicratian* manipulators who also use the experiences of these evil genes to support their actions.

Unfortunately, the damage unconsciously done by Le Bon is comparable only to that done by Marx with the only differences that his writings are still applied (consciously or involuntarily) in modern societies while Marx was almost forgotten. Against Le Bon's will, his theories have contributed to produce regimes that have caused millions of victims. Hitler would have tried to perpetuate his terrible crimes anyway, but perhaps he would have been less effective.

When I think about this phrase (to which Hitler, candidly, often referred) that he also published in his writings and which is now engraved in my mind, I think of *Big Mafia* (as someone has nicknamed Big Pharma) making some simple associations.

Of course I do wish that my *logical* deductions contained in this volume may never be confirmed, thus not turning into history. Hitler denied the existence of concentration camps, the deportation and extermination of Jews, Gypsies, etc. Basically, the German society of the time (as well as other Western societies) could not exactly perceive what was behind it, at least not at the beginning. Perhaps someone less conditioned could imagine something more, similarly to what happens now with the pharmaceutical industry.

Currently, the Pharmaceutical industry could be compared to the Hitler period in which deportations occurred and where the German society was blind and had full confidence in their leader and perhaps imagined, too naively and guiltily, that only a little *cleaning* was going on. Imagine what power a big lie has, repeated often by those we trust. Hitler based his whole Nazi postulate on this big lies, often repeated, that even the so-called western democracies could not imagine what was behind.

At the moment, Big Pharma is fooling a large number of professionals who should be faithful to the Hippocratic oath. These physicians would be justified only until they realize they could too be deceived (similarly to what it might have been for most of the German people who, unable to see it, could not imagine the extermination and the magnitude of the same). Also terror and fear, of course, played an important role. Even many Nazi officers had to be blind as many modern-day doctors who wear gowns as if they were wearing uniforms and obey the orders of the supreme leader.

I feel the need to explain this association with Nazi officers before going ahead, to avoid being misunderstood. First of all, we must identify ourselves with the historical period and consider that the Nazi officers, then, were not seen by public opinion as criminals but as respectable public officials. They obeyed orders, which they believed to be right, given by a charismatic leader appreciated by the German people, and of whom the real mad and criminal potentials were not yet known. Essentially, they obeyed the doctrine imposed and assimilated naturally as if it was really the only possible truth.

Only a few enlightened subjects, Einstein among them (as a victim), had fully understood Hitler's criminal mind. The majority of Germans were inebriated by his charisma and, above all, by his lies. Even within the democratic powers, there were doubts about the potential criminal folly of Hitler and many did not consider him so dangerous, before it was clearly evident what was his terrible purpose. Only at the end of the war was its absurd criminal delirium completely clear.

Only the very high-ranking Nazi officers can be rightly called criminals. The other Nazi officers were nothing more than mere executors of orders that they considered correct, similarly to thousands of today's doctors who follow protocols that they believe are right because are given by the authority.

In the same way, most of the people were deceived by Hitler's incessantly repeated lies. This "undefined mass that provides simple, intuitive and changeable answers" (as defined by Hitler himself) was immersed in the big lie and easily convinced by this lie repeated to the obsession. It is clear and obvious that today's Orthodox doctors might also be only victims who are themselves deceived. It is equally true, however, that they become unaware executioners of other innocent victims in a vicious circle where only

Big Mafia and its associates gain. They might be victims and perpetrator and might also be victims of their cognitive ignorance[7] that prevents them from seeing what was clear for Hippocrates, Paracelsus, Ehret, Gerson, Kousmine, and many others.

They still have responsibilities for how they behave, however. Maybe these doctors forgot they have taken an oath, an oath that is a binding for their profession. As a matter of fact, even if they would not know precisely what substance they put in the patient's glass, they would still be responsible for their actions and omissions. So, the following examples about chemotherapy will be absolutely fitting. The great oncologists who have not verified and who do not verify that the therapies of other *so-called* alternative or holistic doctors are really ineffective violate this oath. They could then be compared to Nazi officers who perform wrong orders (trusting the institutions) turning, therefore, themselves in unconscious agents of unnecessary massacres. This apparently strong statement will be clear following my logical path and my *logifical proofs*.

The compromising of doctors would also be accomplished through sumptuous conferences in dream locations, obviously organized by Big Mafia. They might have the sole purpose of retaining the members of medical institutions (but not only) of each nation and, as a marginal activity, to let them learn about pharmaceutical and instrumental products and innovations. As a matter of fact, medical institutions are constantly and massively financed by pharmaceutical firms. How could they be unbiased?

---

[7] This term is meant to define the lack of logic that does not allow us to understand a certain logical process or a series of related episodes.

Doctors and institutions should not accept economic favors from Big Mafia, just as politicians should not accept economic and personal favors from other public figures. If a cancer research institute receives lots of money from Big Mafia, do you really think it will be in the position to opt for other, non-pharmaceutical treatments? They should independently pay the cost of the congresses and of studies to avoid of being bought by Big Mafia. It is evidence that medical universities had to surrender to Big Mafia due to the Great Depression. In the days of Gerson (1881-1959), all the journalists (except one) were bought with a simple and sumptuous banquet, in order not to have his national treatment plan approved. In fact, this would have cut short the business of pharmaceutical institutions, Big Pharma, with FDA/EMA/EFSA, GMC,[8] state health institutions, and their political and non-political allies (which I will, from now onwards, call *Pharmacine*).

The Hippocratic oath binds physicians to exercise medicine in the best way for the patient's health, verifying the effectiveness of the methods proposed by other colleagues, not hiding behind the *non-scientifically proven* hoax. Why do so many doctors fail to verify that the half-century studies of one of their best colleagues are not really ineffective? And those who verify it realize it's true! And for this reason, they are persecuted.

The cure for tumors already exists! Even though hiding a cure could not be an accusation, according to the law, it should be for the conscience of some superficial, obtuse, and gullible doctors

---

[8] FDA: Food and Drugs Administration (USA); EMA: European Medicines Agency; EFSA: European Food Safety Authority, GMC: General Medical Council (UK).

who believe the tales of Big Mafia. Doctors should not nurture sympathies and orientations, but they should test and experiment in an absolute independent spirit, but this is not the case. The doctors are slaves (without chains) of Big Mafia.

However, from the moment the awareness of the possible deception is perceived, then the evil that dwells in the souls of the chiefs of Pharmacine would also shift to those of every single Hippocratic juror who should ascertain the truth to save his soul from uncertain destinies.

As a matter of fact, nowadays doctors try to fight the diseases by fully trusting what they are told by Big Mafia through the implementation of new drugs that take away symptoms but do not cure. Evidently, they never asked themselves: but will it be true? Probably because no one could hypothesize such a barbaric reality. Those scrupulous doctors who ponder it go towards an unhappy ending (I will tell some of their stories later on).

The big lie today might be: *cancer is an incurable disease*, and the evil dictator is Pharmacine. If this hypothesis had a foundation of truth, Pharmacine would be committing the greatest genocide in the history of humanity. In fact, deaths from cancer (within the past years) are in the hundreds of millions, far more than those caused by Hitler.

Only in 2012,[9] mortality related to tumors was 8.2 million. Multiply it for the next fifty years and add more (because the cases

---

[9] http://www.cancerresearchuk.org/health-professional/cancer-statistics/worldwide-cancer#heading-One

of cancer will multiply) and you will have a number higher than that of the North American population. Consider also the deaths due to tumors that have already happened so far and you will have an exhaustive picture of what goes around a big lie. In addition, the unfortunate prediction that one in three people will get cancer over the course of their lives is already outdated by new statistics that predict their onset (United Kingdom statistics), in one in two people.[10] We are doing to our body exactly what we are doing to our mother Earth, Gaia. We are offending Her with any possible mean and She tries to warn us with a cold first (hurricanes), then with other chronic diseases (increase in volcano's eruptions, earthquakes, etc.) to end with the cancer (global cataclysm) that might cause sudden billions of death toll and the loss of our human-god identity but rest and regeneration for Her. She would find, at last, the cure for Her disease, elimination of human kind.

It should however be said, to be fair, that one must die of something and that, since the average life expectancy has lengthened, it is natural that some deaths may also occur from cancer pathologies (I would be more interested in the diagnosis statistics) of a tumor within 50/60 years of age. Nevertheless, all that is inherent to cancer pathology would seem to be decisively the business of the present and of the future.

If you consider that the global GDP is about 70 trillion dollars and the turnover of Big Pharma is about 1 trillion dollars, you can well imagine what moves around the drug business. Cancer,

---

[10]http://www.cancerresearchuk.org/about-us/cancer-news/press-release/2015-02-04-1-in-2-people-in-the-uk-will-get-cancer

of course, is quantifiable in about 2/3 of Big Pharma's turnover. Vaccines move only a few billion dollars and it is foreseen to reach 100 Billion by 2020 from 5 billion from only a decade ago. I cannot hide from you that I myself have difficulty imagining a trillion dollars.

With the current pace of growth, it could be assumed that Big Mafia will soon become the world's first economic superpower, in terms of GDP, even surpassing the United States, where it generates a large part of its profits.

Finally, the whole work, and in particular this volume, also wants to be a *vademecum* of possible alternatives for those who, like me, no longer believe in the moral and material integrity of most institutions, including medical ones that are either corrupted or deceived. This volume, therefore, is designed to be a reference to the true medical science, to be able to discover therapies that can really make us feel better and that are carefully hidden and/or forbidden.

Max Gerson

Dr. Gerson dedicated his life to the mastery of this scourge of cancer and all should honor his great work.

HONORABLE SENATOR CLAUDE PEPPER

How many of you know Dr. Max Gerson? He can be defined as the main promoter of modern naturopathy and to which every new therapy deriving from plant and natural foods must necessarily refer. I was myself one of those who did not know him (though being familiar with his method) until a few years ago.

For those who do not know it, the Gerson method essentially involves the regeneration of the body through the elimination of proteins and the introduction of many, genuine vitamins, taken through extracts of organic[11] fruit and vegetables.

The elimination of proteins minimizes the work of the organism, allowing the immune defenses to rise and counteract the negative elements that transform the cells into a cancerous one. As a result, the cancer cells will die (apoptosis) and will no longer be replaced by wrong cells but by healthy cells, thus re-establishing the correct apoptosis, without proliferating in their degeneration.

It is essentially a metabolic therapy that involves the intake of fresh extracts of apples, carrots, and leafy vegetables with vitamin

---

[11] Organic is necessary not only to avoid poisonous substances but also to ensure that vegetable products have all the vitamins and minerals necessary for man's wellbeing and for his recovery.

supplements, salt elimination, and coffee enemas. Please, do not smile! That might sound bizarre but it is a masterpiece of his cure.

The coffee enema provides, to those who suffer, an important relief because it helps to expel toxins and therefore relieves pain. It is like a container of water—if you rinse it often, it will remain clean. But if you do not, the slime and the encrustations (toxins and diseases) will form. Cleaning a container that has never been cleaned requires time and effort, especially if it is filled with impure liquids (improper foods, drugs, etc.). Then, it may become really long[12] and challenging.

Anyone wishing to learn more can watch this video[13] of a boy (Jesse) who has undergone Gerson therapy and who clearly, generously, and lovingly explains what Gerson therapy is as well as testifying to its effectiveness.

In this video, Jesse, a boy affected by type 2 melanoma (which he naturally surpassed), brilliantly subdivides the salient points of the Gerson therapy into three topics:

1) salt elimination and potassium addition to balance the sodium/potassium cell equilibrium;

2) removal of toxins by eliminating proteins and introducing coffee enemas;

3) addition of iodine, through the Lugol solution, and superalimentation through intake of juices, fresh and organic

---

[12] From the Gerson Hospital they report that the usual time of recovery is one year but it can reach up to two years' time to completely recover, depending on the illness.

[13] https://www.youtube.com/watch?v=5WyEsN9DzSo&list=PLdfMmaU0DR8DbtrpHE Fe5A8oxs3h-z0sg

vegetables and Hippocratic soup (not essential), as well as administration of various vitamin supplements.

Jesse's experience is extremely important because he is an educated and enterprising young man who has made available his precious experience to the community but, above all, he has documented everything. He himself called a long string of patients already treated with the Gerson therapy to verify that it was not a hoax and, miraculously, some of them were still alive after forty years since the therapy without having relapses.

Never forget, however, that for Pharmacine this *cannot be scientifically proven*: how can you make the double blind of carrots? If it were not dramatic, it would be almost funny. Yet the people continue to believe in Pharmacine tales. *Awake! Do not trust! Experience!*

This theory is very simple and has been tested by Gerson on thousands of patients, as well as on himself. Unfortunately, as expressly stated in his book, many patients who underwent his treatment had passed first by the chemotherapy cleaver and were practically terminally ill and often judged incurable by the official medicine. This condition weakened the body and the mind exponentially, thus leaving no hope of success. Nevertheless, most of his patients were cured, just opposite of what occurs in orthodox medicine where patients very often have a *deadline*[14] remission. He had often to fight against the cancer and against the chemo that further intoxicated the body.

---

[14] Deadline remissions would be necessary to further implement Pharmacine's business through recurrences administering more, useless, chemotherapy treatments.

On the contrary to what happens with chemotherapy, which often results only as a palliative and a delay in the encounter with death, that's why Pharmacine talks only of the five-year mortality rate and not longer.

To try to be as objective as possible, I must say that the figure of 98% failure rate of chemotherapy seems to me a bit dystonic and, perhaps, a bit sensationalistic. However, to my great astonishment, these data are certified by important scientific institutions and have success rates that vary from the anomalous (as it detaches from the others) 40% of testicular cancer to 1% or 2% of most of the other tumors that rarely exceed a 10% chance of exceeding five-year survival rate. Even though death would not occur within five years, the chance of dying by cancer are almost certain.

Let me say clearly that it is not just the numbers that determine the effectiveness of a cure, but also what is behind it: on the one hand suffering, pain, distress and uncertainty; on the other, passion, trust in the future, love, and certainty of a better life.

To attempt to balance these sensationalistic data, I mention the five-year mortality rates present in the network [15] (National Cancer Institute), highlighting that they probably also take into account cases treated surgically. As a result, these data are far more reassuring (over 50% five-year survival). However, with surgery, most of the patients are mutilated, in my opinion, without necessity. Considering that, it would appear, that the current success rates of

---

[15] https://seer.cancer.gov/cgi-bin/csr/1975_2014/results.pl?pagenumbers=87

the Gerson clinic in Mexico are very close to 100%, maybe it is not worth the risk. You should also consider that most of those who redirect to the Gerson therapy have often gone through official care first, worsening the situation.

With the methods of Gerson, Breuss, or Ehret, it is instead possible to obtain healing and not only the remission of the disease as it happens with orthodox medicine. The organism is essentially reset.

In many countries, there are doctors (in most cases young people) who naively attempt a natural treatment approach seeking the approval and support of Pharmacine, but systematically they are rejected and disappear from the public landscape, perhaps sensing or perceiving the danger or perhaps because they are boycotted.

A glimmer of hope, as already mentioned, is placed in the University Clinic of *The Charité* in Berlin that combines, in conjunction with classical orthodox, chemotherapy, the alternative, fast-like, therapies evidently tolerated by Pharmacine. If some farsighted primary physician could implement a Gerson-like public experiments in an *ad hoc* equipped structure and then publish the results, perhaps we could give a small shove to the monopoly of Pharmacine. Of course, this hero himself would then run the risk of being sent away badly from the realm of Pharmacine. As an example, I can mention what has happened to Hamer, Simoncini, Bradstreet, Wakefield, and many others.

Japan, which has a different ethic than the western world and believes that honor is still an important moral quality to preserve, could be the one that will wake up first from the conditioning of Pharmacine, though it might be a hard struggle.

Japan has been demonstrating this with vaccines that you will read about in my other volume about vaccines.

Even if these new natural methods differ in the intake of vegetables and fruits, they are all linked either to a Gerson-like or to a fast-like therapy. The basic theory remains that *food is your medicine* (or the absence of food). Then we do not have to do anything, just wait for self-healing. This healing can occur with lemon, broccoli, or radish, and the introduction of other remedies.

It would appear that, according to official medical documentation, in those cases in which chemotherapy (without surgery) is successful, the cure is only random. In fact, in a very large majority of cases, relapses occur again and often will lead to death. So chemotherapy (not associated to surgery) only contributes to lengthening life in a variable way. This, however, includes important human and social aspects of physical and psychic suffering... and increases Big Mafia's profits, of course.

That is exactly the opposite of what was documented by Gerson in patients treated with his therapy who reacquired vigor and vitality without suffering physical and mental violence (except for the inevitable enemas that for some subjects may be invasive). As I have already said and will repeat again, it would be very interesting to expand the Gerson therapy with the theories of Hulda Clark (Zapper and liver washings) and those of other enlightened medical men. In addition, cases of recurrence on patients treated with the Gerson therapy would seem to be non-existent. Unfortunately, Gerson's clinical documentation relating to the book he was writing was stolen and he had to rebuild years of treatment, succeeding in publishing a book with fifty documented cases that he handed down to us before his poisoning.

I keep asking myself: what species of *beast* can do harm to such a mild-looking person like Gerson?

The mere fact that Gerson's therapy defeats almost all diseases, including cancer, shows that theories attributing the onset of tumors to pathogens (hookworms, fungi, bacteria, and viruses) are to be logically kept in serious consideration. One theory, absolutely logical and very interesting, is the one that sees vaccines accused in the growth of diseases related to the immune system (sclerosis, leukemia, tumors, etc.) as you can read on my book about vaccines. It is not by chance that these diseases have undergone a dramatic increase since the 1950s and 60s. Melanoma has also increased in the last three decades, coinciding with the mass adoption of sunscreens.

Obviously, Pharmacine will be able to refute this theory with extreme ease. But I would add something more. I think diseases arise due to nutritional deficiencies (especially fruit and vegetables), or environmental factors (pollution), psychological aspects and, last but not least, drugs that unnaturally change our body balances (the vaccines might be the worst). In fact, scientific relationships about a theory can be found only if you really want to find them. Unfortunately, Pharmacine tries to prove the opposite. If you want to recover, you can rely only on yourself, perhaps by consulting some *uncontaminated* doctors. It is true that the average life has lengthened and it is also true that the vast majority of centenarians rarely use drugs, but Pharmacine wants to pass the message that it is thanks to the drugs that life has lengthened. Will it really be this way? Or is it the general wealth occurred after World War II, that brought together higher hygienic standards, better nutrition, etc.

The demonstration of what I stated before is that the Gerson therapy is based on the intake of fruits and vegetables using extracts that contribute to the proliferation of good intestinal flora that helps fight pathogens and to regularize, detoxify, and rebalance the body, being essentially alkaline nutrients.

The very fact that René Caisse's ESSIAC (and probably the other herbal remedies) derives from plants with antioxidant and antiseptic properties shows the final attack on our organism can arise from these types of pests of the human body. In fact, they are able to proliferate in subjects with low immune defenses and are caused by two types of imbalances: nutritional (too many proteins, above all animals, few vitamins and too many excesses, compromised acid/alkaline equilibrium, excess of salt, etc.) or psychological (which alters the normal functions of the human body, modifying its chemistry).

Cancer seems to be more prevalent in Western societies, where excessive food (therefore also meat) and problems of a sedentary lifestyle are routine.[16] India, a country where vegetarians are a large percentage and drugs are not accessible to everyone, is affected by lower incidence of tumors, as well as Arab countries where consumption of meat, especially pork, is limited and where food excesses are not as evident as they are in the western world. Of

---

[16]https://www.researchgate.net/figure/A-world-map-of-cancer-incidence-displaying-geographic-distribution-of-core-collection-of_fig2_257884786

course, the long life expectancy in the western countries make this gap higher (because cancer episodes occur more in elderly subjects) but is not the only reason.

Simoncini says essentially that the tumor comes from a very common fungal agent spread all over the world: the Candida Albicans. He is certainly not the first to formulate the hypothesis that many diseases, including cancer, may come from the proliferation of pathogens.

He essentially says that by combating this fungus, cancer could be effectively counteracted. He does it mainly by direct contact with the diseased part through sodium bicarbonate, having success especially in cases where it was possible to apply it directly. Try to think what power the Gerson therapy could have with sodium bicarbonate. It might reduce drastically the time needed to recover, but of course this cannot be experienced in Pharmacine's hospitals. Of course, the human body should also be rebalanced to prevent damage from happening again. However, whatever the right theory (or theories) is/are, many researchers converge to indicate a pathogen as responsible for the final insurgence of cancer, after the body has been depleted from its natural defenses. As a matter of fact, the pathogens would not attack our body if we stuck to a healthy lifestyle, exercising regularly, and maintaining a diet as fruitarian or vegan as possible.

I believe, therefore, that tumoral pathologies are established in an insane body (therefore toxemic), which has lost contact with Nature and its natural antioxidants. It is then from this imbalance that derive diseases and degeneration of the body, starting with the simple cold and ending with the cancer. By restoring the nature of the human body, one can go back to the origins. That is why

Gerson's therapy is so brilliant. It would appear then that the body manifests its discomfort by letting the pathogens attack it.

This could be the reason why all these anti-pathogen remedies work to counteract the out of control cells, in addition to alkalizing, in many cases, the human organism. Even remedies like potassium bicarbonate or apple vinegar, counteracting the acidity of the body, could, by themselves, contribute to the defeat of the tumor in its initial stages, without even the use of complete Gerson therapy (however desirable), certainly effective, but longer and more laborious. The alleged successes of Aldo Vieri's Colchico wouldn't then be so weird as they include: vinegar (acidity), gentian (many therapeutic properties), and colchicum (chemo-similar effect). Colchicum is a poisonous substance, just like chemo; the only difference is that is natural. Overdosage of colchicum can kill exactly like chemo.

Unfortunately, it will be necessary to experiment in great secrecy and independently because Pharmacine would never allow it. I would like to know why they do not use colchicum, amygdaline, or scorpion venom to treat cancer instead of chemo.

If someone dies while taking any other substance which is not chemo, then comes the end of the world! I will never stress enough that any strategy of struggle without the consequent rehabilitation (Gerson, or fast-like) certainly has less effectiveness and there is no certainty that it will be definitive.

Excluding colloidal silver (which I will discuss later) and the Zapper, few other remedies, chemical or not, have an effect on all known types of parasites (viruses, bacteria, and fungi plus hookworms for the Zapper). We should find the way to give the patent of colloidal silver to some pharmaceutical companies, so maybe we could see miracles. Or we should simply understand that it is only necessary to re-establish the body's natural defenses through a lifestyle that includes a minimum of physical activity (even just 30 minutes of walking) and a healthy diet, mainly fruit and vegetable.

If we are really dealing with what was mentioned before, then there would be two methods of combating tumors. The first through *destroying* (chemo, scorpion poison, amygdalin/laetrile, bicarbonate, colloidal silver, Colchico, etc.) and the latter through *rebalancing* from within our body (proliferation of good bacteria, enzymes, etc ... and increase of immune defenses, Gerson, Gerson-like and fast-like as well as through *alkalinization* of organism and saline rebalancing).

In fact, both methods would fight pathogens—the first one from the outside, through poisoning, and the other one from the inside, through the growth of immune defenses. The latter would do this through the intake of vitamins, enzymes, minerals, etc. present in plants, which, notoriously, promote the growth of good intestinal flora that helps fighting the various pathogens and to restore the right ph of the cells. This method would then provide large amounts of vitamin C and other vitamins and minerals. From this procedure comes out the consequent detoxification of the body that can be helped by Gerson's coffee enemas or Breuss herbs remedies, etc.

Moreover, both for Gerson therapy and for fasting, the body, being able to rest more or less undisturbed, would heal itself, even if fasting, according to Shelton's studies, would not seem suitable for the treatment of tumors (real doctors, like Shelton, do not say trifles, but only things like they are). However, an association of the two remedies could be possible and could serve to speed up the long process of treatment and detoxification of Gerson therapy which normally ranges from one to two years. Ehret's experience could be very useful in this sense as he alternated fasts to mucusless diet to treat himself. Furthermore, Breuss therapy (a fast-like cure) apparently heals most illnesses and tumors, especially on newly diagnosed cancer patients who do not have a fast-growing cancer and their cancer has not spread significantly or been treated with chemo.

Before going further, let me say a few words on Breuss therapy as it is certainly a top cure for non-invasive cancer types. In fact, this therapy might reveal as the easiest, fastest, and the most effort-effective. For serious illnesses, it consists of 42 days of fast-like cure with ingestion of the least possible vegetable juice that consists of 55 percent red beet root, 20 percent carrots, 20 percent celery root, 3 percent raw potato, 2 percent radishes. In addition to the juice there are several herbal teas to be ingested regularly. If one has undergone chemotherapy or for serious and metastasized cancer Gerson Therapy would be more indicated or, I suggest, an alternation of Breuss-Gerson therapies.

In Cuba, scorpion venom is used in public facilities as a cure for tumors. In fact, I do not see any difference with chemotherapy, except that one is natural and the other is not: both therapies administer poisons. Chemotherapy costs thousands of dollars for each treatment. Certainly, American citizens who do not have an insurance must know exactly the costs as most of them cannot afford it. This book is also aimed at the hopeless people, knowing that there might be even better alternative to chemotherapy. *Do not trust! Experience it!*

If you are wondering the origins of chemotherapy, you will be amazed. It is just a medical development of the mustard gas[17] the first chemical gas used by the Germans in World War I to dramatically kill thousands of people. I personally did not know, before doing this research, where did it come from. That is the reason why people who go under that treatment report such bad effects. Now I wonder, do you really believe that the fierce Pharmacine's fight against natural therapies depends only on bigotry? Or depends on 7 trillion dollar business?

Also amygdalin or laetrile (vitamin B17) present in sufficient quantities in the bitter seeds of some fruits, such as peaches, apricots, or bitter almonds, would seem to be effective in treating the tumor, since they contain ions-cyanide, then transformed. As well as the Colchico and all other *poisoning* treatments mentioned in this book. But, of course, no orthodox doctor will give you bitter almonds as an anticancer treatment, too little Pharmacine! Think about it: 10, 20, or 30 dollars of treatment against 10,000, 20,000, or 30,000. Furthermore, any inconvenience with these products it would also lend itself to a sure and easy Pharmacine *Pharmainquisition*.

As mentioned earlier, the nutritive principles contained in plants also contribute considerably to the reconstruction of bacterial flora that naturally counteracts the proliferation of pathogenic elements by rebalancing the relationship between good and bad. In fact, it is a commonplace to say that all ills have a root in a bad and unbalanced intestinal flora. This is probably also caused by a wrong

---

[17] https://en.wikipedia.org/wiki/History_of_cancer_chemotherapy

diet as well as by problems related to the psychological sphere that, as known, also affects the intestinal sphere.

The improper feeding[18] also causes important acid/alkaline imbalances, so a good diet should take into account the balance between acid and alkaline foods, thus keeping the right pH. Therefore, the imbalance of modern food towards acid foods (meat and animal derivatives, coffee, and sweetened drinks, etc.) and the indiscriminate use of drugs lead to an imbalance of the alkaline pH in favor of the acid one. The highly alkaline vegetable diet would therefore also help to rebalance the pH of the human body.

If you are wondering why these methods are not used, the answer is pretty easy. Bicarbonate, juices, and other natural substances cost only a few dollars, while chemotherapy costs thousands of dollars per treatment. However, in general, we must always remember that it is not enough just to destroy, we must also restore. Indeed, destruction should be replaced by reconstitution, exactly as experienced by Gerson, Breuss, Ehret, and others.

It would seem, therefore, more and more to take hold, obviously without any support for what Big Mafia calls *scientific* (that is: what can be patented and sold), the idea that combating cancer diseases is something relatively simple, especially if not in an advanced state. Gerson and the other followers of natural therapies have shown that many desperate cases, that traditional allopathic medicine would not even try to cure, can miraculously recover if the body has a minimum healing energy left.

---

[18] According to my theory the human diet has to be logically fruitarian, as you will read in the following chapter about nutrition.

Lastly, *the greatest physician after Hippocrates* documents that his therapy treats most of the diseases including cancer and, since Pharmacine says *it is not scientific*, all his medical colleagues believe and repeat those words exactly as Nazi officers would do. They do not even doubt and do not even need to carry out due verification, that should compulsory be done by a follower of Hippocrates. Otherwise they should swear the oath of Pharmacine and not the one of Hippocrates.

Gerson has documented that his therapy treats an endless string of diseases: cancer (lungs, skin, breast, liver, bone, colon, thyroid, testicles, eyes, leukemia, Hodgkin's lymphoma and also, partially, brain), hypertension (100 % of cases), cholesterol, diabetes, heart attack, obesity, restores glycemia (hyper/hypo), allergies, migraines, chronic fatigue, hepatitis (A, B, C), cirrhosis, eczema, acne, lupus, psoriasis, tuberculosis, arthritis, rheumatoid arthritis, gout, osteoporosis, anemia, fibromyalgia, osteomyelitis, asthma, pulmonary emphysema, bronchitis, cystic fibrosis, hemorrhoids, colitis, candida, multiple sclerosis, goiter, ocular histoplasmosis, macular degeneration, dysmenorrhea, infertility, premenstrual syndrome, benign tumors, depression, panic attacks, neurasthenia, drug addiction, AIDS, herpes, syphilis, etc.

Gerson therapy is therefore the most complete and effective natural and universal remedy that allows the human body to go back to its original state and self-heal itself. Nature does it all. Then it should, always, be used, especially if other natural treatments did not work. In fact, it restores energy and allows the body to regain its natural balance. In one of her interviews, Charlotte Gerson reports that almost all the patients in the Mexican hospital are overwhelmingly resuming their lives.

So, it would appear that multiple sclerosis and many other autoimmune diseases are treated with this therapy, certainly not with other drugs that are, probably, the triggering cause of insurgence. In fact, the accumulation of poisons over a lifetime could eventually determine this type of onset. It is therefore necessary to detoxify the organism from all the accumulated poisons, which are food, drugs, vaccines, pollution, etc. That is why the therapies of Ehret, Gerson, Breuss, Kousmine work. They are natural methods, they are methods that make us find our natural state.

Many diabetics people still believe that there is no cure for diabetes and they carry this scourge, that greatly affects their social life, for a lifetime. Instead, it would take a few months (or a year at the most) of Gerson therapy to return to normal, maybe avoiding, then, the previous abuses.

Yet, famous professors will tell you that there is no cure for diabetes (certainly not a *pharmacinical* one). You may believe that, if you prefer, but be sure that truth might be far from what you are told. *Do not trust! Experience!* Obviously Pharmacine's supporters could argue that Charlotte Gerson lies. Of course, that is possible as well. The care in the Gerson hospital is not free, but I believe this scenario is absolutely unlikely. They do not have trillions of dollars to protect and their morality is certainly higher than the one of Pharmacine.

Of course, even Jesse, the aforementioned guy who treated himself with Gerson therapy and has documented everything, could tell lies. Instead, in your opinion, is it possible that those who have 10 trillion dollars of reasons to lie shamelessly do not do it? In my opinion these can be counted as absolute *logifical proofs*. There is a strong economic interest behind chemo ($7 trillion) and everything is done to keep it alive, even if it is useless, harmful, and often determines future death.

In a just world, every doctor's theory should be kept, however, in due consideration and sincerely investigated by his colleagues has intended in Hippocratic oath. It is evident that fungus responds to treatments with sodium bicarbonate. They also respond to treatments with colloidal silver and probably Hulda's Clark Zapper. And it is likely they respond to treatments with potassium ascorbate or simply with potassium bicarbonate, as already experimented by Pantellini in another millennium.

So, Hamer, Simoncini, and all the others could definitely be a people persecuted by Pharmacine. Thus, the hypotheses remain only two: either they are really charlatans or they are physicians who are disturbing Pharmacine's business. As a matter of fact, sodium bicarbonate could work in many cases, as it does according to the reported cases. It could work the many therapies mentioned in this book all equally treated by the Pharmainquisition. It is an evidence that both bicarbonates mentioned would regularize the pH, being alkaline substances, and, in addition, potassium bicarbonate helps to regularize the sodium/potassium balance (indicated by Gerson and others as a major threat).

Let me stress once again that most of these therapies are used to kill and not to heal. Only Gerson therapy and fast-like therapies naturally heal all diseases, bringing our body back to its origin. It would be, however, improper to say that these last methods cure all diseases, in fact, it is Nature that does it, Gerson therapy or other natural ones are just the means used by Nature.

In essence, it happens as when a pc is formatted because it is malfunctioning and so it returns to its original state. Of course, you can try to uninstall a program to solve the problem (chemo or other) but often this is insufficient. Unfortunately, as already highlighted, the Gerson method is quite long (up to two years), but certainly considerably lower than the long process that caused the disease.

Max Gerson insists on the *knowledge that is the basis of the power of every single human being*. If you entrust third parties, blindly and solely, to manage what each of us knows best, then, what is the meaning of life itself?

In fact, the principle *knowledge is power* is fundamental to correctly implement the Gerson method. Knowing the damage caused by drugs, wrong food, and food additives, electromagnetic fields, alcohol, nicotine, agricultural products cultivated with chemistry, and even the mind is essential to be able to self-heal.

It is no coincidence that Albert Schweitzer, a well-known multi-media genius, said about Gerson: "I see him as one of the most eminent medical geniuses in the history of medicine ... he was strongly impeded in the profession by the contrary political conditions." I would add that he was boycotted, attacked, and finally killed by the political power implicit in Pharmacine.

As evidence of the validity of the Gerson method, I report below some passages of the book *Healing the Gerson way*:

When do patients begin to feel better and have more energy?

Almost all patients, including those who are very ill, feel better after the first week of therapy. Pain decreases, appetite returns and sleep improves; in some cases, the tumor also recedes or becomes softer.

In addition to attacking the malignant tissue, the body begins to heal old wounds, fractures, scars and serious diseases, including perhaps high blood pressure or diabetes due to age. It is impossible to stop or hold back this process, because the body cannot select what to heal! In other words, it does not heal only the present deadly pathology, but also all the other problems, old or new.

All of this is a great psychological stimulus, but this is the moment when the patient should be warned against a possible healing reaction, which will make him feel ill for several days. A true increase in energy could occur after three, six months, depending on the age and status of the patient. At that point, it is essential that the patient continues to rest and does not launch into multiple activities! The new energy is used for healing and nothing else. There will be plenty of time, later on, to strengthen the muscles and recover lost exercise. Trying to do it too soon can cause a serious relapse.

If this therapy is so effective, why is it not recognized by the medical authorities?

As known, the current orthodox medical system is dominated by large and powerful pharmaceutical companies. They come to control, through substantial donations to medical schools, what is taught to students: drugs, drugs and more drugs to suppress symptoms. The drugs never heal, and the result is that chronic degenerative diseases are called "incurable."

The Gerson therapy totally eliminates the consumption of drugs, healing the body from its real problems: the general metabolism disorders, the weakened immune system and the debilitated essential organs. In this way it is possible to heal the whole body, restoring health. The problem is that big pharmaceutical companies cannot make money with organic and natural food like carrots, so they oppose nutritionist therapy with all their strength. However, they know that people begin to understand what is happening.

Unfortunately, Gerson had not considered the succession of generations when he said that "people begin to understand what is happening." More than half a century has passed since his disappearance and the power of Big Mafia is always greater and the deception is far from being unveiled, even if episodes like the one of Jesse (mentioned in this book) give hope. After all, the pioneers see the future and imagine that such visions may occur soon. Unfortunately, this does not always happen in these terms and it takes longer time before it happens.

That these tremendous considerations must be made by the population and the sick is absolutely necessary. However, it does not seem to have changed much since these words were written. People are forced to treat themselves in hospitals run by Pharmacine as they are forced to use the oil of the seven sisters.

I am sure that in the end, the deception will fall, but this depends a lot on our ability to discern the true from the false and the desire and the ability to *renounce ignorance*. It is often easier to discharge the responsibility of our lives on the *so-called professors* then take it on us. I do believe that our consciences will evolve and in the end, the big lie will fall. Whether it will take decades, centuries, or millennia, I can't tell.

We are asked not to trust people like Gerson and his daughter Charlotte and instead we should trust Pharmacine, which loots our bodies. More and more people are unveiling their criminal subterfuges. And yet, the very image of Charlotte Gerson is worth a thousand words: this therapy extends life! How can you not see! Max Gerson has been stolen his patients' medical records and has been poisoned. Bradstreet's house, as already mentioned, was searched after his death by the FDA and not by the police: explain to me why a state drug agency, or even the police itself, should search your home! They did not even investigate his death. *Do not trust! We are all cheated!*

Max Gerson was ready to list all the cases he treated but they prevented him from doing so by stealing his folders. Essentially, you do not want to see because you cannot believe there can be so much barbarism, but what is at stake is much too high.

It is easier to live in ignorance than to live as a scholar and it is easier when they tell us what to do, even if when they say it is for their interest and not ours.

To reveal the deception, perhaps we should self-finance holistic clinics that can really cure us, maybe using crowd funding that can give unexpected results. In fact, with this system of social solidarity many projects could be implemented, including that of the holistic clinic where patients can deal with all the remedies indicated in this book and experiment with new ones. I am sure that many real *Hippocratians* therapist would be happy to serve, even as volunteers.

Unfortunately, people with the actual *institutional system*, do not have chances, they cannot choose, they are bound to be teased. It is not easy and natural to think that who should protect you is instead teasing you. One needs to suspect and doubt first to be able to unveil the deception by thinking logically, experimenting, and realizing to have been cheated.

Dr. Gerson studied thousands of cases in which hypertension disappeared, yet even this is not scientific because, according to Pharmacine, there is *essential hypertension* (when they cannot give pharmacinical explanations they invent unexplainable terms). Unfortunately, following the Gerson therapy, you cannot give a pill to one patient and another pill to the other and see if there are any differences (according to the double-blind hoax that serves only to justify the misdeeds of Pharmacine). In fact, it is not conceivable for Pharmacine that a non-pill can work because they only reason in terms of drugs that can be patented, produced, and sold (the more expensive, the better it is).

I tell you that if there will not be a general scholarship of the people you will never find a remedy for cancer. In fact, the cure for most of the known (and yet to know) diseases already exists but the people (educated or ignorant) are not able to see it and, above all, do not understand that there can never be any chemical treatment for human health.

Furthermore, we should also rediscover the dignity of death. When we get to the end of our journey, we should become aware of it and let it happen naturally, without stubbornly trying to keep whatever is destined to die at any cost. But it is useless to be obsessed over (when in old age) relying on therapies that lengthen the life of a few months but that make it sad and empty. This is often a request from physicians and family members rather than from the patient. We should prepare ourselves to abandon life more consciously, and according to Nature.

As I was writing this volume, I did a bizarre and perhaps risky consideration, even on the basis of a personal experience. You could use as a simple and intuitive diagnostic method a trivial procedure: adopt the Gerson diet, quite rigidly (at least 8/9 juices a day, instead of 13 for cancer patients) for a few days without performing the enemas and check how long it takes to manifest discomfort or pains and the intensity of the same. If the pain appears, soon it is intense or even unbearable, then it could be assumed that the body is suffering from serious diseases and should be investigated with more complete diagnostic tests. However, if the discomfort arises after many days and are mild and bearable, then one could only prefer a short/medium period of Gerson therapy with a detoxifying purpose. That is just a bizarre hypothesis that came to my mind but it needs to be experimented and proved right.

Unfortunately, I realize that many people are not willing to make the least sacrifice, at least until there is a need. However, sometimes it might be too late (though I believe is never too late) and the person should be aware of the lifesaving cures of Gerson, Breuss, and others.

The fact that so many personalities in the medical field converge in indicating the interests of Pharmacine as an obstacle to the development of natural therapies and publicly denounce the misdeeds has a deep meaning.

Unfortunately, there is no weapon that can fight and defeat Big Mafia and Pharmacine except awareness and erudition of the people. Perhaps the only weapon available for the deceived people is that of renunciation. The people should consciously renounce the, so-called, hope that provides Pharmacine, even if they are free, as it happens in many European countries. It should, therefore, renounce chemotherapy and decide massively to treat oneself in another way, then maybe something would change. A bit like what happened with Gandhi's protest fast which alone and peacefully defeated far stronger powers.

Unfortunately, the fear of the risk of life makes people even more fragile and do not let them realize that it is precisely what Big Mafia wants. That is, that the frightened people recur to them, thinking that the only hope of saving one's life is chemo (as I stated before, it is not even certain that chemo lengthen one's life).

Even surgery, although it can help you (only if, after the surgery, you change hygienic/alimentary and or psychological habits), is not necessary except to shorten the psychological sufferings related to the awareness of your state of health.

We should, therefore, have the courage to get informed and consciously decide what to do with our lives and not to further load the conscience of the deceived doctors, who is already sufficiently loaded, allowing to be treated with chemotherapy.

Winning my reluctance to talk and, above all, to question the work of people no longer alive, but to better understand how

Pharmacine permeates and shapes doctors' consciences, I insert, below, an e-mail published in a newspaper, with the response of a respected doctor (who had a congenital defect: he was born and raised professionally in the faculties of Pharmacine).

Anna's e-mail sent to the Professor:

Tuesday, September 14th 2010

Dear Professor, I would love to know your thoughts about Gerson therapy. If it were true that tumors could be cured with substantial amounts of fresh organic fruit and vegetable juices, I do not understand why we continue to treat cancer with conventional treatments like radio and chemo that are so invasive and toxic to the body . Thank you in advance if you would like to consider my message worthy of an answer.

Answer by the Professor:

Tuesday, September 14th 2010

Dear Anna, Gerson's idea that we can have a regression of cancer following a diet and detoxification is *generally considered unconfirmed* (by whom? AN) and *devoid of clinical and scientific findings* (such as? Gerson and his successors have documented and document everything, AN). The Gerson therapy is therefore *not recognized as valid by medical science* (from the science of Pharmacine! AN) *but falls within the so-called alternative medicine* (unfortunately it is not the alternative, but the cure, AN). On this I have already had occasion to express myself several times and I willingly reiterate my position, which is then universally adopted in science (pharmacinical, AN): *the certainty in medicine is based on the results of documented scientific studies* (you cannot do the double blind of carrots? AN). For the validity of a drug or a therapeutic approach to be guaranteed, they must be subjected to *scientific verification criteria* that follow precise phases (scientific verification that only Pharmacine can do with the double-blind farce, AN). Until the research has not covered all these steps in demonstrating the effectiveness of a therapy, we cannot be convinced by messages of other nature, more or less appealing. Precisely because they *lack scientific foundation*. These alternative treatments are in reality *non-cures* that sometimes delude the patient causing him to abandon life-saving therapies (maybe 5 or 10 years life-saving, if lucky).

It looks like a script already written, perhaps by someone else, which is repeated, if necessary, endlessly and always the same.

The tone of the answer clearly shows how the associates to Pharmacine, whether they are aware or unaware, do not even wonder if such therapy may or may not be effective. They already have the pre-packaged answer *considering unconfirmed the Gerson therapy, and free of clinical and scientific findings*. And, for pity's sake, who should provide these clinical and scientific findings? Perhaps, it was enough to ask Dr. Gerson (and his fellows) who among other things, published the clinical results in a book, or even to the thousands of people who have undertaken his cure and got healed with his method.

Gerson was meticulous, careful, and dedicated a lifetime to perfecting his cure. As far as I'm concerned his cure appears absolutely *scientific, logific and documented*. So much documented that, in addition to stealing his medical records with many selected cases, they poisoned him. As Dr. Matthias Rath says: "The pharmaceutical industry market is your body, but until it is sick." So, the interest of *Nazipharm* (also called Big Mafia) is to keep your body sick or make it become. For this purpose they make use of the, often unaware, associates to Pharmacine and if someone rebels against it they are badly kicked out of from its kingdom.

Henry Gadsen, director of the pharmaceutical company Merck, candidly declared in a *Fortune* magazine interview that: "Our dream is to produce drugs for healthy people. This would allow us to sell to anyone." What transpires from these words? The medical interest towards thy neighbor? In your opinion, do they care about the toxicity of drugs and their consequences?

Therefore, the eminent *scientists,* before pronouncing their judgments, commissioned and pre-packaged by the Pharmainquisition, should investigate and document the matter to provide an opinion, this time, *serious and authoritative* to avoid compromising their conscience with Nazipharm criminals.

Imagine if Gerson or Bradstreet had said that the care of this or that doctor were useless, amoral, and harmful towards the sick patients, maybe making some allusive and humorous reference? Yet, this is demonstrated by the same statistics that are incredibly published in some scientific circuits: 98% of patients treated with chemo (without the aid of surgery) often dies within five years and often do not reach their natural end of life without a recurrence.

Who could tell so many lies and get away with it? Yet, even today it happens that the people naively accept the big lies. This is statistical scientific data published by health institutions. Instead, the fact that coffee enemas are not effective are mere denigrations of Pharmacine that does not even have an idea of what it is, but officially sentences anybody who goes against it with the Pharmainquisition.

Characters like Ehret and Gerson (enlightened minds, loving and charitable) can be criticized (without any foundation) by blind and guilty bureaucrats of medicine who have not been able to cure diseases, which they have not even understood. Then the same

Gerson (and others) show what was the right therapy, to self-heal and heal others, and the scientists of Pharmacine can only criticize them harshly, instead of learning the real Medicine. Of course, otherwise they should admit that their pharmacinical world is useless and counterproductive. But they dared to take an oath, inspired by Hippocrates, although they have nothing to do with his thought.

The author of this book, before expressing opinions, has documented and personally experienced fasting, Gerson therapy (albeit for short periods), liver washing, Breuss therapy, etc. I can therefore say, quite authoritatively, that coffee enemas are a powerful detoxifier for the colon, the liver, and for the whole organism. In fact, they allow the liver to produce more bile, opening the bile ducts to facilitate its exit. In this way, an intoxicated liver can get rid of many of its toxins within a few minutes. Hulda's Clark liver washing gets rid of gallstones increasing the amount of bile produced. Breuss's fast-like cure is quite easy powerful, detoxifying and affordable by anybody, as gets rid of most side effects of fasting.

Coffee enemas often give great relief to the whole body, and sometimes make the difference between feeling miserable and feeling good and being more active. Imagine what effect it can have on a suffering cancer patient. But famous doctors deride this cure without even knowing what they are talking about. Maybe they would immediately operate a person suffering from gallstones when, with the procedure of liver washing rediscovered by Hulda Regehr Clark, can be easily released by helping to restore the liver and gall bladder instead of eliminating an organ.

On the side, you can see the image of my gallstones expelled by liver washing. Think, a simple procedure (which can be equated, in the results, to a real surgical operation) that can avoid the removal of an organ such as the gall bladder. Yet if you try to ask any orthodox doctor what remedy exists for gallstones, he/she will tell you that only surgery can achieve this result!

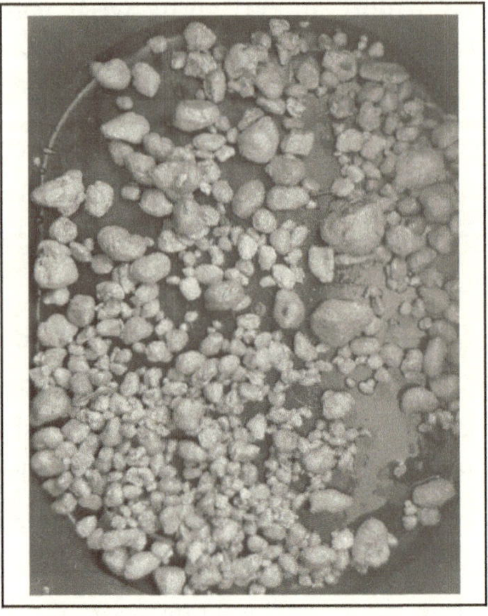

Consider that I could be classified in the category of healthy people, that I have never highlighted problems like that and that I would never have imagined having that stuff inside. Before doing the washing, I also represented to my doctor that I wanted to undertake this procedure to expel gallstones. Obviously, he did not know what I was talking about, but he still gave his answer: "Why should you have gallstones? It is absolutely useless and unnecessary."

Just as you would remove the gall bladder (trusting the luminaries) you also have your breasts removed, part of the intestine, a testicle, part of the rectum and so on and so forth. It would seem, however, that there is no need to be dissected to recover from tumors. Evidently, in all this there is a strong pharmacinical interest. Of course, the methods shown are sometimes challenging, but when you see the results you will certainly adopt them willingly. Having tried most of them, I can put forth my impression for the following cures:

- Breuss: it is quite easy, does not need external help even in cases of cancer. If you are not acquainted with fasting, the first day might be harder. Hunger is not felt (apart the first day) and work can continue regularly (if not seriously ill). Preparation of the juices and teas is quite easy and juices can even be bought bottled (though not recommended). I have tried only 20 days instead of the 42 but I reckon it would not change much as you do not suffer hunger and weakness too seriously. This fast-like therapy is also recommended because recovery from fasting is not traumatic because the body has not stopped functioning completely as food and calories have been introduced over the course of 42 days.

- Gerson: it appears to be tremendously effective even for deadly pathologies. It needs external help (if seriously ill) and work is not allowed for the first few months (depending on the seriousness of the illness). It needs logistic and organizational skills as the quantities of vegetables to be prepared are important. For serious illnesses requires up to four coffee enemas a day. One or two people must be dedicated to the sick person. It might result not a low-priced therapy as the organic food and vitamin supplements cost. It would be extremely improbable that you won't achieve results with this therapy but its implementation can be tricky. For extreme cases it is recommended to visit the hospital in Mexico or the clinic in Hungary, or at least have a contact with the Gerson organization for help.

- Liver and gallbladder cleanse: it is a really easy and amazing procedure that I recommend to everybody just to be certain not to have any gallstones. According to my theory, almost everyone might have some as it might depend on food excess, the kind of food we eat, and the drugs we take. I have been doing it for ten month expelling considerable quantities of gallstones (thousands for about 300gr to 400gr of cholesterol gallstones). Epsom salt has got an unpleasant taste but it is still bearable for the results obtained. Apparently, all gallstones are expelled within one year. Afterwards it will be enough to do the cleanse once or twice a year. I reckon that fruitarian might not be affected by this pathology.

However, I invite you not to trust what I say and what you see, *do not trust! Experience!* Perform the simple liver cleanse procedure described in the book and present on the internet and verify by yourself. Be assured that if you are exaggerating with food and/or you are not fruitarian from birth, you will probably have gallstones (it is essentially cholesterol and precipitated bile pigments) that can cause serious problems, as well as limiting the functionality of the liver.

Unfortunately, Gerson did not have time to experience the liver washing rediscovered by Hulda Regehr Clark, since introduced after his death (I think he would have found it particularly interesting). To have an easy result, it would be enough to make a statistic, very simple and easy to realize, about the average age of those who strictly adheres to the Gerson diet, fruitarians, vegans, omnivores, macrobiotic, etc.

The Gerson therapy allows you to completely regenerate the blood in just three months. I personally did it for a month and a half and I had significant benefits. It is true that it is very demanding, but with a little dedication it can be adapted to your needs. Those who were afflicted by minor illnesses and succeeded in carrying it out for only three months (or even less) would certainly obtain important benefits, detoxifying part of the toxins accumulated during life. Then, keeping a Gerson-like nourishment, you could stay away from illnesses. The most daring could alternate a week of Gerson with three days of fast-like/Breuss like avoiding coffee enemas in the days of fasting.

Dr. Horvath, who runs a Gerson clinic in Hungary with other partners, must have documented himself thoroughly. He probably went to see for himself what happens at the Gerson Hospital in Mexico and he decided, consciously, to carry on a project because the existing scientific or logifical data convinced him. Beata Bishop, who greatly contributed to the establishment of the European Gerson clinic, know very well what the Gerson therapy is. In fact, she was treated and operated for a melanoma that after a year returned and then decided *logically* to follow the Gerson therapy. Well, she is in perfect form after more than 30 years. I suggest you watch her testimony.[19] It may have played an important role in this.

Yes, it is true, there are no patents for this, but it works and works in almost all cases and not only cancer but all the main diseases, including the autoimmune ones (probably caused by drugs, especially vaccines) considered incurable by Pharmacine who has most probably caused them. So if you are told to suffer from an autoimmune disease, or pancreatic cancer or any other incurable disease, *Beware! Beware! Beware!*

Gerson therapy is accessible to everyone without having to go to a hospital, even if it is certainly challenging. However, with the

---

[19] http://www.gerson.hu/all-about-gerson---videos#.WU3jSC5uaUl

help of loved ones, you can do it at home. In most countries they steal our money, paid for the public health service, to give them back to Big Mafia and Pharmacine to be treated in hospitals with no soul. In fact, often, when you enter a hospital, you have an unpleasant feeling of discomfort and the impression that the patient is just an inanimate number or an object. They follow standard protocols, obviously dictated by Pharmacine, treating the patient as if it were not a single entity but composed of many assembled pieces. There is therefore the protocol for the gastroenterologist, the one for the dermatologist, the one for the urologist, etc., and we witness this inhumane and detached treatment and transfer of skills, which, often, could make us ask: why are we in this place?

I wonder who the money we spent on health care in Europe belongs to? Are not they of the people? Should not the people choose how to spend them? Why is there no public holistic hospital anywhere in the world? And why not even a private one in the USA? This could be possible but Pharmacine does not allow it as demonstrated by the Hoxsey and Gerson story.

The interest of Big Mafia is confusing, misdirecting, deceiving, corrupting, training, and taming the audience, especially those characters who have to deal with pharmacological products and it uses any lawful and illicit means.

We have now forgotten Gerson's events, but his story and his therapy had a strong internal and international prominence to the point that he was summoned to the American Congress and his therapy was ready to be implemented at national level.

Then, Big Mafia did everything not to make it happen, and Gerson was relegated to an ordinary doctor, instead of being recognized as that extraordinary doctor that he was. For those who are curious, the chronicle of his times is reported on the internet.

Many good people and conscientious doctors, with years of study and sacrifice, fight for the corrupted ideas of Pharmacine, believing they are real. They still have faith in the institutions and in their fathers, similarly to officers following orders. Sometimes, when I happen to consult with orthodox doctors, I am delighted to quote Dr. Gerson or Dr. Clark, colloidal silver, phages, etc. Even if they have no idea who/what they are, they are still able to miraculously pronounce the magic words: *these are not scientifically proven theories; one must rely on science.* Try to do the same with your orthodox doctor. I am pretty sure you will get the same answers.

MEDICINE AND PHARMACINE

Be strong enough not to believe in what they want you to believe. You determine both the origin and the end of the disease.

GAIA STRAUS

The deception perpetrated on the medical field is the one that I do not tolerate and suffer from most. I consider deception to be one of the worst crimes imputable to man, perhaps second only to murder. However, I found out only before the publishing of this book that the worst deception of all has been taking place since several decades and might disclose to us soon: the deception of soul and spirit. In fact what is more evil that hiding the existence of your brothers. That is exactly what is happening with our non terrestrial brothers. They asked the governments to meet and hug their terrestrial brothers and help them in their evolution but that was denied, because the evil (governments driven by financial lobbies) have to further implement their satanic plans of destructions, forgetting that the Nature and God will always have the supremacy.

In fact, Eugenio Siragusa, in one of his channeling from the non-terrestrial counterpart, was informed that five discs landed in 1954 at the military base of Muroc Fields (now renamed Edwards Air Force Base), in California, meeting Eisenhower. In this meeting they showed their abilities and expressed their willingness to help the Terrestrials by providing their technology to us (which included free energy for all) and material and spiritual help... Of course, the later answer was negative as the finance institutions that govern the Earth could not accept to lose the oil money and the political power.

In this volume, I do not want to recommend remedies or cures, although the references to them are obvious. I want to denounce the naive blindness of the people (including the writer, until recently).

When Hitler ruled Germany, people hurled themselves against his fellow Hebrew citizens because a malefactor made them believe, in a convincing way, that Jews were inferior and unworthy beings. So harmless, conscientious citizens turned into persecutors of their fellows just because Hitler was much more prepared than many and had guessed that "the way of feeling of the people is not tortuous but simple and elementary" and that a "lie of hyperbolic proportions" would have been fully accepted, "especially if repeated often," because "the people will not even think that it is possible to construct such a profound falsification of the truth."

Let me clarify this last concept related to the people because I could be accused of being discriminatory towards the people itself, of which, among other things, I am also a part. The people (educated and not, rich or poor), as I have already said, think and act in a different way than a single individual does. Le Bon has clearly highlighted it in his pioneering study. All the dictators have shown it and still prove it.

The chiefs of Pharmacine, but especially Big Mafia, must have well studied Hitler and his criminal successes to be able to implement such a plan of world conquest through chemotherapy. Now it happens that a *lie of hyperbolic proportions* is almost fully accepted by the people and also by honest and educated physicians "who cannot even think that such a profound falsification of the truth can be achieved" (Hitler).

It also happens that those who try to treat themselves in a different way from the pharmaceutical one are often mocked and humiliated and the poor doctors who try to help these people are treated as enemies of the people and of medicine. My vision about this last topic is: a mass extermination to gain power ... and money, of course. Probably, you will think that this association with Nazism is crazy and out of place but wait until you get to the end of the book. I too thought it was crazy and absurd when I theorized it, but then logic opened my eyes and I fear that what I have described is even inferior to reality.

As I have already mentioned, medicine is, in my opinion, one of the vocational fields *par excellence*, just as politics and religion should be. In fact, wanting to bring relief to those who have a suffering body can certainly be part of the vocational disciplines, similar to politics and religion.

With the advent of modern pharmacology, the relationship between patient and physician has radically changed. In the old times, we tried to treat with the few means available, but above all without effective diagnostic tools.

However, there was, probably, a better harmony between patient and doctor. Perhaps physicians used trivial and artisanal methods, but, somehow, often effective, such as bleeding (including cupping), enemas, or other elementary remedies that largely contributed to the elimination of toxins. These methods may appear primitive or unsuitable today, but certainly were not at those times and would still be effective if combined with a different awareness of the disease and a holistic approach to it.

Unfortunately, at that time, these remedies could not be supported by other therapies, now available, and could not, therefore, be effective for all existing diseases. In ancient times, when they did not know how to intervene, bleeding was prescribed, regardless of the disease, as a panacea for all illnesses. It was effective for many diseases, as it helped to regenerate the blood and eliminate toxins

Today, doctors are completely unaware of those ancient methods that worked and focuses solely and exclusively on modern pharmacology, and more and more resemble mere *prescribers* of drugs imposed by an increasingly powerful and authoritarian pharmaceutical lobby. Most modern physicians are interested only in surgery (*cut and sewing*) or in the *magic pill*.

The level of influence reached by the international pharmaceutical lobby is unprecedented; it has even surpassed that of the oil lobbies and who knows how far it will go.

Natural therapies, which I will describe later, in the modern age have been opposed, boycotted, and denigrated with various stratagems and procedures from a lobby whose behavior increasingly resembles that of the mafia or a terrible dictator who annihilates all his enemies with every conceivable method. It is, in fact, evident that these natural therapies that work could really bring down Big Mafia's *paper castle*, determining its collapse, similarly to what was the defeat of Stalingrad for Hitler (the beginning of the end).

Unfortunately, the Orthodox medical class, educated according to the teachings of Big Mafia, is completely drowned in the big lie and does not even consider other hypotheses of cure, because that's the way it should be. However, providentially, an increasing number of people and, perhaps even doctors, are starting to wake up, freeing themselves from the big lie.

Nowadays, to call this science medicine is a contradiction in terms, perhaps we should call it Pharmacine. In fact, there is very little medicine left and so much pharmaceutical. To dictate how we must be treated are no longer doctors but Big Mafia and the FDA, in association and support, with all the other *cronies* of the rest of the capitalist world.

To demonstrate the *logical* nature of these words, every national authority in the health and/or pharmaceutical field is associated with Big Mafia, through the FDA or similar institutes of other countries, in an absolute league. They renounce their role as protectors of the people and thus create a formidable, unbeatable, and unassailable world drug cartel.

Whoever has the misfortune to meet or, worse, to clash with Big Mafia is annihilated, miserably passing, suddenly, from being an illustrious doctor or scholar to become a charlatan, perhaps questioned by the various medical orders or even by their judiciary. Some have even been more unfortunate by being poisoned twice with arsenic as happened to the most illustrious Dr. Max Gerson (1881-1959). (An entire chapter dedicated to repudiated and contrasted doctors and scholars will follow). Even the EMEA (European Medicines Agency), although less known by the public, certainly does its part by conforming (in an unwritten mandatory code) to the behavior of the powerful American sister, in perfect *twin sisters* style.

Unfortunately, as the video *The Forbidden Cures* by Donald K. Ranvaud[20] shows in an efficacious and discouraging way, many ignore that the Great Depression of 1929, besides bringing so much misery, has greatly contributed to the defeat of Medicine ... the one with the capital M. As a consequence, medicine universities *surrendered* to what would have become today's Pharmacine (Big Mafia, FDA, EMEA, medical associations, ministries of health, political institutions, etc.). In fact, due to the lack of funds to support American universities, in 1933 the pharmaceutical companies massively entered in the funding of universities, first on tiptoe, and then colonizing and imposing, more or less veiledly, their wills and later their business, until they became one body… and one soul. Since the starting of financing by pharmaceutical entrepreneurs medical universities have lost their autonomy and the physicians their independence of judgment.

Today, doctors that do not follow the doctrine imposed by Pharmacine are exposed to the public inquisitorial judgment by the national medical boards. This judgment could be further amplified by the blind (or accomplices) mass media and sometimes even by the judiciary.

This inquisition is therefore unsustainable for any honest doctor who deviates from the doctrine. Obviously, this type of attitude is less significant for the purely technical disciplines that do not disturb Pharmacine—surgery, orthopedics, etc.

---

[20] https://www.youtube.com/watch?v=BTGye7kA6rM

Today's medical universities teach new doctors they should not accept *non scientifically proven theories* (through the double-blind[21] *hoax*) and they do what they are told. Should we be upset with doctors? They are innocent victims too! Doctors who are logical enough and do not believe in this *fairy tale* try to *escape*, but often it ends badly.

Even Mr. Harry Hoxsey, although he was not a physician, had to succumb to the extreme power of the pharmaceutical lobbies who, methodically, scorched the earth around any unfortunate person who runs into their clutches.

Mr. Hoxsey was a Texan businessman who received from his father a similar recipe to the one of René Caisse's ESSIAC (which I will describe later). Unlike René Caisse's character (softer and gentler), he had a strong combative one, important economic resources, and he was not afraid of anyone.

The origin of his remedy is traced back to his great-grandfather. One day, he sent his precious cancer-afflicted stallion to die in the fields. After a few weeks, the great-grandfather noticed that the stallion had stabilized by eating herbs that he normally did not eat. After about a year, the stallion was completely healed and the great-grandfather began to use this herb, together with other traditional remedies, to cure other animals. Hence, the Hoxsey cure originated.

---

[21] A testing procedure, designed to eliminate biased results, in which the identity of those receiving a test treatment is concealed from both administrators and subjects until after the study is completed.

Hoxsey, in the years in which he lived, fought one of the most epic battles against what he called *organized medicine*. He was therefore defined by Pharmacine's associates as *the worst charlatan of the century*, despite having compiled clinical data on thousands of cases treated with his remedy, as did many others before and after him.

In the time I have dedicated to this research, I noticed a common thread: all the professionals (doctors or similar) who harm the interests of Pharmacine are ostracized as *charlatans*, regardless of the proposed treatment and regardless of the evidence. They are then undergone media pillory, similarly to what must have happened with the witch hunt. Then it will be the people "simple and elementary" (Hitler) and naive to shout: *fire to the witches!* Also in these cases, the strategy of a "lie, often repeated" is adopted by addressing the unwanted as charlatans, a word that thus becomes an identifier for the "simple and elementary people," similar to what happened with the Jews.

No medical institution linked to Pharmacine has even ever thought to verify these therapies. They just ignore them! In fact, as you will read later, René Caisse, Gerson, Hoxsey, etc., were all sacrificed to the altar of public opinion, without any clear scientific proof, or even logifical proof, of the unreliability of such non-pharmaceutical remedies. As a matter of fact, there were thousands of people who could testify to the effectiveness of these cures.

In fact, natural therapies will never be able to provide scientific evidence as that is the absolute prerogative of Pharmacine. A scientific proof for Pharmacine, as I will repeat endlessly, is just something that can be patented and sold.

They even invented the *double-blind fairy tale* to be able to get rid of the poor unfortunate doctors who will never be able to prove their studies and their remedies with that technique. In fact, those who do not have a *magic pill* to prescribe to their patients will never be able to provide any scientific evidence. Even if someone could provide a natural pill, however, it would be annihilated from Pharmacine.

Pharmacine has never supported non-patentable scientific evidence. It is not in its interest, thus it tries to hinder them by any lawful or illicit means. So, who has the responsibility to provide scientific evidence of something that is not patentable? National health institutions? Can you just imagine it?

If it is true that the scientific method is relevant to the science on natural cures, it would be enough to simply take the most renowned cancer orthodox hospital and compare it with a Gerson-like hospital, checking the results and statistics of care.

It would be very easy to compare the results, verifying how many relapses would be present in one hospital versus other and so on. Paradoxically, the greatest hopes of disillusionment lie in countries condemned by history, such as Japan and Germany (these two nations are among those where the *olicracy* is, perhaps, less rooted; Japan especially has a sense of honor unseen in other countries). Moreover, *pharmacinized* governments could not implement such policy as it would not be allowed by Big Mafia.

Moreover, in countries where healthcare is free, those who pay for the National Health Service are practically obliged to the treatment decided by Pharmacine with its inhumane protocols. One cannot do otherwise, if not paying out considerable amounts, as no public health institution would ever recognize natural therapies. The

Americans, however, might include this condition in their health insurance to ensure it is treated in a *human* way. But even this possibility would not be possible because it would cut Pharmacine*'s* income. However, those Americans who do not have insurance and can't afford medical cures (though often useless) can certainly undergo the therapies listed later on this book, especially Breuss therapy in addition to ESSIAC herbs. If the time is not enough to heal with this therapies, then, Gerson therapy might complete the healing. If the readers want to take care of their own lives, they will have to be ready to become their own physicians.

In most countries, health cures are free but natural therapies will never be granted because they are effective and might dismantle the Pharmacine business. Obviously, a holistic (or Gerson-like) hospital would also disturb Pharmacine's dirty business. It would also upset the dirty dealings of the evil chemical lobbies, linked to Monsanto and the six sisters. In fact, the considerable supply of biological vegetables would generate healthy and sustainable organic companies around the hospital. All in all, *Pharmacine* would initially lose only a few profits, but certainly could not tolerate the spread of doubt. In fact, just that little seed could determine its end with a battle that would hardly be painless for the poor unfortunates who will need medical facilities.

On the contrary, today, in most countries, it is decided politically that only Pharmacine medical facilities can operate. That's why the Gerson hospital had to escape to Mexico and you can hardly find any important natural therapy facilities around Europe. I would not be surprised if these *pundits of Pharmacine* would implement new strategies to fight effective natural therapies.

At the moment, the contrast is only through the media action which is sufficient to guarantee Pharmacine supremacy. But, should it not be enough anymore, then, someone might have the idea of obscuring websites and other actions like this. Basically, Pharmacine says that vaccines are safe and do not cause autism, SIDS, etc. and that chemotherapy is the only hope for cancer treatment. But it's not true! It is a huge lie! They do not respect those who died for our medical scholarship, such as Gerson (defined by me as the greatest doctor after Hippocrates), Breuss, Shelton, Kousmine, Bradstreet, etc.

Unfortunately, it is equally true that people are confused by the same institutions which, instead of protecting them, act against them, being themselves a true source of misinformation. What would these websites gain, instead, in spreading hoaxes (according to Pharmacine) if not insults and defamation? Maybe they have fun defaming honest public officials? Who knows!

The anti-Pharmacine websites report that the FDA opposed Bradstreet in any way possible until he committed *assisted suicide* on himself. It is documented that, even after his death, the FDA perpetrated a strong Pharmainquisition on him, seizing his studies, data, computers, etc. What were they looking for? The hoaxes? Or the documents proving that some vaccines cause autism? Or even the production processes of GcMAF, which apparently cures not only autism but also tumors. This alone would be an excellent reason for an *assisted suicide*. Do you really think that it was not the ending point of an obviously unsuccessful Pharmainquisition?

However, the authorities you trust so much have immediately dismissed the case as a suicide. Bah, maybe it is this way! I will tell you that, because *the big lie* is wobbling, this war of position between information and disinformation, natural and unnatural, simple and artificial, will become more and more cruel and only the people will finally decide who will be the winner. This will depend on the people whether they can transform from a "simple and elementary crowd" (as defined by Hitler) to a thinking and reasoning one. In fact, it is more than obvious that the Bradstreet suicide and GcMAF is *logifically* [22] a pharmacinical intelligence operation to eliminate the product from circulation, as well as eliminating its creator using a similar strategy to that already described with the *Emergency* episode.

If I were sick with autism or cancer, being unable to trust anybody, I would grab as many packs of GcMAF as possible before Pharmacine would be able to remove it effectively from the trade. This is something that institutions that are supposedly protecting us can make happen, pretending they are defending our health. In most countries around the globe, politicians tell us how to behave and who to trust. But can we really trust them, first of all?

I learnt not to trust anybody, but to experiment by myself with harmless treatments and any other affordable subject to be able to judge by myself as I sincerely believe that health institutions protect (fraudulently or not) Pharmacine's business. In fact, I've learned to think that one should do the opposite of what they say. Institutions keep on repeating that chemtrails are hoaxes, like the association between vaccines and autism. Because of this, I'm even changing my mind about chemtrails, which until recently I thought

---

[22] See *logific*

were nonsense. I know now that one cannot trust anybody and I believe that the powerful, to become even more powerful and rich, would do everything, not only change the climate with chemicals but even spread drugs to maintain and increase cancer diffusion to support their multi-billion dollar business. That is why I do not trust anybody anymore. Money and power corrupt almost anybody.

Often the institutions do not even know these scholars, but they find the courage to condemn a dead person only by hearsay. Who knows why only the alternative or holistic doctors shoot themselves in the chest or die in a weird way? This happens very rarely to corrupt politicians. Would we feel the same displeasure?

So, in this case, the epilogue is simple and only two hypotheses are possible: either these politicians are also part of Pharmacine or are part of the large group of deceived people who fight unknowingly, blindly, and obtusely for Pharmacine. Trump, who is certainly not stupid and must have also studied Le Bon's theories, could contribute in an important way to the anticipated disappearance of humankind, not caring about the greenhouse effect and disseminating weapons indiscriminately.

This is to prove that the *high Nazi officers* belonging to Pharmacine are seldom in the medical field, but more frequently in the highest institutional environments (especially health) and in all those areas where Pharmacine is involved.

I hear the powerful of the Earth who say that global warming cannot be attributed to human activities in order to be able to continue to pollute and enrich themselves with oil. Certainly, in this case, they are not completely wrong; as it is a cycle of natural thaw. However, just as certainly, it is accelerated by human activities.

So, yes, man is causing his misfortune in advance. There is no doubt about this.

What about terrestrial axis change? Could it be caused by man with underground nuclear explosions? Apparently God Himself (Adoniesis) [23] and the Celestial beings, through their messengers, (Eugenio Siragusa, first of all) has been repeating that we have already reached a hypercritical status[24]. If, or when, we will be reaching the hyperchaotic status, our mother Earth will have to get rid of her cancer: Man… and the relative pollution of air, water and soil. Now, you may say that he might be a crazy man but if you use your intellect and read God and other Celestial messages you will realize, logically, that a man cannot have all that fantasy. Those words must necessarily come from an Entity who knows the creation. Furthermore, had he written a fiction it would have been a worldwide bestseller. Why insisting on saying that his messages come from God and the celestial hierarchy? Certainly we do not need to use atomic power to destroy humanity. By doing so, however, not only might we destroy humanity but we would dramatically offend our mother Earth even more than we are already doing. Why don't we firmly demand all nations leaders to dismantle all atomic bombs? What are they for? Nations have already demonstrated that they can destroy each other without atomic power (see Second World War). It appears that we are doing everything to disappoint our Father and Mother and let the evil

---

[23] The Father, not to be confused with the Creator of everything, who we call the Holy Spirit.
[24] See message received on 17 September 1976.

prevail. I do not doubt that God might have regretted having created the man. He has provided us with divine intellect that we do not use. We let the evil operate freely and do not love our neighbor. We are very close to the judgment day and we have not learnt to love our neighbor yet, which is the only universal law. We are asleep in our coward numbness and let the evil undisturbed in his diabolic plans. LET'S WAKE UP!!! World is at the final stage: we are going to see the Promised Land but we must wake up and love each other otherwise the price for the Promised Land will be catastrophically heavy.

We certainly do not need God to tell us that by exploding thousands of nuclear bombs on Earth we may cause a self-induced apocalypse, but we keep on doing it and let the evil work almost undisturbed. Why do not we disarm our nuclear arsenal? What do we need it for? To let the devil destroy Earth?. Let's ask firmly, but loving our neighbor, to dismantle nuclear armament all over the world and let's ask even more firmly to meet our non terrestrial brothers. LET'S BOYCOT THE DEVIL UNVEILING HIS PLANS! Do not let him deceive you, don't you know that he is a master in deception?

Since the deception involves everyone (rich, powerful, poor, defenseless, cultured or less cultured) I hope that at least Germany, a nation perhaps less bigoted and gullible and an expression of genes of the medical field (but not only) will redeem us from holocaust by unveiling the great deception. The fact that Berlin's Charité clinic is hopefully testing natural cures (though in association with pharmacological ones) bodes well that the wall of indifference might collapse. Moreover, the widespread use of *heilpraktiker* (empirical doctors, with similar dignity, respect, and consideration of traditional doctors) integrated into the German national health care structure means that there is no excessive jealousy and contrast with the official medicine of Pharmacine.

What has been said so far means that any further natural remedy (or rather, non-pharmaceutical, therefore patentable and sellable) against tumors and other illnesses will have to be tested only in secret, perhaps with word of mouth, similarly to what happened with the secret societies. Also old remedies already known or new ones must be experimented with quietly without giving prominence that could disturb Big Mafia and Pharmacine. I wonder, what else is there to be experimented? There are already dozens of very effective natural therapies available to combat tumors (Gerson, Breuss, Kousmine, etc.), but nobody cares.

It is certain that any new discovery that is not chemical, and therefore sellable and patentable, will be defamed and its inventors will be prosecuted with the Pharmainquisition.

Moreover, do you really believe that Pharmacine is an ethical organization? Then, why is it allowed to sell a life-saving drug to about one million dollars per kilogram (over 20 times the value of gold). Yes, you understood correctly! I assure you, it is not a hoax; it is the drug against hepatitis C. Think about it, one million dollars! Of course, research costs are definitely important and must be amortized, bla ... bla ... bla ... but charging tens of thousands of dollars on a single cure seems enough to classify Pharmacine as a bottlenecking agency similar to *The Octopus*. It is estimated that the cost of production of a cure cycle of Sofosbuvir, marketed by Gilead, is about 200,00 dollars, while the cost of therapy is around $100.000,00. But obviously the costs are justifiable by research, bla ... bla ... bla ....

It must also be said that it is not even certain that this drug was really necessary. In fact I suppose no one ever thought to test colloidal silver, the Gerson therapy, or the amazing Zapper of Hulda Regehr Clark against the Hepatitis C virus. Maybe it was not even necessary but who would have earned 150 billion dollars by selling colloidal silver producible at home or simply using the Gerson therapy or the Zapper (kills any pathogen instantly)?

The release of this drug has transformed a stagnant pharmaceutical company, which was worth about three billion dollars, into a company that enters fully into the realm of Big Mafia and, consequently, of Pharmacine. In fact, with the astonishing sum of a hundred and fifty billion dollars in turnover (about the GDP of a small/medium country like Hungary, New Zealand, or Romania) obtained thanks to a single drug, it has climbed the rankings. Ironically, the Gerson therapy cures almost all illnesses (including hepatitis C) but has never been considered because it does not bring any money, on the opposite it would make pharmaceutical company useless. The Zapper with three single treatments could defeat it, but only pills or serums are considered in this realm.

Tell me how anyone can trust Pharmacine if one of its associated companies charges 100,000.00 dollars for a single treatment. How can ordinary people still believe in Pharmacine? Do you think they really want to cure you? Or that they care for your health? Or are they just looking after their interests neglecting everything else?

Do you sincerely believe that a single doctor who formulates meaningful theories with empirical evidence would be more corrupted than Pharmacine with its ten trillion dollars in turnover to be protected and increased with lies? Or do you think that

Bradstreet, Simoncini, Gòrgun, or anybody else can make fun of you by really jeopardizing their reputation?

It is a certainty that Big Mafia is doing everything to avoid the side effects of chemotherapy, not so much to alleviate the suffering of patients, which would be insignificant for them, but to be able to sell the new anti-cancer drugs at a higher price. New cancer drugs are expected to cost up to 4-5 times more than today's chemotherapy, yet the cure may be there for all to see, as Gerson and others have documented. However, the targeted disinformation successfully deceives most of the people.

From time to time we hear about natural food, herbal cures, etc. to fight tumors. Yet it has all been written and handed down. Even nowadays some doctors, perhaps unaware, believe they have found the cure of the century, the decisive one that has, however, been known for millennia. In fact, Hippocrates used to say: "Cancer is not treated with the iron of the surgeon but with the vegetarian diet and the medical herbs." This concept is similarly repeated somehow by Gerson, Ehret, Breuss, Kousmine, Nacci, and a long string of *crazy* misunderstood medicine men. Furthermore, Gerson and Ehret were not even vegetarians when they implemented their therapies. If they did so, radically, they did it only to heal their diseases; Ehret, however, continued to experiment with meat and other foods, to completely be sure that the human diet is logically fruitarian.

The obvious paradox is also in the Hippocrates oath that the doctors took inspiration from. Now, often, they do exactly the opposite of what it is stated in it and they fill their patients with, often, unnecessary drug. All the real great doctors say that each of us is the best physician of himself/herself, and I urge you to consider these words. If you really want to treat yourself, the only weapon is renunciation. I am not astonished about what happens in the medicine field, as the same happens with religion (adepts, often, do the opposite of what was taught by the Masters). Politics is not far behind as politicians do not practice what they preach.

These kinds of natural therapies (Gerson, Breuss, etc.) can, maybe, integrate with and improve the original one of Hippocrates but the basic theory is always that: *only the Nature cures*. In fact, usually, natural therapies regulate the acid/base ratio of the body, reduce mucus, and regulate the intestinal flora.

Nowadays, they still tell us that it *is not scientifically proven* and a lot of other *hoaxes* when it would be enough to simply try, test and experiment. We also insult the memory of Hippocrates (who, if he only could see, would turn in his grave) by giving his name to an oath that is regularly violated by a congregation, often closed and obtuse, like the one of physicians who are unconsciously corrupted by Big Mafia.

During the last century, we have witnessed, also in the medical field, an endless series of studies and incredible discoveries. This is due, as well, to an effervescence that modern society, driven by technological progress, has impressed on modern life. Therefore findings such as colloidal silver, DMSO (dimethyl sulphoxide) or MSM (Methylsulfonylmethane), the therapy of bacteriophages (or more simply phages) have become almost unknown (or worse are snubbed and ignored by members of Pharmacine) among a large part of the world population.

The drug has become the faithful friend who saves us when we need it. Do not dare, however, to read the contraindications and undesirable effects that somehow occur, and not in low percentages.

Let's not mention their worst fault: they isolate only the diseased parts and treat the symptom but not the cause, leaving out the consequent intoxication of the body that often leads to worse illnesses. In this field, the well-established oriental medicine could, instead, help us, by circulating our Primordial Energy in a more fluid way.

Unfortunately, the holistic approach to treatment is hard to take root in the official medical field. We face with doctors who often indicate a cure without the possibility of detours or additions, perhaps causing a worse illness to arise. I do not want to say that those doctors who treat patients with Ayurveda, homeopathy, acupuncture, traditional Chinese medicine, psychotherapy, herbal medicine or other natural therapies use the best care available, bearing in mind that food is our main cure. However, a holistic approach that includes more remedies, counting allopathic medicine, if necessary (hygienists, please, do not hate me) could help to treat the human being in its entirety.

Using *logic*, are we sure that the explosion of allergies in recent years (to which we are all accustomed because almost in every family there is an allergic individual) does not depend on the excessive use of drugs or GMOs? Or still (almost certainly) from pollution or all these factors in association? We are looting the earth and making it suffer, without realizing that it will survive to any outrage we can commit, while we will not.

It would be interesting to see who is allergic to lactose and check how many of these subjects have used drugs and of what kind. For example, how many women allergic to lactose have taken the contraceptive pill or other drugs for a long period, before manifesting the allergy? However, it is evident that the allergy to lactose may be a condition probably linked to the evolution of the species. In fact, milk is the last food introduced in the human diet, about 10,000 years ago, and milk consumption has not spread in the same way among all peoples. This does not exclude, however, that the onset of the allergy could also depend on the drugs (which often contain lactose as their excipients) that alter the chemical composition of our bodies.

Celiac disease is so widespread in the modern age. Are we sure that it only comes from excessive consumption of cereals (improper food, according to my theory, supported by brilliant characters of the past)?[25]

Can we be completely sure that it does not depend on the excessive use of certain drugs, chemical pesticides (Roundup)[26] or, even worse, genetic changes in the wheat we eat every day?

Even in this case, the *expert scientists* have no doubt in determining *scientifically* with absolute certainty that what has been generated by the Creator will not be affected by the superb modifications of man. It would be interesting to check how many people who use seeds that are not genetically modified or chemically treated (few are left) have contracted this type of food disorder.

Modern society is corrupted and rotten and everything keeps revolving around money and power. However, as long as people will not wake up from this *great deception* and claiming to get clean air,

---

[25] Theory explained in the chapter *fasting and nutrition*.
[26] https://responsibletechnology.org/category/glyphosate/
https://www.maurizioblondet.it/ma-quale-celiachia-chiamatela-roundup/

genuine food, honest politicians, etc., evil will keep on spreading around the world.

Those who advocate GMOs are so certain of the goodness of their theory (or more likely they do not care) that they do not even wonder how to turn back from a possible catastrophe caused by GMOs. Who knows if they planned to safeguard an appropriate sample of grains not genetically modified to recover from a possible catastrophe. However, it will be difficult, even impossible, to go back because the GMO grains have contaminated almost the entire globe even in countries where they are not allowed.

According to the doctors, fomented and educated by Pharmacine, antibiotics are absolutely indispensable, and probably it is this way, at least for some diseases. Then why do we fear a harmless remedy like colloidal silver, which many readers probably do not even know, to the point of not even allowing its marketing as a food supplement but only as a tonic?

The official answer of Big Mafia sounds more or less like this: because there are no experiments (and there will never be because the recognized valid trials are only those of Pharmacine and, of course, Pharmacine has no interest to damage itself), it cannot be marketed as a supplement food because its effects are not known. At this point, the question arises: who can experiment on these remedies? Perhaps a private citizen? Or the medical institutions associated to Pharmacine? Yet, in this case, it would be very simple to implement the double-blind experimentation, already mentioned in the text, but as usual, there is no interest in doing so.

I personally drank gallons of colloidal silver, among other things self-produced, and I'm still alive, as well as having solved minor problems of mine and of those close to me. I would have no fear to take it intravenously if needed, in spite of their experiments, as there is already scientific evidence.

So, it should be the same health institutions, often associated (knowingly or unconsciously) to Pharmacine, to carry out such experiments. It is just an excuse not to let us use products that could damage their business regardless of their effectiveness and life-saving effects. They obviously have no intention of doing so and they will never do it voluntarily. Among other things, there is medical documentation of an important use of colloidal silver (in ionic form, not comparable to the one currently available) up to the 1930s, even intravenously, that is scientifically documented.

Since we have not yet found a drug that can effectively treat osteoarthritis and all arthritic and rheumatic forms, MSM and the DMSO are still allowed as supplements (I will dedicate a chapter to these remedies).

The specter of super bacteria, which until very recently appeared as pure science fiction, seems now to be a reality. As Alexander Fleming himself (inventor of antibiotics) prophesied, it is the worst scenario.

His words: "Pay attention! Do not abuse it otherwise this weapon will no longer work" have not, unfortunately, been considered and not only have we used them inconsiderately on humans, but we have also over-abused on animals. Consequently, we ingest, with their meat and derivatives, important quantities that could contribute to the emergence of new super bacteria, nullifying what this important medicine was for. Maybe, in a catastrophic scenario, we could go back to colloidal silver to test (or better, retest) its properties by experimenting on it consistently and methodically. In fact, colloidal silver has only one defect for pharmaceutical companies: it cannot be patented, like Graviola (Annona Muricata) and other remedies offered by Nature.

It would appear that Pharmacine's members justify their misdeeds in a rational and acceptable way for their degenerated consciousnesses. Hitler invented the Aryan race *fairy tale*, to *enchant* the innocent and naïve Germans, convincing them that they had an enemy. So, he justified the extermination of millions of Jews in order to take advantage of the credulity of the masses.

So, a great part of the pre-war German society had assimilated the sheer lie about the *purity* of the Aryans and the *impurity* of the Jews, Gypsies, etc. that, for this reason, had to be purged from society. Similarly, today it happens that a large part of the population of this globalized world is daily beguiled by the *huge lie* that *cancer is an incurable disease* or *there is no alternative to oil*, or yet, *vaccines are necessary*. These lies are endlessly repeated by important public and convincing characters, normally associated with Pharmacine or *Petroline*.

I wonder then, logically, why so much hostility towards natural medicine? Why cannot one die in a Gerson clinic or stuffed with sodium bicarbonate if he/she has chosen it freely? Perhaps because he/she could heal? And in many documented cases it does ... and forever, without the almost certain relapses of cases treated with official medicine

As documented by thousands and thousands of cases during the last century, the percentage of healing (not remission) with the

Gerson method was well over 50%,[27] even considering that many who tried the Gerson method did it as the last resort, so had more difficulty recovering. Exactly the opposite of what happens with chemotherapy, where only a few people get a remission over five years after treatment, as it was allowed to publish to some doctors, probably in good faith, in their official statistics.[28]

However, this will never be recognized by any of the so-called *medical scientists*. In fact, the statistics are valid only for the scientific data produced by the Orthodox medical institutions financed by Pharmacine. But please, you absolutely must not believe my words, *do not believe me*! And *do not trust me*! But, above all, *do not trust anybody else*—neither the writer, nor those who claim to heal you. Do not trust those who are in bad faith but, but above all, who is in good faith, because they believe in what they say and are convinced that what they say is true. I warmly invite you not to delegate your lives to others. *Get informed! Do not trust anybody! Experience yourself!* Nowadays it is increasingly difficult to hide the truth and the reality (if one wants to find out). To state: "if they said so, it must be so," it is not a justification, because doctors die of cancer and other illnesses exactly like we do and they are deceived as well. Unfortunately *pharmacinical scientific theories* and *medical scientific theories* are contrasting and it is difficult for someone who is not very logical

---

[27] Currently, the Gerson clinic (through Charlotte Gerson) describes successes close to 100% of remissions, against the single-digit percentages of chemotherapy (without surgery) of Pharmacine. Reoccurrences are evidently not happening as they would be reported either to the Gerson hospital or to the orthodox facilities that would certainly make a big fuss out of it.

[28] http://www.mednat.org/cancro/MORGAN.PDF

and informed to understand where the deception is. Profit promotes the deception towards everybody, including therapists that, usually, do not even suspect they might be deceived.

From statistical data published in important medical journals close to *Pharmacine*, in most cases, the percentage of successful cancer remissions would be in the single digits. Translated into common language, it would seem from such orthodox scientific studies that only this percentage of patients who have had cancer and have been treated with chemotherapy (but without the aid of surgery) would not die of the tumor. However, the confusion about therapies is necessary for Pharmacine to implement its deception through propaganda, hiding and boycotting alternative therapies and pretending their cures are the only effective ones. So, the Gerson therapy's successful cures (and not remissions) are, apparently, close to 100%, while chemotherapy, in most cases does not reach 10%, but it looks just as the opposite.

Do not be surprised! It is typical of propaganda. The widespread common opinion is that, actually, chemotherapy can cure cancer diseases, but it's NOT SO! And it is not me to state it but the same scientific institutions belonging to Pharmacine. However, the masses believe the institutions.

For the propagandists, a won battle equals a won war and a lost one by the opponent is tantamount to a defeat. I keep on being amazed at how the propaganda messages easily pass on TV and are still believed by so many people. *Pharmacine* throws the media against cases of deaths due to tumor diseases treated alternatively, while Pharmacine itself kills most of cancer patients with impunity. It is true that there are types of cancer that reach even 40% of remissions, such as testicular, but for most of the other types we often move to single-digit numbers. Believe me, I do not care if you decide to treat yourself with chemotherapy or naturopathy; I care to help uncover the deception, if it really existed, and consequently contribute to saving lives. I would like to see a world where we face each other to establish what is best for a patient and not for the coffers of one side or the other.

How long can this deception continue? Perhaps a long time, but the acceleration that took place in modern society bodes well for the unveiling of deception. The Internet could break down the big lie, and therefore also Big Mafia and Pharmacine.

Obviously, those who realize the deception will not have the power (nor the permission) to build clinics to treat themselves naturally. However, sometimes, destiny, Nature (for believers), or the Lord (for religious believers) could put a hand on it. After all, if it is true that in the end the good triumphs, so it will be. In fact, with the advent of the internet, it is relatively more difficult to hide, misdirect, misinform, because information and misinformation face themselves with the same means of information (i.e., the network). At the same time traditional means of information (radio, TV, and newspapers) are an absolute monopoly of Pharmacine.

However, the power of those who want to disinform is disproportionately greater, but this does not mean that it is disproportionately effective. Its current effectiveness is given by the fact that the majority of people still trust the established power (perhaps more the medical than the political power).

The last century saw the birth of the internet, the revolutionary new technology we are discovering, day after day, with its incredibly good and malicious potential. In fact, in just over twenty years, the internet has radically changed the way of thinking, of relating, of socializing, of self-education, of living, of publicizing, of committing crimes, etc.

Cyberspace has become a new dimension in which the physical world is replicated in good and evil: cyber criminals and cyber policemen, virtual bullies and virtual saints, etc. This means that we can hypothesize a real new environment of competition and information and/or disinformation. Before the advent of the internet, anyone suffering from a fatal disease could only contact the doctor or consult books and various libraries. Now one only needs *to Google* and the world opens up in front of you. Almost everything that has been produced in millennia of humanity is now available to everyone instantly. Of course, we must also know how to read it and how to deal with a great mass of information.

The internet could really be the novelty that will defeat the *big lie*, or it could be the one that will definitely validate it. However, distinguishing information from disinformation is not always simple and requires a thorough understanding of human dynamics. Nevertheless, this is an era where we can choose, more or less consciously, even with the help of the experience shared instantly by other people, not to accept what is imposed on us and to choose our path. If it is true that good finally triumphs, it will not be long before deception is revealed (however, manipulations of media is still a great wall to pull down).

In fact, similarly to what happens in a couple, as soon as the suspicion of deception insinuates itself, then everything changes. Be assured that if there is the awareness of the possibility of being deceived then, sooner or later, the deception will be unmasked by an ever-larger audience. The hoax about cancer, *the incurable disease*, therefore, will not last long.

It should also be said that if these diseases are not curable naturally, they will hardly be treated with chemotherapy. Surgery, on the other hand, is a different matter, but does not solve the problem of recurrences. According to Charlotte Gerson, almost all patients receive definitive cure at the Gerson clinic in Mexico. They also treat cancers that are defined as incurable or rarely curable by Pharmacine, i.e., pancreatic cancer (minus 55 of video[29]), liver cancer, and others, as well as treating the so-called autoimmune diseases defined as incurable by orthodox medicine (min. 43 of the video). The latter were in practice unknown before the implementation of vaccination.

But do not forget that, of course, Charlotte Gerson (daughter of Max) could be lying! This would certainly be the thesis of Pharmacine, while the members of Pharmacine would not have $10 trillion of reasons to lie. Gerson is probably the greatest doctor since Hippocrates but *illustrious* orthodox doctors allow themselves to judge his therapy, in violation of the Hippocrates oath, without even knowing what they are talking about and without even having tried it on themselves and/or on their patients

These luminaries send people home to die, saying that they are hopeless, even taking away the illusion of the cure while there is still a concrete hope of full cure of the disease, as Charlotte Gerson herself states in the afore mentioned video.

If you really think that Big Mafia would not do anything for $10 trillion, you're wrong. People's greed is usually limitless. In fact,

---

[29] https://www.youtube.com/watch?v=UL5qSegu2ds&t=46s

usually, the more money one owns the more he/she wants to get. Trump will be a good example of this theory. We will have proof of this in a few years time, watching his increase in capital.[30]

Fortunately, Charlotte does not need words, just look at her: born in 1922, she still goes around lecturing and spreading hope for those who have lost theirs and her image is worth a thousand words. It would take very little to see if the Gerson therapy (and many others) is effective but the Pharmainquisition will never grant it, even on trial. Who knows what went behind the scenes not to implement it at that time, why should they do it now?

Of course, it is not a 100% miraculous therapy, but it is, apparently, very close to it. What I find almost amusing, if not tragic, is the publication with great emphasis of the business that Big Mafia generates, almost as a reason of pride, instead of shame.

The hundreds of researchers, scholars, and willing people who are struggling to find new anti-cancer treatments have no hope of convincing the established order about the goodness of their treatments unless it is a chemical one. Not even if they produce all the possible evidence because Pharmacine institutions look only for the best way to oppose them. At best, the alternative remedies proposed by these unaware and courageous pioneers of medicine will only be ignored. In the worst case, they might occur in fatal accidents, like the great supporter of naturopathy, Max Gerson. If

---

[30] Just before the publishing of this volume, media spread the news that the highest budget since the Second World War was allocated by Trump for armaments, with a reduction of environmental and health expenditures. Do you think there could be the possibility that he is pursuing his own interests by favoring warlords for predictable reasons? Obviously, these weapons will also need to be used; otherwise the business is not optimal.

not so, they might be jailed or condemned by the established order and by the deceived public opinion, as were the witches in the old times.

The cures to overcome cancer pathologies have been existing for a long time, and are within reach of many, if not all, because they require very little money, but, unfortunately, sometimes a little more time (of course not all might get healed, but almost, apparently). In the average patient there is a sort of modesty or shame of the disease that prevents people from sharing and communicating, as well as *a dull faith in the authority that is the worst enemy of truth* as Einstein brilliantly affirmed.

Today people die in dignity, in silence, obviously treated with the only remedy accepted in institutional care where dying is normal. In fact, there is only one way of dying accepted by orthodox medical institutions, completely normal and that does not create any scandal: chemotherapy. Over eight million deaths a year worldwide are, in the vast majority of cases, treated with chemotherapy, but this is not outrageous.

It is not outrageous that 98%[31] of patients treated with chemotherapy (not associated with surgery) still die of cancer, and it is not outrageous that even those who are not treated in any way have three or four times more chances to save themselves than

---

[31] Clin Oncol (R Coll Radiol). 2004 Dec;16(8):549-60. The contribution of cytotoxic chemotherapy to 5-year survival in adult malignancies. Morgan G, Ward R, Barton M. http://www.mednat.org/cancro/chemio_nonrisolve.htm

those who are poisoned with chemotherapy.[32] But it is scandalous and provokes indignation that patients can be treated alternately and consciously decide to possibly die in a different way from that of chemotherapy death. Perhaps there are also those who would prefer scorpion-like death (scorpion venom),[33] less expensive for the coffers of the state (and citizens), and also more natural and less invasive.

To protect the interests of Big Mafia and Pharmacine (because Big Mafia will have to grease the members of Pharmacine abundantly), a very long string of professionals are brutally attacked by the press, fomented by the various institutions linked to Big Mafia and Pharmacine.

Anyone wishing to be treated with the Gerson method, Di Bella, Simoncini, Hamer, or anything else, can do it only by oneself without support and the assistance of a public structure. Essentially, most of the anticancer treatments that are alternative to pharmacological death are based on fundamental principles: the tumor establishes in an unbalanced body, depleted of nutritive principles, and/or in psychologically fragile subjects. In fact, more

---

[32] In 1975, prof. Hardin Jones, of the University of California, demonstrated for the first time, in a large-scale study lasting 23 years, that for those with cancer who have refused to undergo surgery, radiation, and chemotherapy (following free nutrition, without special diets) the average survival is 3-4 times higher, compared to those who have undergone standard medical treatments such as surgery, radio therapy and chemotherapy. [Walter Last, "The Ecologist," vol. 28, No 2, marzo/aprile 1998] Source:http://www.rethinkingcancer.org/resources/magazine-articles/2_1-2/cancer-cures-more-deadly-than-disease.php

[33] It is a treatment used in Cuba (because, fortunately for them, chemotherapy drugs have unsustainable costs). The treatment is effective for many types of cancer, so as to have activated a "medical tourism" to be treated with this method.

and more studies and research converge on the fact that the transformation of a healthy cell into a sick one can occur due to imbalances that allow pathogens/malevolent parasites to proliferate at the expense of good ones. The fact that remedies that fight them seem to have the effect it could be a demonstration of this theory.

Even in this case, only a few alternative, enlightened, scholars converge towards a more holistic treatment to contrast this deadly degeneration. In fact, usually a doctor or a scholar focuses almost exclusively on his method, just as it is right and logical. But let us wonder: what if the various methods experimented on in the last century and treated so far individually were instead put into a system? For example, using a Gerson-like basic therapy in conjunction with colloidal silver, Marie Cassie's ESSIAC, DMSO, Hamer therapy, potassium ascorbate or one of the many other therapies mentioned in this book, would the result be even greater than a single one.

Imagine if one could enter a health facility where he/she could be treated following the therapy developed by Breuss or the Gerson method and that this clinic was inclined to experiment other natural treatments in combination, such as the colloidal silver, the Colchino, the Laetrile (Amygdalin or vit. B17), or be treated with the Gemm of SecKiner Gòrgun, the phage therapy, the amazing Biotron of Albert, the Zapper, the Hamer method (if necessary), and so on and so forth. The demonstration of the logical bad faith within Pharmacine is that if such natural and alternative methods to the *chemical death* were essentially hoaxes perpetrated by charlatan doctors, then they would be easily unmasked if there was the possibility to document them according to the canons of Pharmacine. But such concessions have never been made, nor will ever be done because even doing nothing, as demonstrated by some

 MEDICINE AND PHARMACINE

scientific studies of the last century (previously mentioned), is more effective than chemotherapy. So, any attempt at experimentation would be tantamount to determining the end of Big Mafia and Pharmacine, together with 7 trillion dollars. In the majority of cases, chemotherapy only serves to lengthen our life for a few years to be able to tap more money, even with other unnecessary treatments. I would not like to be in the place of gullible doctors who trust Pharmacine, as they have responsibilities towards other souls and the oath the swore.

What would be more truthful, official, and scientific than hypothetical experimentation done in the same hospitals managed by Pharmacine following the Gerson therapy or similar one? Following this method, results could be published and visible to everybody, but are we sure that is something agreeable to Pharmacine? Perhaps the risk is exaggerated for the coffers of Big Mafia. Moreover, the scientific data on the effectiveness of the Gerson therapy (and also others) already exist, but they are not accepted. There is no deafness worse than that of a person who doesn't want to hear.

As evidence of what I state, with problems of blood values out of the norm for a hint of metabolic syndrome, in repeated periods of my life, I had triglyceride levels and cholesterol out of the norm (despite being vegetarian) and exactly about 300 (mg/dl) for triglycerides and 250 for cholesterol. Well, after only three weeks of a Gerson-like diet, the values were exactly halved.

Yet the doctors say that there is inheritance, predisposition, etc. This might also be true, but it does not mean they cannot be kept under control. Hereditary comes into play only when the levels of toxemia are so high that the body cannot do anything other than to manifest the disease, as Arnold Ehret and others have magnificently demonstrated.

So, I want to challenge you: if you have values out of the norm, try to do only three weeks, or even two, of a strict diet that includes only fruit and vegetables (even in juices, unless you suffer from diabetes) with a tablespoon of flaxseeds oil for lunch and dinner in the quantities that you like most. For example, for lunch and dinner you could eat Hippocratic soup,[34] adding salad, broccoli, aubergines, peppers, and courgettes in the quantities you like most. At the end of three weeks, check your blood values again; if they are not within the norm, I am ready to make public apologies.

All these characters who, according to Pharmacine, are charlatans should then be sent to court for a public trial, facing evidence and justifications. The same should be done for those who cause millions of deaths from tumors and other diseases in Pharmacine's hospitals.

Everyone should be free to take care of oneself as stated in many modern constitutions and be free of choosing the doctor and the therapy he/she likes most. So I do not see the controversy in the fact that people who treat themselves in natural ways die exactly as those who are treated with chemotherapy and other orthodox methods. Fortunately, however, the percentage of success of the firsts is, apparently, much higher than the latter. People choose a doctor according to their consciousness, and according to the law. The doctors are even trained in Pharmacine's schools but in *betraying*

---

[34] Leeks, potatoes, tomatoes, onions, celery, parsley.

their masters, they must pay the punishment. It was essentially Pharmacine's error that gave him/her a medical degree and raised a rebel doctor.

Fortunately, these *errors* are always more frequent though Pharmacine still tries to solve the problem, first warning the unfortunate dissident physician promoting only short suspensions, that may, eventually, get to the radiation if the subject insists and does not give up. For doctors living in the US, however, life is also at stake.

Many volunteer themselves to fight this war of information and fail to understand they are also sacrificial victims voluntarily offered to Pharmacine's devil. Many others, however, might be mercenaries hired by Pharmacine that use improper weapons, such as false pseudonyms in social networks, trying to influence or disorient those who do not have a clear idea. So be careful not to trust what you read on social media, unless you or other reliable participants know the topic personally, as there may be infiltrators paid specifically to throw you off.

Today they try to change the opinions of people for a specific reason, often selfish, and/or for a personal benefit: that is, the desire to be elected, to grab a customer, or obtain the purchase of a product, the war that one wants to fight at all costs, etc. Thus, these theories about hired social influencer, which to some less world-wise would seem fanciful, would already be more than real and certainly are already used at least in the field of politics.

History shows that the first science fiction writings were, by far, outdated by reality. *1984* by George Orwell does not appear anymore as pure science fiction but as a science almost entirely realized. The existence of extraterrestrial life is now taken, logically, for granted by an increasingly large audience and the governments evil deception about its existence is going to be unveiled soon.

After this brief digression, let me say that the only positive results obtainable from orthodox medicine are surgery, which however, in the case of tumors, does not eliminate the cause of the evil that could recur (as often happens), and, partially, antibiotics and antihypertensive drugs (for those who do not want give up salt).

From the medical statistics, we can monitor the cases treated and the deaths toll. However, few say, perhaps unconsciously, how many of the cancer patients treated then die of natural death and not of a recurrence that, with the chemotherapy alone, is almost certain.

Instead, as previously mentioned, the cases taken care of by Gerson and other doctors who adopt the Gerson-like method, if they do not die because the tumor was far too advanced or was one of the few for which the natural cure was not feasible, they heal without traumatic interventions. As a matter of fact, it would appear that in almost all cases treated naturally, the person dies of other death different from cancer and not from a recurrence.

The sites of the deceivers can effectively misinform, but rarely manage to create a network of experiences that spread in blogs, as it happens for the sites of the deceived. All over the chemotherapeutic world, happens that *all* those doctors or personages who go against Pharmacine are passed through the Pharmainquisition without even bothering to verify if that specific therapy is valid or brings some benefit. Pharmacine's sentence is only one: *there is no other cure than chemotherapy*. It is helped in spreading the propaganda by the, often guilty, mass-media owned by the influencing people

Watching the shows on TV and how they are usually anchored, I am almost certain that we do not assist at an unbiased confrontation. In fact, usually, the mass-media belong to the world's VIPs who have strict connection one each other. The dark powers of evil origins are in all those fields where money and power is involved. It would not be possible otherwise for them to be so blind. Journalists are men and must also obey to the owners who are usually also masters of the world. As a matter of fact, today's medicine is the unique prerogative of Pharmacine. Therefore, its strategy is indeed successful since it dumps to the natural cures the patients no longer treatable with its methods. However, even under these extreme conditions, many are saved. In this way, they could then condemn the natural therapies when they fail, using the *scientific/non-scientific* hoax, acting as *sons of Pharmacine*! This strategy is comparable to the one used by political opponents when they want to get consensus.

Most people are confused by this ping-pong between *supposedly good* and *supposedly evil* and they are fooled by what they watch and believe to be true. Even famous TV shows are affected by this media ping-pong, which is often (certainly in the case of medicine) one sided.

I wonder: is it simply possible that so many journalists are so blind? ... Or is it valid as stated by Mark Twain? "The journalist is the one who distinguishes the true from the false ... and publishes the false."

The public audience who often experience these types of scandals are indignant when they hear about a doctor suspended or investigated by the respective medical boards for this or that *supposed* crime. But will it really be like that? Or it is a process that is always similar: first the news of miraculous cure (non-pharmaceutical) comes out, then the curiosity with dangerous insinuations of possible success, after the doubt and then again the inevitable condemnation, ALWAYS, of the Pharmainquisition.

I wonder often why those responsible for millions of murders caused by chemotherapy and other treatments authorized by official medicine are not charged or expelled by the medical boards. Incidentally, only those who propose unorthodox remedies (which rarely do new damage and which in the worst case are not very effective, however less and less than chemo) undergo this type of treatment. I will let you, dear readers, find out the answer. Now the Pharmainquisition is focusing on anti-vaccine doctors, even promoting immediate radiation. Big Mafia does not renounce to anything, even just a hundred miserable billions of dollars.

Always following the theory related to my logific *method* (which, I repeat, can be assimilated to an exact science, if well interpreted) can explain a lot, if not all. For example, for what bizarre reason so many doctors who have spent a lifetime of studies and personal sacrifices should throw them away, along with their reputation, and often their social life, to support something absurd and far-fetched? Why should a reputed doctor suddenly become a trickster? (see Bradstreet, Wakefield, Simoncini, etc.).

Of course, there might be individual cases of some professionals who want to get suddenly rich or who, more or less quickly, go crazy. But fortunately, those are rare exceptions, easily detectable. It must be said, however, that these holistic doctors must necessarily experiment on people, as should do, and do, those of Pharmacine. That is the real essence of medicine itself. The only difference is that the doctors belonging to Pharmacine do it exclusively to sell Big Mafia products. Instead, Gerson has experimented a lot, first on himself and then on the other patients. This is the true spirit of a juror of Hippocrates, not to sell drugs to replenish the already huge Big Mafia's lockbox.

More easily, these so-called charlatans would make unnecessary or unethical surgery operations or sponsor very expensive treatments. Certainly with these preaches they would not get rich. In fact, sodium carbonate, cabbage, and herbs are available to everyone, unlike chemotherapy. So, would it be plausible that the continually repeated mantra *the only valid therapy to fight cancer is chemotherapy* would be similar to a big lie, repeated often, as taught by a great liar and evil character in history.

Should I become known and my work reach notoriety, they would certainly try to find a connection of some kind with some holistic doctors (which does not exist at all, at the moment) to try to apply the Pharmainquisition on me.

It should also be said, to be fair, that unfortunately the scoundrels and the profiteers dive where they smell the scent of money and therefore also natural cures abound of real charlatans who are ready to sell remedies or miraculous books at totally inconsiderate prices. Evidently these people do not have a natural conscience. Beware of them.

In some countries, there is already a large group of fake doctors without the necessary academic qualifications, who cheat many people with their hoaxes. But why, logically, a respected oncologist should invent the theory about sodium carbonate and plot the death of his patients, or advertise healing herbs that kill the patients, at least more than chemotherapy? In any case, he could ask for an honorable parcel without having to invent the story of sodium carbonate or other unusual cures. Could it perhaps be that they have a conscience? However, it would also be plausible that among many trained doctors there might be some single, rare and isolated case of real charlatanism. However, on my opinion, charlatanism is more widely spread within the realm of Pharmacine. In fact, it happens not so seldom that doctors make unnecessary surgical operations or do other acts against their hoax.

I do not know Dr. Simoncini personally. I do not know if he is guilty of being a compulsive sodium carbonate diffuser or if maybe he owns a sodium carbonate factory but certainly logic tells me that it is suspicious that all those who theorize, study, and implement (either being doctors or not) cures distant from the pharmacology ones are discredited, annihilated, and put to the public stake. Besides, as often happens, it is not even the first to theorize about bicarbonate, in that case of potassium (or better potassium ascorbate), theorized and documented by Valsè Pantellini[35] in the second part of the last century with results that would seem to be absolutely effective.

In fact, systematically, each of these non-aligned physicians passes under the cleaver of the board of the national doctors (or FDA, if the case). In fact, national board of doctors resembles modern court of the Inquisition where those who have the misfortune to stumble are first sentenced by the Pharmainquisition and then passed to the *media pillory* and, sometimes, the *media burning*.

---

[35] See chapter The Forbidden Cures

Moreover, even to the most bigoted of doctors should raise the doubt that perhaps such treatments could be effective, if not for all types of cancer, at least for some. In fact, if so many treatments that kill parasites (worms), fungi, bacteria and viruses have success on tumors will want to say something (and maybe not that they are all charlatans!) It is documented, for those who want to see, that there have been successful cases with the following treatments that are also antiseptic: sodium bicarbonate, potassium ascorbate, colloidal silver, DMSO and MSM, ESSIAC, Hoxsey herbs, scorpion venom, the Zapper by Hulda Clark, etc. However, I will never repeat enough that Gerson and Breuss (for minor cancers) therapies are those that give more chances of success.

Moreover, Pharmacine will never find a remedy against tumors because there is no chemical, aggressive, poisonous, and unnatural remedy to counteract them. The only remedy is the natural way and has existed since it was rediscovered and perfected—after Hippocrates and Paracelsus—almost a century ago, by Gerson.

Hippocrates, more than two millennia earlier, had already discovered that man can be treated effectively through food. Gerson has only perfected a method, and many after him try, sometimes succeeding, to implement it furthermore.

This topic is so vast and complex that it would require a book just to describe these cures and this is not the purpose of this volume.

Cancer... An Ever-Increasing Business

> *Cancer is not cured with the surgeon's iron but with the vegetarian diet and the medical herbs.*
>
> HIPPOCRATES

A single cycle of chemotherapy costs tens of thousands of dollars either paid by insurances, governments, or private citizens.

I have always wondered why there was so much fury against those who offer legitimate care but who deviate from the official medicine and pharmacology. I often ask myself if today we can still choose how to die. Those who are affected by cancer pathology at the moment have three choices: either get cured/die with orthodox medicine, die without any care waiting for their end (which may be late or not arrive as expected), or independently try to self-heal, which appear as being pretty easy certainly for non-advanced pathologies according to Gerson, Breuss, and other doctor's experiences, but also for advanced one following the Gerson cure. However, it must be said, that for those who are already in critical health conditions, this option might be somehow challenging, if not supported by family.

The average citizen could not afford weeks or months of Gerson or Gerson-like therapy in a private facility. He/she should therefore undertake a path of solitude with the total or partial distrust of those close to him/her overcoming technical and logistical significant difficulties. In fact, the procurement and treatment of food (large amounts of organic juices) and the frequent coffee enemas (absolutely necessary) would not allow the patient to take care of himself. He/she would need at least one person completely dedicated to him/her, making it complex for most of the people this type of therapy (personally experienced, and considered absolutely effective). However, one could, in full autonomy, adopt simple precautions such as those that I will describe in the course of the book (potassium ascorbate, apple vinegar, ESSIAC, COD Tea, aloe of Father Zago, Zapper, and liverwashing by Hulda Clark or, even better, try the relatively short Breuss therapy etc.).

I have always wondered: why is it not possible for a cancer patient to be cured or die on their own terms? The media have great power. They have the power to make a single case appear as a multitude of cases. On the other hand, they can hide thousands and thousands of deaths that occur daily in hospitals around the world, making them pass as ordinary administration or as *things in life* (as the previously mentioned disinformation case about Chavez shows). But be careful not to cure yourself and, above all, not to die with other treatments, otherwise an endless media ruckus will be unleashed.

This practice is comparable to the millions of deaths that occur around the world in wars and barbarities of any kind that do not belong to us and, since we do not talk about it, they do not seem to exist. While, in the homeland, any death seems to matter. In my eyes no death is justifiable or simply understandable, but not even that of thousands and thousands of Africans who die drowning in the sea trying to reach a *better world* or bombed Syrians or Iraqis leaping into the air. A human being is a human being wherever he lives and life should have the same value for everyone. Unfortunately, it does not seem so.

There are very few alternative holistic structures around the world. As far as I know, there is a well-established Gerson hospital in Mexico, a minor Gerson clinic in Hungary, and an orthodox hospital with natural openings in Berlin that also combines chemotherapy with natural therapies (as probable compensation to be paid to Big Mafia in order not to suffer attacks). For the latter German structure, it would be interesting to see the epilogue of a clash between *Medicine* and *Pharmacine*. Who would win? Imagine: a billion-dollar giant against Charlotte Gerson. I laugh just thinking about it! No wonder that the Gerson clinic had to be exiled to Mexico. The positive side is that Charlotte is still alive and approaching her hundredth birthday.

Unfortunately, I fear that Pharmacine is still too powerful and the weapons used for the struggle are still disproportionate. As long as the awareness of the deception will not spread among the people but also, and above all, among the doctors themselves, then the fight will be unequal. We will continue to witness these media battles leaving Big Mafia to watch the bitter fight while Pharmacine enjoys, having profit, ready to intervene in favor of its members, should it be necessary. In all this, millions of people keep unnecessarily losing their lives.

Moreover, this orthodox/unorthodox association that is still being tested in Germany would, most probably, allow the great lie to come out stronger. In fact, the successes of the treatments would certainly be attributed to chemotherapy while the alternative therapies would only go with, providing a note of sympathy to what certainly is not pleasant. It is, however, difficult to understand how it would be possible to associate the devil and the holy water. Can both things live together?

    Cancer... An Ever-Increasing Business

Not according to Gerson. In fact, he said that the natural way is incompatible with the artificial way. According to Gerson, who had already undergone chemotherapy and decided to take the therapy developed by him, a patient will have fewer benefits and should first detoxify from the same chemotherapeutic care. However, never say never. Better the devil and the holy water in conjunction than only the devil. If this was the price to pay so that we can recover from tumors, then *welcome evil!*

It must be stressed, however, that physician are grown in Pharmacine medical universities, so, most of them might be heavily conditioned and it will be very difficult for some to get rid of this kind of brainwashing.

I am certain that most of the readers will have mourned someone with cancer who was treated with chemotherapy that did not work and was denied even a dignified death. Were they accidentally investigated by Pharmacine and the Pharmainquisition (national boards)? No, everything is in the normal logic of life: at life follows death. You might have been answered: *we have tried the impossible* (false, because the impossible is Gerson or others) or *we have tried everything* and then ... The unwary doctor will really be sorry and heartbroken but the members of Pharmacine will rub their hands, smelling the money. In fact, the longer the cure the more revenue will be made. But when the possible and the impossible are tried by somebody not associated to Pharmacine, then, it is the end of the world. It is an effective strategy. Those who control the media have the power to make us believe what they want, at least until the people do not realize that they are just an instrument.

To make this colossal deception perceptible, I have to push myself into a field that I will deal with in another volume, the energy one. Imagine a world without oil and with means of transport that only run on water. I think the reader would feel pleasure and satisfaction. Maybe you are wondering who could not want the good of all humanity, free energy for all and more without pollution, and even with economic savings?

Now try to put yourself in the shoes of an oilman or of a company that treats profits as the only reason for living. You will realize how the perspective changes radically and how a beautiful dream turns into a terrible nightmare. Even the States would have to lose the conspicuous fuel taxes. Just try to imagine the desperation resulting from the cessation of the use of oil that would fall on these people.[36]

In the same way, try to imagine if suddenly we find out that potassium ascorbate, colloidal silver, DMSO, or more simply the Gerson, Breuss, and other therapies actually heal the tumor pathologies. What would happen to about seven trillion dollars (about China's GDP) of cancer treatment?

This eventuality would, in all likelihood, cause the failure of many pharmaceutical companies that have made chemotherapy and cancer drugs their primary source of income. Many thousands of jobs would be lost and we would probably devolve into global turmoil. Imagine if China declared default or, even worse, the United States[37]. What would happen to the world economy? If it happened in a small/medium state, it would be an absorbable

---

[36] It has been realizable since ages with hydrogen (Brown's gas, Joe Cell and Stanley Mayer's water fuel cell).

[37] The international debt is a sand castle that will, sooner or later, definitely fall.

  Cancer... An Ever-Increasing Business

trauma but if it happened to a superpower, it would leave an indelible scar in the world, probably causing a revolutionary situation like the disappearance of money. So, if the possibility of such an unlikely hypothesis should be highlighted, we must make sure that this happens very gradually through a happy decrease or simply let it happen and see where the chips fall. However, at the moment, millions of people cannot avoid being *killed by cancer* because otherwise there would be a global pharmaceutical bankruptcy. That could not be acceptable, but, on the other hand, neither is the alleged deception and criminal activity adopted to cover this cruel business that will soon end with the rest of the devil's activities.

Every greedy and selfish person is willing to make false documents to maintain the social and economic power achieved. Probably, some are even willing to commit homicides ... oops incidents or unexplained/casual deaths. But these are only, in some cases, logifical evidence. Of course, it was a logifical evidence, which later became certainty, that Max Gerson could have been murdered.[38]

However, logifically, without wishing to bother the FBI or Interpol, the mere fact that people who support uncomfortable truths die prematurely more than other subjects of the same age, sex, and social conditions seems to be a logifical evidence. Charlotte Gerson documented his father killing with the poison by doing the

---

[38] http://www.doctoryourself.com/charlotte.html

autopsy. Unfortunately for many other cases, including Stanley Meyer (hydrogen), such information is not available.

Today conspiracy is something not seriously considered. As the FBI founder, J. Edgar Hoover, might have said about communism: "The individual is handicapped by coming face-to-face with a conspiracy so monstrous he cannot believe it exists. The American mind simply has not come to a realization of the evil which has been introduced into our midst. It rejects even the assumption that human creatures could espouse a philosophy which must ultimately destroy all that is good and decent.[39]" Probably Hoover had more than an idea about conspiracy, having been the creator and long-time director of the FBI. After all, what do you think they thought of Hitler and the concentration camps before their existence was discovered? And of mass genocide? No, it's not possible...

Do you really believe there is no conspiracy behind the pharmaceutical business? These words also comfort me because, although I have not seen with my own eyes what is behind it, I am supported by unequivocal logific proofs of conspiracy. So, the idea that made me compare Pharmacine to Hitler and Nazism is now less and less absurd and, unfortunately, much closer to a possible reality.

The extreme practices put in place by Pharmacine (especially Big Mafia) seemed to have become obsolete and overcome by the

---

[39] https://www.metabunk.org/debunked-a-conspiracy-so-monstrous-he-cannot-believe-it-exists-hoover.t330/

media demolition and the subsequent social annihilation that happens to the awkward characters. Unfortunately, it appears that they have had an unprecedented resurgence. From 2015 in the United States, there has been a generalized death epidemic of holistic doctors apparently attributable to suicides and strange incidents (including death by dehydration). This is worrying, but also encouraging, because it would mean that Pharmacine might start having difficulty controlling this epidemic of non-aligned doctors in other ways. We just have to thank these missionaries and martyrs of true medicine for their sacrifice.

It would seem, however, to have consolidated the method of giving to the public opinion all those who sustain uncomfortable truths, thus obtaining mass-media resonance. In fact, the chronicles are dotted with episodes where the Pharmainquisition has started the witch hunting season through its modern tribunals: the medical boards.

It is also quite bizarre that these accidents/suicides occur almost exclusively in the United States. It would seem, in fact, that the American approach is based more on a far-west style and that there would be fewer scruples in physically eliminating the uncomfortable subjects. In Europe, instead, the legal factor is preferred (inquisition, trials and, if necessary, incarceration - Hamer, Simoncini, Wakefield, etc.) in harmony between States that does not fear borders, demonstrating that Pharmacine is a globalized entity.

The case of Bradstreet (the doctor died for the vaccine/autism association) shows that when you insist on wanting to fight Pharmacine at all costs, then you risk your life.

Enlightening, in this regard, is the 2015 film, *Concussion*, based on a true story, with Will Smith, which deals with a brilliant pathologist who makes an exceptional discovery by attributing psychiatric crises in American football players to the traumas suffered during their sporting life.

Well, after the initial euphoria, shared by those who still believe in the real Medicine, there has been an oppression to the limits of tolerance with the intrusion of FBI and other actors that should not normally appear in such situations. In this case, thanks to a dramatic epilogue (a former player wrote in his will that he wanted his brain to be dissected), the end was not too dramatic as the doctor was voluntarily exiled. This is a relatively happy ending, but be sure that usually does not end this way, but the way it ended the Bradstreet event, found dead in a river with a shot in the chest (if you really want to understand how Pharmainquisition works, watch it).

This is what happens to those who clash against Pharmacine, either absent-mindedly undergoing some imaginative accident (from the clash with a criminal, to the road accident, to the heart attack, to suicide - perhaps the most popular) or being socially annihilated. All in all, this story had a happy ending but it is not usually so and accidents cannot be documented, because there are, as a rule, no witnesses.

Some of these brave pioneers died to defend their ideas and for the good of their neighbor, simply because they dared too much. Their studies and their convictions were too bothersome. All those who support uncomfortable truths sooner or later, especially when they become known, are hampered in all ways by the pharmacological power. Often, if they do not die prematurely in unclear circumstances, they are declared as charlatans by the mass media to the public.

     Cancer... An Ever-Increasing Business

A few years ago, I naively thought that an alternative energy did not exist and that everyone would be happy to travel by putting only water in the tank (without polluting, with great economic savings). Therefore, the fact that *apparently* we have not found an alternative energy source should have been just a technological problem. Probably 99.9% of the people would be happy about clean and free energy, but not the powerful people who own the world. They probably or never have heard the phrase: *God blesses those who are poor and realize their need for him, for the Kingdom of Heaven is theirs*, or, more likely, they cannot even imagine a kingdom of heaven.

In the same way, in the medical field, the vast majority of the world's population would have low-cost medicines/remedies available to everyone. Instead, poisons such as chemotherapy, which further damage the patient's condition, are sold at disproportionate prices with huge revenues.

These revenues occur on the skin of unsuspecting and confident patients and doctors, also passing the subtle message of favoring only the patient. Pharmacine does not care when someone dies (on average about 10 to 30 times[40] more than patients treated with natural cures) with these poisons, which are even worse than doing nothing, as already shown before.

Chemotherapy could prove to be one of the biggest lie in the history of mankind, even bigger than those pronounced by Hitler. It would be probably second only to the one of extraterrestrial presence on earth that, if undisclosed, would

---

[40] http://stopalcancro.blogspot.it/2011/10/il-potere-della-natura.html)

determine the end of satanic activities directed by the devil trough financial institutions that control global politics, pharmaceutical industries, energy institutions, lord's war, etc.

Many people, including the writer, trusted the established medical powers, only to then to become suspicious. The very fact that the former FDA Commissioner, Dr. Herbert L. Ley, said: "The thing that bugs me is that the people think the FDA is protecting them - it isn't. What the FDA is doing and what the public thinks it's doing are as different as night and day," denotes that it is difficult to suppress remorse in those with a minimum of conscience and who knows what's behind it.

However, I also realize that some unsuspecting, gullible doctors, not inclined to the medical vocation and the oath of Hippocrates and/or completely immersed in the big lie, can bite to this farce of modern medicine, or rather of modern Pharmacine. They then abdicate to the true function of the doctor, they trust what they are told and, often, imposed by their masters clearly violating Hippocrates oath.

Orthodox doctors tell you not to consult the internet because it is misleading. I tell you the opposite; do not consult orthodox doctors because they are the servants of one master, Big Mafia, and report only what they were taught in Pharmacine's schools. If you suffer from cancer or a serious illness and want to stay alive for a long time, I recommend you not consult orthodox doctors but to rely on your skills and those of real doctors, as reported in this volume. The economic interests are too important for them to care about your soul. Chemotherapy is *the business.*

In modern medicine, only a little vocational attitude is left, except in rare cases, and in those medical disciplines that do not give too much trouble to Pharmacine.

The very fact of being raised and educated, as doctors, in the institutions of Big Mafia changes the mind and the reasoning of most learners who become their followers and are no longer, therefore, *independent* and without even realizing it. I myself have had the opportunity to debate with young doctors about unorthodox practices and the most common feeling is that of mistrust and not wanting to even hear about it without even wanting to refute the data collected and the available evidence.

I remember once talking to a young family doctor about colloidal silver. His first reaction was looking smugly at me and saying immediately that it was toxic, because it was a metal. He then ridiculed this remedy without even wanting to deepen, repeating, like an automaton, Pharmacine's mantra: *it is not scientifically proven.* On another occasion, I talked to a nutritionist about Ehret and his mucusless diet. Guess what she replied? "I have read about it but... *there is no scientific evidence*". I cannot believe it! It's like a format instilled in their brain. Now I realize how brain washing works.

In my opinion, medicine should always be holistic (not excluding *a priori* the pharmacy that, in some cases, might provide important aid), adopting for each individual case what is best for the patient. Therefore, for some pathologies and for certain types of subjects, the most appropriate therapies for that person and that spirit should be used. Acupuncture in one case, in another the Ayurvedic medicine or traditional Chinese medicine, homeopathy, herbal medicine, psychotherapy, naturopathy, or whatever is best for him/her. Except then use allopathic medicine or modern surgery where necessary or, again, a mixture of the medical arts known in a synergy that can only favor the condition of the patient leaving aside unnecessary sectarianism (mainly dictated by profit), where at the base of everything stood the studies of Gerson, our modern Hippocrates.

To do this, it would be necessary for the *new doctors* to be trained by having a basic knowledge of all types of existing treatments and then specializing in one or more of those methods.

The current trend is instead to boycott any possible new or old natural remedy. They do this through the *unscientific* (non patentable) hoax, not testing (therefore never making it scientific) them. When tested privately by willing and courageous doctors, they discredit the results because, in fact, *not scientific* (since not approved and carried out by Pharmacine's official medicine). So the studies, lasting decades, carried out by Gerson and other enlightened doctors would be thrown away, because not scientific, negligible, useless and, I would add, annoying.

It is evident, in fact, as a doctor who departs from the stereotypes of the doctors associated to Pharmacine faces, generally, a not happy ending. Doctors of disciplines belonging to other cultures, such as acupuncture, Chinese medicine, Ayurvedic medicine, etc., are perhaps more tolerated, but not those that can undermine Big Mafia's income. However, if one was to find out that acupuncture or homeopathy can cure tumors, then he/she would most likely see an acrimonious contrast from Pharmacine that would trigger Pharmainquisition even for these disciplines.

I am more convinced that in the contemporary world, it is scientific all that can be patented and sold, possibly at a high price, and that it is, instead, *not scientifically proven* all that does not bring an income and for which there is no commercial interest that can be patented.

In the Amazon, which we are destroying, there are thousands of plants only partly known or perhaps still to be discovered that could greatly improve our health. It is said that Graviola (Annona Muricata) was tested as an antitumor in the 1970s by a pharmaceutical company but then abandoned because accessible and exploitable by everybody. Graviola is a vitamin bomb, so this would prove that the theories and studies of Gerson, Pauling, Rath and other are not science fiction.

I am so critical about Pharmacine, I have often asked myself if it were not just cultural and egoic bigotry and not a Hitler-style killing conspiracy aimed at the wealth of those who plot. Big Mafia may decide not to interfere in natural cures, but only for treatments that are ineffective and do not disturb its business. It is instead furious with those that undermine its interests. I have come to the point of thinking that the more an unorthodox therapy, and the doctor who proposes it, is hindered and attacked, the more effective the cure is and the doctor himself, competent.

Gerson, who died for this reason, would have rediscovered (incidentally, as the most important discoveries usually happen) and implemented the greatest cure against cancer and most of the known and not yet known diseases of the human being. Even Bradstreet may have discovered something really effective with his GcMAF. However, Gerson is not the first to hypothesize and scientifically prove that nutrition can be a source of cure. In fact, Hippocrates said: "Let food be thy medicine and medicine be thy food" and Paracelsus, after him, "The art of healing comes from nature, not from the physician."

As Rita Levi Montalcini says in a letter to her sister: "Cancer is not an illness but a rebellion of the cells." In fact, the cells rebel against all the abuses that we perpetrate against the human organism and especially the improper foods, acidity, salt, and the functions of the psyche that influence the functioning of the human body. For this reason, the bicarbonate theories are not funny or ridiculous theories at all, nor is it the Gerson theory, who should be awarded the Nobel Prize, post mortem, for medicine, if we lived in a just world.

Also Hulda Regehr-Clark would have deserved this award for the invention of his Zapper but, of course, the Nobel Prize is easier to assign to those who discover an often useless new chemical molecule and not to the real pillars of Medicine.

The danger of salt is certainly underestimated. In fact, salt is not the one and only cause of hypertension, as demonstrated scientifically by Gerson. In fact, it is also the principal defendant for the onset of the mutation of cancer cells that see their sodium/potassium equilibrium unbalanced. From this derives the efficacy of the Pantellini remedy which helps to restore, besides the acid/base ratio, the sodium/potassium cell balance. It is not by chance that Gerson introduced a potassium solution in his therapy. As I will state often in this book, if you really cannot avoid table salt, use at least natural integral salt (Himalaya, Atlantic, etc.).

The Forbidden Cures

This chapter is mostly taken from the release Andromeda 49/1998[41] (published in Italian language) and other major websites related to natural cures. I address to these players my personal praise for the work done in the disclosure of the hidden truths and my gratitude for the effort to unveil the big lie.

I decided to include this chapter because I think it is an excellent way to remember those who dedicate/dedicated or who offered their lives in the quest for truth and the good of their neighbor. Another reason is to avoid scholars of the specific subject to repeat studies already carried out from others. Unfortunately, the efforts of these *infidels* have been thwarted, for the most part, by the fierce opposition of Pharmacine which by all means, lawful and illicit, has been hindering their implementation on a large scale.

This chapter can also be a reference for those who are disgusted by Pharmacine's behavior, like me, and who would prefer to give up one's own life rather than enter a place of degradation run by Pharmacine, with the certainty of receiving not medical

---

[41] http://www.edizioniandromeda.com/media/2/32.pdf

treatments but pharmacological ones. However, I want to point out that not all the treatments listed are, or have been, hampered by Pharmacine. The degree of opposition probably depends on their effectiveness: the more effective they are, the more they are hampered.

Unfortunately, it is not possible to know if, among all the names present, there is also some true charlatan, but the experience teaches me that if these characters have been persecuted by the Pharmainquisition, it means that there is some good in them. In fact, Pharmacine pursues the good ones, leaving undisturbed the real charlatans, those with neither art nor part, without titles and ready to escape as soon as discovered.

Out of curiosity, try typing *forbidden therapies* on YouTube and you will see what comes out. This testifies that the big lie falters, perhaps as never has faltered so far. The advent of the internet could be the novelty that will give the final push, if Pharmacine does not invent some stratagem before it happens.

ALBERT - Biohelp or Biotron (90s)

The pseudonym used is *probably* related to Alberto Mondini (died in 2015). He was persecuted as others like him were. Albert is/was an Italian engineer inventor of the Biohelp (also called Biotron, from the producer's name), a device as big as a pack of cigarettes that would send electromagnetic messages to the tissues allowing them to rebuild themselves in a normal way and thus eliminating cancer cells, probably fighting pathogens. His reports on the clinical cases and his scientific communications were constantly ignored. A dossier about him was published by the Italian ARPC Association (Association for Research and Prevention of Cancer).

Albert's Biotron is probably one of the best devices to fight cancer. It must be somehow similar to the Hulda Clark's Zapper and Görgün's Gemm. Unfortunately, only the Zapper is easily obtainable on the internet. The other two devices are difficult to find.

ALESSIANI Aldo (1925-1999) - Water (90s)

This is a Roman doctor who would have developed an anticancer treatment based on a natural product at no cost called precisely Alessiani Water. It seems that he reported the positive results to the Italian health minister of the time and that he was then contacted on 29 July 1993 by the office of the Public Prosecutor of Rome who made him understand that continuing on that path could end badly. His hypothesis, formulated as early as 1981, is based on the consideration of cancer as a deficiency disease and that its incidence goes hand in hand with the increase in the average height of the population. In its water are dissolved soils rich in natural substances that we no longer take through food. A dossier about him was published by the Italian ARPC Association (Association for Research and Prevention of Cancer).

Also this experience is the proof and the demonstration that we are facing a cartel headed by Big Mafia branched all over the world and with invisible but strong and persistent connections. It also demonstrates that the theories related to vitamin deficiency (related to impoverishment of human diet also because of the use of chemicals in agriculture) are not so weird.

ARMSTRONG John W. (1886-1968) – Urinotherapy (40s)

He is a doctor who, together with other innumerable therapists, collected a long series of cases with an ancient system: urinotherapy. It is a therapy based on the assumption, internal and external, of your own urine. He has written the book *The Water of Life: A Treatise on Urine Therapy*. In recent years, many other books have been published on the subject.

I suppose that in this case, the urine has the function of a sort of vaccine that immunizes us from our own illnesses present at the time of the assumption. Yet the theory is similar to the natural practice of organic composting. Fallen leaves, when dug back into the soil, provide valuable mineral salts to nourish new plant life. The same principle holds true for the human body.

There is also a similar theory with homeopathy where you take a teaspoon of urine and pour into a small bottle of 0.5 l, then fill it halfway, rinse it and throw it away, repeating the procedure three times, and then you drink in homeopathic quantity.

BARONI Father Vittorio (1911-1990) - Phytoradiesthesia (90s)

He was a priest who would have worked for many years through phytotherapy and radiesthesia applied to the diagnostic investigation. It is said he has achieved important results by discovering the still unknown properties of some plants. In concomitance, he would have developed a marked radiesthesic sensitivity that he exercised particularly in the diagnosis and treatment of the ills of the century and in particular of cancer. He wrote a book entitled *Dodici piante per i mali del secolo* (Twelve plants for the ills of the century) (not translated) in which he describes the therapeutic properties of laurel, burdock, cypress, madder, wormwood, periwinkle, calendula, boxwood, colchicum, thuja, navel of Venus, and juniper.

It is a very interesting treatment that is somehow similar to those of René Caisse, Hoxsey, and others.

BARTORELLI Alberto - Uk 101 (90s)

He is/was a doctor and a university professor who studied an anti-cancer product which gave the name of Uk 101. The Uk101 distinguished itself in scientific contexts in 1995 and can be ascribed to the category of immunotherapy. It is, in fact, a protein that counteracts the tumor pathology, with particularly positive results in breast and colon cancers. Obviously, this remedy was bitterly opposed. However, it was admitted to experimentation thanks to the involvement of an Italian Health Minister. On Wednesday, December 24, 1997, the editor of the newspaper *La Repubblica*,[42] speaking of the Di Bella case, states: "Thirty years ago another doctor, or rather a veterinarian, Liborio Bonifacio, noticed that the goats had no tumors and distributed widely his serum. To say that he was strongly opposed is a euphemism, but it is above all thanks to his intuitions that today there is the experimentation of the Uk101."

There were rumors that, after his meeting with the Minister, Bartorelli wanted to go abroad. As a matter of fact, this remedy is unknown to the public. Wonder why?

---

[42] A major Italian newspaper

BEARD John (1858-1924) - Enzymes (70s)

He is a doctor who first experienced cancer treatment by digestive enzymes. Kelley, an American non-medical therapist from the 1970s, promoted its use through a treatment based on massive doses of pancreatic enzymes that are (not by chance) still used in the Gerson therapy. Starting from these premises, Dr. Nicholas Gonzales, from New York, developed what he called individualized metabolic therapy, with which he obtained positive results. Other enzyme-based products used in cancer treatment are two German preparations: Carzodelan and Wobe-Mugos.

Gerson therapy uses pancreatin and daily supplements and vitamins such as Lugol (iodine), liver extract, potassium solution, niacin, vitamin B12, and others.

BENETTI Roberta (year 2010)

She is an Italian researcher who has discovered, together with colleagues from the University of Udine, some molecules that would block tumor proliferation. These molecules, attacking only the diseased cells, could represent a valid alternative to chemo and radiotherapy. The study was published in the journal *Cancer Research* by the American Association for Cancer Research. The question is: can it be patented? If so, we may have found the cure for cancer that is welcomed by Pharmacine. However, there are seven trillion dollars' worth of reasons that make me think that also this remedy will be boycotted.

BONIFACIO Liborio (1908-1983) – Bonifacio's Serum (1960s)

He was an Italian veterinary surgeon (1908-1983) who in 1950 devised an anticancer drug, obtained from goats' sigma colon. Initially, it was ignored by science and orthodox medicine, which looked at its discovery with disregard and suspicion. It looks like his remedy has treated thousands of sick people. His experience has been the subject of journalistic inquiries and scientific communications. Even the most skeptical had to admit that there was something precious in Bonifacio's serum. In 1970, the Italian Ministry of Health was finally forced to take into consideration the results obtained and experiment the serum. Because it probably undermined too many economic, scientific, and prestigious interests, the experiment was liquidated in 15 days. The outcome is therefore negative and a couple of people appear to have died after being given the drug. Bonifacio's cure is related to the UK 101 and the product of the oncologist Giuseppe Zora. Does it look like a Pharmainquisition operation?

I have the feeling of reading a book already written, always the same strategy repeated endlessly, and yet you still believe the hoax of the *non-scientifically proven? Do not trust! Experience!*

BRADLEY COLEY William (1862-1936) - (early 1900s)

He was a doctor considered to be the father of anti-tumor immunotherapy. For about 40 years, he used a cocktail of bacterial toxins (Serrata Marcescens and Streptococcus Pyogenes) in cancer therapy, obtaining remission in 45-50% of cases. These toxins caused a strong febrile reaction in patients, which stimulated the immune system. His therapy ended up (who knows why?) in oblivion and nobody uses it anymore.

BRADSTREET Jeff (1954-2015) – GcMAF

The GcMAF of Dr. Bradstreet probably cost him his life. Apparently, it is effective not only against autism but also against cancer. It would appear that the doctor's death was necessary to safeguard Pharmacine's business. In fact, if we could just get rid of cancer, $7 trillion would go up in smoke in an instant. Among other things, the GcMAF, produced by human blood from a British company, would not even seem a complicated product with derivations from vitamin D. It is incredible how everyone including the BBC so uniformly condemned products that do not come from Pharmacine and that go against its interests. It is always the same whole spiel: *it is not scientifically proven*, *the effects are not known*. Well, then let's experiment it scientifically and prove that it is really not effective! Remember, only you can save yourself.

BREUSS Rudolf (1899-1990)

In March 1990, at the ripe old age of 91, he published the incredible book *Krebs, Leukemie und andere scheinbar unheilbare Krankeiten mit naturlichen Mitteln heilbar* (translated in English as: *The Breuss cancer cure*). It is a fast-like therapy that includes the administration of a glass of vegetable juice cocktail to be drunk during the day. It includes, as well, administration of several herbal teas. It is said of having healed about 45,000 cancer patients (most of them reputed to be incurable by Pharmacine) since 1950. This theory is similar to that of Ehret (great character of real medicine) integrated with the juices of Gerson and the phytotherapy of others. It is exactly what I hypothesized before reading these theories that I fully agree with. This is the proof that almost everything is already written, but nobody wants to see and above all Pharmacine wants us to ignore it. Were I affected by cancer, this would be the first therapy I would try (as it is easy and short). I would then combine the Breuss system with the ESSIAC tea as it might be a tremendously effective combination. Branded ESSIAC or ESSIAC Formula products are relatively expensive but if you let your herbal shop assemble the herbs for you, it is certainly a cheap cure.

BUDWIG Johanna (1908-2003)

She was a German doctor who based her therapy on nutrition to restore the natural balance destroyed by toxic elements in the modern world. She paid particular attention to degenerative diseases and the perverse effects of fat metabolism. Precisely on the carcinogenic effects of fats she wrote an interesting text in 1959.

BURZYNSKI Stanislaw - Antineoplastons (90s)

He is a doctor who runs a clinic in Houston, Texas, which states that antineoplastons can normalize cancer cells. According to his statements, he would have helped many people affected by cancer to heal or get better. His theory is based on the belief that parallel to the known immune system, another biochemical system exists that is made up of substances that he calls antineoplastons, which would be able to reprogram cancer cells. Therefore, the cancer would be the simple consequence of an excess of these substances, and its remission would also manifest itself with a reduction of the rate of this secretion. As you can see, all theories converge somehow and somewhere (adding or removing something from the body — bicarbonate, vinegar, alkaline food, herbs, juices, salt, fast, etc.). If doctors like Simoncini, Burzynski himself, and others can raise some money with their method, they will probably do. Who wouldn't? (maybe Gerson). Anyway, they don't live on air; that is not a crime! (though price moderation is a good indicator to find a really caring doctor). All kinds of modern orthodox doctor do the same, and even worse, but they are not blamed for this.

BUZZI Silvio (1930-2009) - CRM197 Therapy (80s/90s)

He was an illustrious professor who died in 2009 who was completely ignored by the Italian health institutions and his research was obscenely boycotted and blocked by bureaucratic impediments, aimed at masking the strong interests of Pharmacine. He wrote a book titled *My anticancer toxin*, obviously also snubbed by Pharmacine. Above all, Pharmacine's business did not allow this therapy to be implemented.

CAISSE René (1888-1978) - ESSIAC (20s-60s)

René discovered in the Twenties an ancient herbal infusion used by the Ojibwa Indians (other names are Ojibway and Ojibwe) of Canada having heard about it, also by chance. ESSIAC is the surname of the Caisse on the contrary. Since then, hundreds of terminally ill cancer patients were successfully treated. Numerous books have been written on the subject. René had doctors and people on her side and for this reason intimidatory acts were necessary with the sending of ad hoc commissioners.

This story seems to me to be very clear of how the early Pharmainquisition worked. It has not changed much since those times, the methods used are still very similar. In fact, it is a nefarious example of how a meek person as René was persecuted by the

Pharmacine's inquisition perpetrated by evil people belonging to the system. As I said before, a clear example of how Pharmainquisition works comes from the film *Concussion* with Will Smith and the French film *150 milligrams*. It is unbelievable, how the Pharmainquisition can effectively be successful. The film was shown at the cinema only for a very short time and it is not so easy to buy the DVD or watch it on streaming. That is a demonstration of how censorship can still work very effectively in the 21st century. The producer should display it for free on YouTube with voluntary donations.

I highly recommend anyone to use the ESSIAC, consisting of: sorrel, inner husk, slimy elm, burdock roots and Indian rhubarb, both to prevent and to treat cancer and other diseases as there is clear evidence that it works.

CEVALLOS Edwin - BIRM

BIRM is an extract of the plant Solanaceae-Dulcamara discovered, researched and produced by dr. Cevallos and comes from Ecuador's folk remedies. There is some very convincing research that BIRM is an effective alternative Cancer treatment. This remedy goes on the strand that supports phytotherapy (Caisse, Hoxsey, Tamas, Breuss, and many many others).

DELBET Pierre (1861-1957) - Magnesium chloride (30s/40s)

He was a doctor and academic of France who discovered the properties and potentials of magnesium chloride, which until then was considered a waste product of salt. His studies are based on the assumption that magnesium deficiency in food can play a role in cancer development. His research, and those of his medical colleague, A. Neveu, are widespread and practiced all over the world. This theory, absolutely logical, is linked with the theories of Pantellini, Gerson, Pauling, Rath, and also with my own that sees induced vitamins and minerals deficiency as the main problem in modern society. In fact, I believe that the huge amount of refined salt used in modern society (that leaves only sodium taking away potassium, magnesium, and other minerals) might be an important co-cause of illnesses. Moreover, modern agriculture prevents the optimal variety and quantity of minerals in fruits and vegetables because of the use of chemicals. So, the arbitrary and artificial introduction of excessive sodium obtained through the refined salt present in almost every food, might seriously contribute to create an imbalance of the equilibrium of the four body electrolytes (sodium, potassium, magnesium, and calcium).

DEOTTO SALIMEI Mercedes

She is an ontogenetic dietician who bases his theory on a biological methodology based on the strengthening of the immune system through the practice of fasting and the administration of minerals, vegetal-minerals, vegetable, organic, and natural vitamins supplements according to specific detailed protocols for each type of tumor degeneration.

As you can see, theories are repeated because the cure is simpler than expected. Shelton was not able to cure the tumors only with fasting because the period of a fast is too short to allow complete regeneration. However, increasing this period with alternating short fast and super-feeding (mineral and vitamins) will shorten the healing times that could take more than a year for Gerson therapy and others. However, Breuss has shown that a fasting seed of forty-two days, supplemented with juices and decoctions can have, in many cases, tremendous efficacy, especially in less serious cases.

DI BELLA Luigi (1912-2003)

He was a doctor and a university professor. I think it is superfluous to describe his therapeutic protocol because it was already widely reported by the mass media at the time. Di Bella, despite the thousands of patients witnessing the positivity of his methods, was opposed by all means—moral, material, and physical—so much that he had to move, changing nations. His son, also a doctor, continues the work begun by his father in Argentina.

He too will one day be forgotten and his care accessible only to a few people. It is clear that the strategy of Pharmacine aims at this. It does not give publicity to the remedies that really cure, otherwise their business would fail. I purposely avoid using the term *alternative* because it is not an alternative to anything. Orthodox medicine does not cure cancer, at the most takes it away surgically, hoping it will not come back. Chemotherapy is essentially a justification for extorting money from the people and the States.

DIDO Emilio (1909-2000) - BORGHINI Francesco - Informed water

Their remedy uses solutions based on distilled water treated in order to receive specific electromagnetic frequencies of a tissue: those of the nervous system, the endocrine system, the immune system, and so on. While in the drugs energy is given by the drug molecule, in this case the energy is in the hydrogen ions of the water. The water is *informed* to achieve the goal that has been chosen.

EHRET Arnold (1866-1922) - Fasting and mucusless diet

He was a professor (not a physician) and proposed a series of short and reasonably balanced fasts, with his *Diet without mucus* stating that the mucus would be a substance totally unfamiliar to the human body. It would then be produced by unnatural food and should be expelled little by little. He also proposed a new physiology of the human body.

He seemed to have had a riding accident but there are rumors that he was killed because his method worked too well. Nowadays, something has survived in the United States, thanks to his disciples, who would create currents of thought inspired to him.

This theory also coincides with others (Breuss, Shelton and others) by finding a meeting point. In fact, fasting purifies and the diet without mucus is nothing but an alkaline diet, quite similar to that of Dr. Gerson. As you can see, everyone thinks they have discovered something new while, in most cases, all these methods are already known and the theories have been thoroughly tested.

He was dumped by the official medicine of his time because he was deemed not to have any hope of survival because of the bright disease. Despite his illness, he investigated the older naturopathy and the more recent one to completely restore his health. He then undertook several fasts and realized that his disease was improving rather than worsening. He later developed his mucusless diet studying the foods producing mucus until he found what he calls "the perfect health."

He made repeated demonstration fasts for forty-nine days. His writings are exciting. He disdained, understandably, orthodox medicine, similarly to other real Scientists of Medicine.

FANELLI Mirco - FUSI Vieri - Maltolo (anticancer molecule)

They are two precarious professors at the University of Urbino (ITA) who, in 2010, discovered the healing properties of some molecules deriving from the chemical modification of maltol. These molecules could be used for the development of new treatments for the inhibition of tumors. They are certainly not the first to have carried out studies on antitumor molecules. They are probably the last ones on the list of the ignored ones, and hopefully will not be persecuted by Pharmacine (as long as they will not become sufficiently known, they can sleep peacefully). Evidently, they also thought that there was not already a cure for tumors.

Of course, even these very recent studies are completely ignored by the *pharmacinated* institutions that have no reason to eradicate cancer as it is their primary source of income. The two poor researchers may have, by now, realized that they have no hope of convincing the pharmacinated institutions. I advise them to use crowd funding, internationally, always keeping in mind that cancer is an absolutely curable disease, through nature.

FERE Maud Tresillian (d. 1965) - (1960s)

She is a doctor from New Zealand who in 1963 wrote the book, *Cancer, its dietetic cause and cure,* explaining the biochemical causes of cancer and its formation in the body. She developed the theory that all the cellular forms of our body have their own center in the brain.

Then, the cells overstimulated by alkaline irritants send the message back to the cells to quickly multiplying at extreme speed.

In this way, any cell of any part of the body can be struck, adopting an abnormal growth mode and give rise to the formation of tumors. She considered cancer as a constitutional disease, like a rheumatism or a simple cold.

It is therefore difficult to hope for a definitive cure through the eradication of tumors, or by destroying them with radio or X-rays. The treatment of Dr. Fere is based on the firm belief that cancer is almost always due to an excess of sodium, combined to a weak state of health caused by non-compliance with the laws of health.

GERSON Max (1881-1959)

He is a doctor of German origin, but emigrated to the USA. He developed a treatment for cancer and most of the known diseases, based on a particular diet rich in fruit and vegetable juices. The regimen is comprised of no added sodium, raw liver juice, coffee enemas, administration of mineral solutions (potassium and iodine), thyroid hormones, and some vitamins.

Gerson therapy appears to be healing almost 100% of patients (even those in precarious conditions), is accessible to all and also heals the tumors judged incurable by Pharmacine. There would be no need for anything other than Gerson therapy, maybe integrated with the other remedies and tools mentioned in this chapter. Perhaps some of these methods could be tested on the most difficult cases where even Gerson therapy has difficulty. I have dedicated, further on, an entire chapter to Gerson and his method of treatment.

GÖRGÜN Seçkiner - Gemm (80s)

He is an extraordinary and unique Turkish researcher and inventor who has developed a very low-power electronic device for the treatment of solid tumors with surprising results. This machine was seized several times and for long periods by the judiciary, following various complaints. Everything has always been solved with acquittals or no place to proceed. Despite this, Alberto De Renzo, the Italian doctor who has been collaborating with Dr. Görgün, has been expelled with infamy by the parallel judiciary system: the Italian medical board. For this invention, the Minister of Culture of Turkey declared that he would work to get him the Nobel Prize. That was in 1972! How many people could have been saved with this device for the last years? Dr. Görgün was also a victim in a murky affair. Evidence of attempts to steal his invention have also been reported. I reckon his device might be something similar to the Zapper of Hulda Regehr Clark and Albert's Biohelp.

GRAVIOLA (Annona Muricata)

It is said that this plant, native to the Amazon, is a very powerful antioxidant and has been tested by an American pharmaceutical company in the 1970s as anti-tumor but then abandoned because it could not be exploited for commercial purposes.

HAMER Ryke Geerd (1935-2017)

He was a brilliant and generous German doctor who often volunteered. He graduated also in theology and physics and had a wonderful and close-knit family with four children when one summer day, while he was on holiday in the waters of Corsica, a tragedy shocked him and his family. During this holiday, in fact, his son Dirk was killed by Victor Emmanuel of Savoy (The son of Italy's last king) while he was drunk.

Then both he and his wife got cancer. Unfortunately, his wife did not survive this tragedy. He later questioned the basic paradigms of official medicine, attacking the entire medical class in an extremely polemic way. He says in one of his first books, Genesis of Cancer: "I had looked for cancer in the cell and found it in a coding error in the brain." At the end of the book, he explains in detail the origin and reports the examples taken care of by him (tens of thousands of cases!) according to his new theory. He reports the *Table of the Law of Cancer*, which specifies the location of cancer, the tenor of the conflict that would be the origin of its appearance, the terms of its manifestation, the position of the tumor focus in the brain and the subsequent steps up to the possible recovery. He was later banned from the German medical board after countless attempts to make him *abjure* the theories of his Medicine, to the point of trying to intern him in an asylum. He consequently went to live in exile in Spain. He was sentenced by the French court to five years on appeal, but took refuge in Spain where he worked for a few years, then was arrested in October 2004 by local authorities on the orders of a French court and imprisoned in a prison security in France, the country that has as its motto: *Liberté Egalité Fraternité*. Health dictatorships are obviously present in many western pharmacinized countries as USA, France, Italy, UK, etc. (the films *150 milligrams* (French) and *Concussion* (American) are proofs taken from true stories). In 2006, he was finally released from prison. He has recently passed away.

HOXSEY Harry (1901-1974) - Healing Infusion (40s/50s)

He received the formula of a phytotherapeutic treatment from his father, which was for decades the thorn in the side of the AMA (American Medical Association). Eventually the AMA succeeded in having his cancer clinics in several American States shut down. Many Hoxsey-like formulas are still widespread in the US.

Unlike Mrs. Caisse, though, Hoxsey had a lot of money, and he was not afraid of anyone. No one more than he could therefore have given the measure of the real obstacles faced by anyone who promotes a cancer remedy outside the rails imposed by the dominant pharmaceutical caste.

In his case, it was not enough to have the enthusiastic support of senators, lawyers, judges, journalists, preachers, and even doctors, nor were the repeated judgments confirming in court the validity of the cure. At the end, the FDA, which should protect the citizen from therapeutic frauds but instead deceives them by *protecting* them from existing therapies, denied the experimentation and authorization.

It makes a certain impression to see, even at those times, an arrogance that we know very closely now and that seems to have increased over time, instead of gradually decreasing. The official Hoxsey website describe Hoxsey's recipe in detail.

Unfortunately, if Hoxsey failed to successfully fight and defeat Pharmacine, it will be difficult for anybody else doing it. Everything is in our hands. We have to work like the Masons, in secret, and take care of ourselves, maybe by organizing dedicated structures. For those who pay for the National Health Service, there should be the possibility of being assigned to other care facilities or perhaps make a private insurance that also includes the centers that actually care.

Finally, if Hoxsey was named by Pharmacine as the greatest charlatan of the century, you can be sure that he was the most annoying one, even more than Gerson, and therefore it means that his herbs really work.

KADNICHANSKY Emil - (Enterosgel)

Enterosgel is a detoxifying product born in the former USSR that selectively binds toxic substances and removes them naturally within 12 hours of taking the product. It also reduces the negative effect of alcohol in case of abuse. It is a selective enteroabsorbent medical device originating in the former Soviet Union, created by the Soviet Ministry of Defense at the time of the USSR/US nuclear-biological-chemical war scenarios and subsequently converted to medical-civil use. The birth of Enterosgel dates back to the late 1970s, when the team of military researchers took the idea of developing a new molecule based on silicon in response to the various weak points of the enteroabsorbents available on the market at that time. The Ministry of Defense of the USSR, assigned to develop the new molecule, immediately started testing the patients of four state hospitals—Tashkent, Kiev, Vilnius, and Dushanbe—conducting studies for the treatment of hepatitis, intestinal infections, poisoning, postoperative complications and burns, testing it on over 5,000 cases. Subsequently, on the occasion of the Russian-Afghan war (1979-1989), Enterosgel proved to be highly effective. In particular during the 1986 Chernobyl disaster, it was administered for two years to the military personnel employed in the area of the fourth reactor, with therapeutic results defined as excellent in 75% of cases and satisfactory in the remaining 25%.

So this remedy, if tested with an open mind and with the true spirit as a juror of Hippocrates, could support detoxification treatments such as Gerson or other therapy.

I realize that I have made free publicity for some of the products mentioned in this book, but in any case, they are natural products that can be replicated, if not protected, by patents (the zeolite could have similar effects with much lower costs).

KOUSMINE Katherine (1904-1992)

She was an amazing doctor of Russian origin who was later naturalized Swiss. She based her therapy on nutrition to restore the health balance destroyed by toxic elements in the modern world. She directed the foundation created by herself in Lausanne and has thousands of successes to her credit.

KREBS Ernst (1911-1996) - Laetrile (1960s)

He was an American doctor who proposed substances such as pangamic acid and Laetrile as a cure for cancer. These substances were obtained mainly from apricot pits and bitter seeds of the fruits (citrus fruit excluded), containing hydrogen cyanide. This acid, according to him, thanks to an enzymatic difference between healthy and cancerous cells, would be toxic (at the dosages recommended by him) only for the latter. The therapy became very famous and was also the subject of some studies in official institutions (such as Memorial Sloan-Ketrering Cancer Center) which, despite the positive work of dr. Sagiura, they found it ineffective. Ralph Moss, director of public affairs at the MSKCC and science divulger, wrote in 1977 an official press release condemning the Laetrile. Later, however, after reviewing the data, he called a press conference during which he announced that the MSKCC officials would deliberately conceal the positive results of the therapy. He was fired for the next day, on the grounds that he acted in a way that conflicts with his fundamental job responsibilities (i.e., protect Pharmacine).

Unfortunately, people forget, trust naively and tend to remain ignorant. I repeat: *do not trust anybody!* What other proof do you want? Here it is not just a matter of evidence, these are facts, they are licensed criminals!

KREMER Heinrich (80s/90s)

He is/was a doctor who has developed a biological recovery therapy where the importance of the *mesenchyme* (or connective tissue) purity is highlighted for the good health of all the organic cells. Dr. Kremer was one of the first physicians in Germany to take an interest in AIDS, as medical director of the Interregional Hospital specializing in addiction-related diseases and minister in charge of health care policy in five German regions (including Berlin). In 1988, he resigned from the official positions for disagreements with the federal government's drugs and AIDS policies and the ostracism manifested by the medical-pharmaceutical establishment in relation to its positions contrary to the official theses that HIV causes AIDS. According to him, and four-thousand-year-old Korean medicine, the disease is due to the loss of proper movement and poor breathing. So the cure is based for 80% on the restoration of these functions and only for 20% on the use of medicines to compensate for the lack of substances consumed during the period of deficit. This treatment must therefore be oriented towards increasing the energy in the affected area, not the attempts to destroy the tumor. His conclusions are very logical and provided with common sense. Tell me how could a doctor preaching to decrease drugs survive in that environment? He published the book, *The Silent Revolution in Cancer and AIDS Medicine.*

IMPERATO Saverio - Sintherapy (90s)

He is a professor who has discovered a cure for cancer patients that has successfully applied for thirty years. He called it sintherapy. It stands for synergy between therapies. Alliance, not war. A synergistic strategy. It consists of a targeted and personalized enhancement of the body's natural defenses by selective immune activations which the patient must undergo before and after each chemotherapy, radiotherapy, hormone therapy or surgical operation. In short, unlike all the other prophets of alternative therapies, Imperato does not take cancer from conventional care. So, he would not be stealing anything from anyone. He has apparently appeared on the death list of a terrorist organization present in Italy until the late 1980s and was ignored by the official science and opposed by his colleagues.

It would appear like a sustainable strategy, but the doctors who are victims of Pharmacine's tricks do not realize what they are doing. Most of them are unsuspecting executioners, like most of Hitler's officers who blindly obeyed because they were deceived by the big lie.

LARRAZ Joaquin Amat - Amatrisan (90s)

He is a doctor who worked several years in Spain where he ran a day hospital. The product he used for both diagnosis and treatment was called Amatrisan. It was based on urea (pee). He said to destroy the tumor by autolysis, setting in motion the inflammatory mechanism that engulfed this dead meat and intervening on the pH rebalancing the acid/base ratio. It appears that in the year 2000, he was sentenced to 14 years in prison for making patients die by using an unsafe product (his Amatrisan). He wrote a book (which seems to have sent to all the most important medical faculties of Europe and the two Americas) entitled: *Cancer, biochemical theory, and clinical practice.*

The harder the sentence is, the more interesting the theory. Should they condemn all the doctors of Pharmacine who kill someone, there would not be anymore around.

MARCHESI Luciano - Orgone orange juice

He is/was working in Piedmont (Italy). His cancer therapy would be based on an orgone orange juice. He held numerous conferences on the subject and declared that he had numerous positive results. His remedy was boycotted, making it difficult to find anything about it on the net. According to the logic with which Pharmacine works, therefore, this discovery could be extremely significant. Essentially, it should be primordial energy transfused through orange juice. Probably Marchesi will also have well understood that having too much publicity would be tantamount to leading Pharmainquisition to the public gallows.

MORI Nello - Isopatinic method

He was a doctor and university professor of bacteriology at the Royal University of Palermo (Italy). Between 1912 and 1930, he obtained remarkable results with the isopatinic method in the fight against tumors. His method can be considered as part of active immunotherapy.

MURGIA Salvatore (1906-1988) - Medical hypnosis

Coming from a Sardinian family of modest conditions, he undertook first the technical studies and then moved to the scientific high school. In 1933 (already married with three children), he enrolled in the medical faculty. In the meantime, in collaboration with his brother James, he selected over twenty boys, mostly in precarious financial conditions, and took them up to the highest qualification. After obtaining a degree in medicine and surgery in 1939, he served in various municipalities as a general and internal doctor. In 1949, he became the owner of a medical consortium in Sardinia. After his retirement, although already seventy years old, he kept on working around the theory of the psychic cause of all diseases, which he called the Law of Health. For this purpose, in 1976 he founded the Center for Study of Mind and Health and, from 1980 until the end of his days, he published the periodical *The medicine of the future*. With the publication of Vol. I of *Zero Medicine*, he insisted stubbornly on the urgency of an accurate theoretical and practical revision of official medicine, immersed in an incurable crisis, so that it could become scientific and really healing.

This theory is absolutely logical and logifical and meets also with those of Louise Hay and Hamer. In fact, the psychosomatic aspect of diseases is undisputed. As an example, the Indian holy men, while ingesting poisons, do not get sick or die.

These assertions might appear to the superficial public as if they were new ideas, but again there is very little new. Even later, in many historical periods, famous people continue to say always the same things: the causes of the disease are food and psyche ... and I would also add the karma carried in this life that influences our body and mind.

NACCI Giuseppe

He is a doctor suspended by the Trieste (Italy) Medical Association as he treats his cancer patients not with chemotherapy but with natural treatments.

Dr. Nacci is a doctor specialized in nuclear medicine. He also contributed with his patented discovery to the diagnosis and treatment of tumors, as described in his book *Cancer Therapy with Gadolinium 159 in Magnetic Nuclear Resonance.*

Considering that normal tumor therapies (radiotherapy, hormone therapy, and especially chemotherapy) have strong side effects, he has developed the study for the treatment of cancer according to the metabolic Gerson method.

All this is amply illustrated in his book *Become a Doctor of yourself* which was awarded by the Mare Nostrum Association of Wildon (Austria – City of Graz) as the best scientific book of the year 2006. For his studies, the mayors of two major cities in Italy awarded him the seal of their cities. The Rector and the Academic Senate of the University of Padua awarded him the City of Padua Award 2008.

Despite the high recognition for his studies and the successful outcome of his therapies, the Medical Association of Trieste has decided to suspend it further because his treatment is not in line with the official ones.

This is a nefarious example of how Big Mafia in conjunction with Pharmacine conducts its aggressive, intimidating, arrogant, blackmailing, and mafia-like actions.

What other proof you need? I would like to know ... *Do not trust anybody! They are licensed criminals!*

ORRICO Mariano - Lamina BIOR (80s/90s)

He was an accountant, but also a scholar of medicine. He invented a simple but extraordinary therapeutic tool amazing in its applications. It is a synthetic lamina (the **BIOR** lamina: a term deriving from his surname **OR**rico in combination with **BI**os) formed by the merger of three different types of resins which, rubbed on a specially treated sheepskin, rebalances the cellular function. The benefits are obtained simply by bringing the lamina closer to the body. Like all brilliant ideas, we are faced with something extremely simple, inspired by the knowledge already spread by Talete from Miletus in the sixth century BC.

From the studies of Dr. Orrico on bioelectrology was born Bioelectrotherapy, which is applied by approaching the body with an instrument in the form of a blue resin sheet and which does not involve any side effects. Its BIOR sheet, rubbed on a sheepskin, is charged with negative electricity and, moving closer to the body, goes to load the cells of the negative charges that the serotonin has reduced, together with other factors, especially the food related ones. Thus the cells of the treated area resume their normal functioning.

As evidence, there are many people who, suffering from diseases like cancer, leukemia, gangrene, cirrhosis of the liver, asthma, osteoporosis, thrombocytopenia, diabetes, encephalopathies, cardiopathies, etc., would have been healed.

This is also a very interesting theory that should be explored. Unfortunately, the work of Pharmacine makes everything more difficult.

PANTELLINI VALSÈ Gianfranco (1917-1999) - Potassium Ascorbate (60s/70s/80s)

He was a well-known biochemist in the Tuscan village where he lived in. In 1947, he was asked advice from a goldsmith living in the same village about his stomach tumor. He suggested drinking a lemonade with bicarbonate daily to alleviate his pains. After a year, he met the goldsmith again and discovered, to his great surprise, that he was fine. He also realized that, instead of ordinary baking soda, he had used potassium bicarbonate. From that point on (1947), he started his research. In 1970, he sent a dossier with his research, his experiences and his results to the Italian Ministry of Health. There was no experimentation on this, but there was an important result: the potassium ascorbate (alkaline product) entered the official pharmacopoeia as a galenic product. Since then, tens of thousands of people have used it both as prevention and as therapy. The product has not yet been officially recognized as an anticancer (and never will be), but there have certainly been heals or/and improvements.

In this case, as in many other, potassium, together with other minerals, such as calcium and magnesium, acts as an alkalizing agent of the human body, as well as counteracting and rebalancing the presence of sodium. Disequilibrium is certainly a major cause of disease.

POGLIO Achilles

He was a phytotherapist who is considered the world's foremost scholar about the propolis of bees.

He identified in the propolis a fundamental support to counter all degenerative diseases. He passed away a few years ago leaving for his disciples the protocols he identified. He has implemented natural remedies against the onset of cancer that are thoroughly described in his book: *The Therapeutic Properties of Propolis*.

This study reconnects to the theories of pathogens as last cause to the insurgence of cancer. Propolis, in fact, would also have a positive effect as it would counteract pathogens.

PONTIGGIA Paolo (b. 1941)

He is and Italian chief physician of the *City of Pavia* Clinic. He works with immunotherapy according to three modalities of stimulation of the immune system: a chemical derivative (metisocrinol), an antiviral and the *corinebacterium parvum* which is a bacterial stimulator. Following his method, he declares to have obtained, in a substantial percentage of his patients, regressions or disappearance of the tumor often transforming serious clinical situations (tumors, etc.) to chronic diseases such as those that can be observed in diabetics.

Tell me why these therapies must remain taboo! In order to defeat Pharmacine, it would be necessary to activate a parallel network of care, avoiding Pharmacine becoming aware of it.

Father **PRADILLA**

For decades, he has been using an herbal treatment that has been actively used for a long time in Burkina (Africa) for AIDS. It has been used in many naturist environments in Madrid and Barcelona and also in Italy.

In this case it might be a product that counteracts pathogens, evidently active against viruses. As a matter of fact, many herbal remedies appear to be tremendously effective against cancer and other illnesses, but they are ignored as other methods. After all, as Gerson says: "The organism cannot differentiate what to cure first," so it cures everything, even AIDS.

PUCCIO Giovanni (90s)

He is a researcher from Palermo (Italy) who produced a study with which he formulated a serious scientific theory, very well explained and with its protocol. His theory was applied in several hospitals, without too much publicity. His research was filed in four copies at the Prefecture of Palermo and recorded on May 15, 1999 and November 25, 1999. He was, then, of course, arrested but 46 scientists and researchers helped this researcher keep a low profile that would not bother Pharmacine. Many foreign institutes are continuing his research, endorsing his findings from month to month.

This case too is a demonstration that cancer treatment cannot be made public because it ends badly. One has to work like a secret sect and treat oneself in secret. It is paradoxical that real criminals sometimes do not go to jail and innocent people are imprisoned quickly and without appeal.

Trust me, or better, do not trust my words either, but be sure that you can verify that Pharmacine is in absolute bad faith. *Do not trust! Experience!*

RATH Matthias (80s onwards)

He discovered that cancer growth and metastasis can be prevented with an optimal supply of lysine and other natural substances that block the enzymatic digestion of connective tissue by cancer cells. He also found that arteriosclerosis, heart attack, and stroke are an early form of scurvy caused by chronic vitamin deficiency in the vascular wall. He discovered that a prolonged vitamin deficiency is also the primary cause of arterial hypertension, heart attack, circulatory problems linked to diabetes, and other related cardiovascular diseases. Rath also considers that the establishment of cellular medicine, which includes the optimal intake of vitamins and other bioenergetic molecules, is the great medical discovery that will allow the prevention, treatment, and eradication of the most widespread pathologies. He collaborated with the two-time Nobel laureate Linus Pauling, passing down his studies on vitamin C.

The vitamins that bear his name are, apparently, sold at a higher price (like everything that makes a name, after all). The one he sells are optimized according to his studies but one could buy basic substances like I did. The cornerstones of its treatment for hypertension are vitamin C and E, arginine, magnesium, calcium, and bioflavonoids. You can have a complete list of vitamins from his famous book *Why Animals Do Not Get Heart Attacks ... But People*

Do! downloadable from his website. Obviously Rath is opposed by the official medicine, as much as possible.

REGEHR CLARK Hulda (1928-2009) - Zapper (80s/90s)

This doctor starts from the hypothesis that degenerative diseases appear because a series of parasites always present in the various organs are combined with chemical substances resulting from the intake of solvents, various pollutants and mycotoxins. Dr. Regehr Clark's cure is based on the assumption of a meticulous herbal remedy plan and the Zapper, an electronic device for external use that can eliminate almost any parasites.

She has also rediscovered liver washing with Epsom salts, which seems to be an enlightened procedure to improve our state of health. I would find it interesting to evaluate the integration of this procedure in Gerson therapy.

Also in this case, the theory of pathogenic germs returns. The Zapper is on the market at a few tens of Euros since it is an easily producible electronic device.

If you have children or relatives with strange, rare, and/or incurable illnesses you may try, in addition to following a Breuss fast-like therapy or a Gerson-like diet, Hulda Regehr Clark's Zapper, but the professional one that scans all the frequencies of the various pathogens, since our bad eating habits cause the disease to attack our body through the action of these agents.

HEPATIC WASHING (perfected by Andreas Moritz)

From Monday to Saturday morning, it is recommended to drink one liter per day of extract of apple or simply organic apple juice (to soften and reduce the gallstones), to be distributed at will during the day (last liter to drink on Saturday morning). During the week, it is preferable to avoid all foods that fatigue the liver (foods of animal origin, sugars, dairy products, fats, etc.) and, if possible, eat only fruit and vegetables.

SATURDAY

- In the morning, drink the last liter of apple juice and take an enema[43] with at least 1.5 liters of water. Use the appropriate devices for enteroclisms available at the pharmacy (not the pumps). The enema should also be repeated after washing (possibly on Sunday or, in any case, within three days). The enema allows you to visit the bathroom less frequently while doing the wash.

- 2.00 pm - do not eat or drink after two o'clock in the afternoon. If you do not observe this rule you may experience discomfort later. Prepare the Epsom salts by dissolving 4 tablespoons (about 80 gr.) In a jug with 720 ml of water. You should get 4 portions of 180 ml each taking care to mix well the mixture (do not worry about any slight excess of salts as it does not compromise the result).

- 6.00 pm - drink the first glass (180 ml) of the contents of the carafe. Who cannot bear the bitter taste, can plug the nostrils or keep a slice of lemon in the mouth, or, again, add a few drops of lemon to the solution or drink a sip of lemon juice after drinking it.

---

[43] Alternatively, coffee or chamomile to be hold, if possible, for at least 12/15 minutes. Please consider that if you take frequent coffee enemas you should adopt this simple rule: three fresh extracts (250ml of apple, carrots, green) for each enema taken.

- 8.00 pm - repeat the operation with the second glass of salts. The emptying of the intestine varies from subject to subject, so it is advisable to have a bath always close. Do not delay. It is important to stick to schedules.

- 21:50 - squeeze two pink grapefruits (about 200 ml), put them in the blender with half a cup of extra virgin olive oil (about 100 ml) and blend for a few seconds until a homogeneous mixture is obtained.

- 22:00 pm - drink the grapefruit and oil mixture while maintaining a standing position. Dr. Regehr Clark recommends taking 4 capsules of ornithine to facilitate sleep while drinking the mixture (those who have no sleep problems may avoid them). Lie down immediately for the night as soon as you finish drinking and do not stand up if not necessary). If you need to evacuate before 06:00 in the morning, do it as needed but stay for at least twenty minutes lying without getting up to facilitate the expulsion of the gallstones. Sleep on your back, with your torso slightly raised and with your head up on the pillow.

SUNDAY

- 06:00 am - drink the third glass of salts, taking care not to get out of bed before the indicated time (unless necessary). Afterwards, you can relax by reading or going back to bed if you are sleepy, although it is better to keep your body in an upright position.

- 08:00 am - drink the last glass of Epsom salts. From now on you will begin to evacuate more frequently. This activity can continue in the morning and also in the afternoon (varies from subject to subject). If you want to verify the output of the gallstones you can put a colander, or other device, in the cup. The gallstones are green, similar to peas, and of varying size. Those of a brownish color also contain other substances (calcium, etc.). Gallstones float because they are mainly formed by fat (cholesterol).

Well, the procedure is over. After two hours, if you do not resist more, you can take some fruit juice. The more gradually you are able to resume the consumption of meals (preferably fruit and vegetables) the better it will be. Remember that you have just avoided a possible surgery without undesirable effects (and without impairments and costs.

The days indicated are, of course, interchangeable. If you work on the weekend, you can do it any other day. It is advisable to do the washing on new moon, avoiding full moon.

REICH Wilhelm (1897-1957) - Orgone (40s/50s)

He was a collaborator of Freud and made an essential contribution to psychoanalysis from which he later distanced himself to concentrate his research on the orgone (vital energy). An important part of his studies also involved tumors. The cancerous mice put in his ORAC (orgone energy accumulator) according to him were healed. He then discovered (anticipating of some decades the theories of Murgia, Hamer and Luise Hay) that stress and conflicts were of great importance in the genesis of this pathology. Reich was also harshly persecuted, imprisoned, and his books were burned. Moreover, the use of his scientific equipment in the democratic America of the 1950s was forbidden. For those wishing to deepen the topic, he wrote many books including *The Cancer Biopathy* (The Discovery of Orgone, Vol. 2).

I find it easier to describe orgone energy as the source of all energies, the primordial energy upon which we can draw freely. This also applies to locomotion, as Teszla and the scholars after him have shown. It is, then, in all probability, the same energy that the true healers draw from. In the East, the term *Prana* is used to indicate the primordial energy that animates everything, including ourselves. Here, perhaps, the Orgone can be understood as a synonym of Prana. Being able to concentrate and accumulate it would be a divine experience. Unfortunately with Pharmacine, it is not allowed to experiment with anything that disturbs its business.

RIFE ROYAL Raymond (1888-1971) - Microscope (1920s/30s)

He is known for its very high-resolution microscope. He built a device, in the '20s and' 30s, for the treatment of cancer and other diseases through the emission of specific electromagnetic frequencies. He obtained sensational results in the treatment of several cases of cancer, attracting the ire of official medicine. His laboratory was mysteriously destroyed (both the machine and the microscope were then lost) and he ended up in jail. Several researchers in the USA are trying to recreate the Rife apparatus today. The best results, up to now, have been obtained from what is called the Rife-Dare apparatus (named after Dr. James Dare who conceived it).

SHELTON Herbert M. (1895-1985)

He was an American doctor of German origin, born in 1895 in Texas, who in his long life wrote dozens of books and was an important reference, together with Ehret, in matters of fasting. He implemented a method against degenerative diseases that is fundamentally based on fasting as a therapeutic element. Fast, obviously, to be carried out under the control of an expert therapist.

There are tens of thousands of documented cases with fasting therapy. His book *Fasting to renew life* is a cornerstone in the discipline of hygienism. He honestly admitted that his method could not cure cancer, but this obstacle was later (for non advanced cases) improved on by Breuss with his therapy. I would like to emphasize now that alternation between Breuss and Gerson therapy (42 days Breuss and one or two months of Gerson) might be the fastest healing path.

SIMONCINI Tullio - Sodium bicarbonate (years 2000)

He is a Roman oncologist and diabetologist. After studying the etiopathogenesis of cancer for years, he reached revolutionary conclusions. According to this researcher, in fact, cancer would have its root cause in Candida Albicans, a species of fungus that is widespread in all geographical areas of the world and in all human bodies, as an indigenous non-invasive form. However, when its natural antagonists (indigenous bacteria) disappear due to chronic bowel dysbiosis, it can immediately colonize a large part of the intestine and then, starting from that place, invade all the inflamed and acid zones of the organism. For this reason, his therapy would consist of spraying cancer areas with water enriched with 5% sodium bicarbonate. He would have obtained positive results on several patients, but also aggressions by the Italian Medical Board (which he was radiated from), and he was investigated and sentenced for fraud and manslaughter. Now he operates in Albania encountering various controversies.

In addition, I would like to add that, beyond the contrast to the fungus, bicarbonate would also act as an alkalizer of acidic processes. So, in the end, all the theories meet at some point. Furthermore, the mushroom theory has already been known for ages, but obviously everything must remain hidden.

SIMPSON Rick - cannabis oil

His treatment is essentially based on the oil extracted from fresh cannabis flowers. Having suffered family deaths from cancer, after a serious accident that caused him severe migraines he began to smoke cannabis. Later, to avoid the problems related to smoking, he decided to extract the oil from fresh flowers and used the latter to treat himself. A few months after being completely healed from the migraine, he was diagnosed with three melanomas in different parts of the body. One of these, close to the eye, was immediately treated surgically.

Even after having removed it, about a week later the same melanoma recurred again larger than the previous one. This is how he also tested cannabis oil for melanoma, applying it directly in contact with the skin, using special patches, where the melanomas were present.

Within a very short time, all the tumors had disappeared and the examinations that followed shortly thereafter did nothing but confirm what Rick already knew: the tumors were gone and he was out of danger.

This treatment also indicates that the theory of Dr. Simoncini to topically treat melanomas with iodine tincture is not madness and that they respond to skin therapy. Certainly you could experiment with other types of topical treatment such as strips of silver placed on melanoma or other remedies, but you will have to do it yourself since no orthodox doctor will ever give you attention. Cannabis is certainly a plant with a thousand resources, a divine gift, leaving out the easy humor. The fact that many countries are authorizing their consumption and cultivation bodes well for the near future.

SOMMER Daniel - Injections of animal cells (90s)

He is a naturopathic doctor and legal advocate of German *Heilpraktiker* medicine. He uses a biological therapeutic program that encompasses many types of therapy: gut regulation and care, nutrition change, homeopathy, ionized oxygen therapy, ozone therapy, thymus gland fetal therapy, mistletoe therapy, cellular therapy, infrared hyperthermic therapy, prof. Humprey (Selten) immunotherapy, trace elements, copper, and selenium.

TAMAS David - COD Tea

Dr. Tamas tea™ is an herbal compound, probably from the Amazon, which helps control the proliferation of malignant cells and the formation of metastases. Some patients have reported significant improvements and some have even reported complete remissions.

In two cases where I recommended using this tea, both treated with chemotherapy, there was, in one case, a total regression of a stomach tumor (according to the patient, attributable only to COD tea) and, on the other, a regression of 70% in a month of a tumor to the rectum (then operated for fear over one's life). Unfortunately, all these experiences were then lost, because they are not handed down in medical science as it is a monopoly of Pharmacine and not of real medicine. Fortunately Dr. Tamas proved to be a very clever person, not publicizing his remedy as an anticancer (which it might easily be) but, rather, as an adjuvant in chemotherapy discomfort (which is absolutely true).

TREBEN Maria (1907-1991) - Swedish herbs

It is said that the recipe of the Swedish bitter comes from the brilliant invention of an exceptional doctor and botanist: Paracelsus. It was rediscovered later by Urban Hjarne and Calus Samst and became public knowledge at the death of the latter. In fact, among his papers, a manuscript was found with the secret formula of eleven miraculous herbs used for its preparation. Samst died at the age of 104 falling from his horse. We owe to Maria Treben the diffusion of this exceptional remedy which she published in her book *Health Through God's Pharmacy*.

This remedy is absolutely amazing to treat an endless string of illnesses and it is, apparently, miraculous for wounds and scars. Apparently it makes it impossible for human beings to get sick. I would not be astonished at all if this remedy were the fruit, as they say, of the brilliant mind of Paracelsus. It can be produced at home by buying herbs and putting them in 1.5 liters of wheat or fruit distillate. In my opinion it should be tried before any other remedy and for any pathology, especially at a topical level

---

VALNET Jean (1920-1995)

He is universally recognized as one of the world's masters of herbal medicine. He proposed and practiced protocols to treat tumors using only this discipline.

This theory also reconnects to ESSIAC, COD, Hoxsey, 12 herbs, Swedish herbs, etc.

VIERI Aldo – Colchico (60s)

It is a cure based on wine vinegar and colchicum (colchicine: also known as saffron of meadows, belonging to the family of *liliaceae*) in 95% alcohol. The recipe included: colchicine tincture, 1 drop; gentian tincture, 1 drop; pure wine vinegar, 1 drop; 95% alcohol, 10cc. The dosage included 9 drops on the tongue, per day. Of course, he was also reached by the Pharmainquisition.

Dr. Aldo Vieri, in the 1960s, came to the fore in Italy and in some countries around the world for the administration of his anticancer with which many patients (even considered close to death by the so-called official medicine) were saved. Of course, he was heavily boycotted by Pharmacine. Despite this, in 2007-2010, honest Canadian researchers, have instead finally rehabilitated his cure after various experiments carried out in their University of Alberta. Colchicum is a toxic herb and must be carefully handled, there is no antidote for this substance. This cure would probably go on the one that poisons the cancer (similarly to amygdaline, scorpion venom, chemo, etc.) Though, apparently, very effective, I always suggest the detox one (Breuss, Gerson, etc.). Maybe this cure might be added to those just mentioned to accelerate the healing processes. Holistic doctors have a lot to experiment from the information present in this book.

However, I foresee that *everything changes so that nothing changes*. Even these Canadian researchers will be annihilated by Pharmacine, it goes for its survival. Until there is a rejection of chemotherapy and some part of orthodox medicine, then, cancer will not be defeated.

VIGO Carlo Alberto (70s/80s) - Musicology and Chromology

He is a doctor of musicology and chromology (Visplenus method) applied to health. He is also an expert in Traditional Chinese Medicine and a homeopathy researcher. He bases its therapy on a vaccine type mixture. This cure is supplemented by magneto-stimulating therapies aimed at electrically recharging cells. He has obtained positive and documented results.

VINCENT Louis-Claude (1906-1988) – Pure water (40s/50s)

He has implemented a bioelectronic system to assess cancer risk and the effectiveness of any other therapy. He has published sixty thousand measurements, the result of decades of research by scholars all over the world that were naturally neglected by official medicine. Vincent's bioelectronic technique was developed in 1950.

He affirms in his studies that the mortality rate for each type of disease—and in particular tuberculosis, cardiovascular diseases, and cancer—is directly linked to the quality of the water distributed to the population. It grows particularly when the waters are very mineralized and artificially potable after physical treatment and with the addition of oxidizing chemicals.

After 10 years of research, he came to the discovery of bioelectronic laws to purify it, applicable to all aqueous media. Around 1946, he defined that an aqueous solution can be qualified and represented rigorously by three factors: the pH, which measures the degree of acidity; rH2, which reflects the redox power; and "r," the electrical resistance that measures the ionic concentration.

From 1952 to 1953, he spent twelve months in Lebanon and quickly obtained important successes in numerous villages in the grip of epidemics. He had succeeded in establishing that, having available good quality water and not polluted, all the epidemics ceased instantly, without any other remedy.

Vincent's technique consists in measuring, with the help of an electronic device, the three parameters: pH, rH2 and r, on blood, saliva and urine of the patients. The representative values of these three fluids are shown on a graph and a series of calculations made on these nine parameters (3x3). It leads to data that allow to characterize, objectively, the biological tissue (healthy factor) of the patient. This would seem to be the only clinical test so far to provide a truly objective assessment of the efficacy, harmfulness or harmlessness of any therapy, regardless of the symptomatic results, which are often misleading (see Bioelectronics).

This study gives further prominence to those of Max Gerson, Andreas Moritz and others who says, unequivocally, that we must avoid fluorine, chlorine and other toxic substances, which are used industrially to treat drinking water.

Father ZAGO Roman – Aloe by Father Zago (90s)

He has brought therapies used for a long time in other countries: the treatment of tumors with Aloe Arborescens. This method has been widely used in Italy for some years.

INGREDIENTS: half a kilo of bee honey (organic acacia honey); 40-50 ml (about 6 tablespoons) of distillate (brandy, cognac, whiskey, etc ...); 350/400 grams of leaves of Aloe Arborescens.

It is prepared as follows: remove the spines from the edges of the leaves and the dust deposited by using a dry cloth or sponge. Cut the leaves into pieces (without removing the peel) and put them in the blender together with the honey and the selected distillate. Blend well and the preparation is ready for consumption. It should not be filtered, nor cooked, but only carefully stored in the fridge inside a dark, well-closed jar and quickly consumed.

ZORA Giuseppe - IMB/Adiuvant Plus (70s/80s)

He is an oncologist. In 1975, in countercurrent and hindered by all, began a series of experiments in test tubes or on living cells, following the immunological experimental lines. His research continued with experiences on immunomodulatory products, already known or otherwise used (BCGm Corynebacterium parvum, Levamisol and others). In 1978, he managed to obtain a harmless, non-toxic biological hybrid that allowed a wide spectrum of total immunological modulation easily applicable. After that, he began Experimentation on the patients. In 1979, he had the opportunity to analyze the Bonifacio serum at the University of Messina, with his wife Anna Tarantino as a biologist, and to ascertain its positive qualities. In 1982, in conjunction with Bonifacio's decision to abandon the administration of his serum, he began distributing his product (which was then called IMB, nowadays Adiuvant Plus) to patients. From 1982 Giuseppe Zora will bear a long series of judicial persecutions that will also lead to his arrest in 1992. Today Zora's product has been registered in Switzerland as a medicinal product. His nightmare is over, and tens of thousands of patients in Italy and throughout Europe use it with excellent results.

Food, fasting and illness

> *Fasting is the first principle of medicine.*
>
> RUMI

*L*ogically, if it is true that we are *monkeys brothers* with a soul,[44] created from the feathered serpent, it was logical that at certain times of the year we could fast or at least partially fast, because the food supply was not the same all around the year.

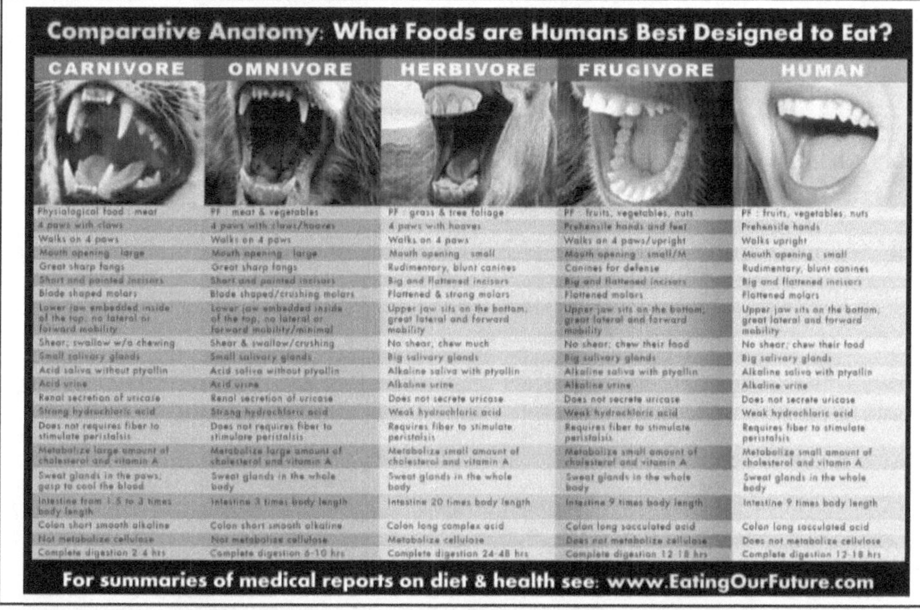

Comparative Anatomy: What Foods are Humans Best Designed to Eat?

	CARNIVORE	OMNIVORE	HERBIVORE	FRUGIVORE	HUMAN
	Physiological food : meat	PF : meat & vegetables	PF : grass & tree foliage	PF : fruits, vegetables, nuts	PF : fruits, vegetables, nuts
	4 paws with claws	4 paws with claws/hooves	4 paws with hooves	Prehensile hands and feet	Prehensile hands
	Walks on 4 paws	Walks on 4 paws	Walks on 4 paws	Walks on 4 paws/upright	Walks upright
	Mouth opening : large	Mouth opening : large	Mouth opening : small	Mouth opening : small/M	Mouth opening : small
	Great sharp fangs	Great sharp fangs	Rudimentary, blunt canines	Canines for defense	Rudimentary, blunt canines
	Short and pointed incisors	Short and pointed incisors	Big and flattened incisors	Big and flattened incisors	Big and flattened incisors
	Blade shaped molars	Blade shaped/crushing molars	Flattened & strong molars	Flattened molars	Flattened molars
	Lower jaw embedded inside of the top, no lateral or forward mobility	Lower jaw embedded inside of the top, no lateral or forward mobility/minimal	Upper jaw sits on the bottom, great lateral and forward mobility	Upper jaw sits on the bottom; great lateral and forward mobility	Upper jaw sits on the bottom, great lateral and forward mobility
	Shear, swallow w/o chewing	Shear & swallow/crushing	No shear, chew much	No shear; chew their food	No shear; chew their food
	Small salivary glands	Small salivary glands	Big salivary glands	Big salivary glands	Big salivary glands
	Acid saliva without ptyalin	Acid saliva without ptyalin	Alkaline saliva with ptyalin	Alkaline saliva with ptyalin	Alkaline saliva with ptyalin
	Acid urine	Acid urine	Alkaline urine	Alkaline urine	Alkaline urine
	Renal secretion of uricase	Renal secretion of uricase	Does not secrete uricase	Does not secrete uricase	Does not secrete uricase
	Strong hydrochloric acid	Strong hydrochloric acid	Weak hydrochloric acid	Weak hydrochloric acid	Weak hydrochloric acid
	Does not requires fiber to stimulate peristalsis	Does not requires fiber to stimulate peristalsis	Requires fiber to stimulate peristalsis	Requires fiber to stimulate peristalsis	Requires fiber to stimulate peristalsis
	Metabolize large amount of cholesterol and vitamin A	Metabolize large amount of cholesterol and vitamin A	Metabolize small amount of cholesterol and vitamin A	Metabolize small amount of cholesterol and vitamin A	Metabolize small amount of cholesterol and vitamin A
	Sweat glands in the paws; gasp to cool the blood	Sweat glands in the whole body	Sweat glands in the whole body	Sweat glands in the whole body	Sweat glands in the whole body
	Intestine from 1.5 to 3 times body length	Intestine 3 times body length	Intestine 20 times body length	Intestine 9 times body length	Intestine 9 times body length
	Colon short smooth alkaline	Colon short smooth alkaline	Colon long complex acid	Colon long sacculated acid	Colon long sacculated acid
	Not metabolize cellulose	Not metabolize cellulose	Metabolize cellulose	Does not metabolize cellulose	Does not metabolize cellulose
	Complete digestion 2-4 hrs	Complete digestion 6-10 hrs	Complete digestion 24-48 hrs	Complete digestion 12-18 hrs	Complete digestion 12-18 hrs

For summaries of medical reports on diet & health see: www.EatingOurFuture.com

[44] Eugenio Siragusa channeled by God Himself, Adoniesis, let us know that we descend from the ancient feathered serpent and that the gorilla's body was not suitable for us. Of course gullible man who is not able to discern the true from the false might laugh at it instead of logically study and discern truth from lies.

We did not have yet the capacity to conserve foods for periods of famine. So, the fact that many experts say that fasting is harmful to humans or that an exclusively vegetarian or fruitarian diet is just as much makes me smile. I wonder: but are these experts in contact with God? Because, as they speak, it would seem so, and it would look as if they know all the, still secret, mechanisms of life.

The same experts say that meat and proteins are indispensable, and it is true that they are indispensable for man and also for all other animals.

All vegetable foods, in fact, contain protein in different amounts that are absolutely sufficient for humans to live well and grow in good health, but also for the elephant, the gorilla, the monkeys, the hippopotamus, the rhinoceros, etc. It sounds like an absurdity, therefore, to say that man, which is omnivorous, cannot live without animal proteins; this appears to me as a great hoax.

To amaze you, I would even venture to say something that for many may seem scandalous: even carnivorous animals could survive without meat. I remember the image of a lion at the feet of an Indian guru who had lived a whole life on a vegetarian diet. Perhaps this statement could be ridiculed by some medical scientist, but it is a fact.

I remember my great mother who always said: you must eat meat, because it is necessary. But she said this only because the Professor/Doctor/Primary/etc. said so. But my mother, also endowed with so much popular wisdom, never wanted to get into a hospital because she knew that often you come out worse than when you entered, if not dead.

I have always wondered: but how is it possible that, according to such luminaries of science, a vegetarian diet is unbalanced and harmful and at least three hundred million Indians live well as vegetarians? In addition, Mahatma Gandhi has survived for 80 years without meat, with an enema a day, in an era where the average life was much lower. In addition, he regularly fasted. Who knows how old he would have died if he had not been killed?

I am sure that in the contemporary world, it is scientific everything that can be patented and sold, possibly at a high price. On the other end, is not scientifically proven anything that does not bring an income and for which there is no commercial interest (patentable). I would like you to understand clearly that when it is said *it is not scientific* they mean this: if a patient heals by taking apples and carrots this is due to a miracle, or to chance, but not to scientific care since he/she has not taken any *magic pills*. So, let me redefine the meaning of the scientific method: *method that allows the administration of chemical products prescribed by Pharmacine*.

They consciously adopted a term that was the one of Galileo, of Newton, and of Einstein to have their poisons accepted by the people. Today the scientific term is immediately associated with the reign of Pharmacine, but it is not this way, scientific is something different that does not have anything to do with Pharmacine. I write what I am writing because I feel the moral obligation to do so and if it will serve to save even only one of you from the jaws of Pharmacine it will be worth it. I understand, however, that people identify themselves with the film that Pharmacine is playing as they are immersed in its reality. That is why it is so difficult to see the truth.

As I have already pointed out previously, the nutritional aspects of the *animal man*, which is considered to be similar to the monkey (leaving out similarity of the intestines, mouth, etc.), had to be logically and necessarily similar to those of the apes. Primitive man, therefore, had to feed exclusively on fruits, nuts, seeds and some grass/vegetables. But then, I ask myself, why bother the logic when it is also written in the Bible that God said: "Behold, I have given you every plant-yielding seed that is on the face of all the earth, and every tree with seed in its fruit. You shall have them for food" (Genesis 1:29). Then, mankind took the forbidden fruit and was abandoned in this valley of tears. If the logic and the Bible were not enough, an enlightened Son of God on earth, Sri Yukteswar, a disciple of Lahiri Mahasaya (who was, in turn, of Babaji) clearly indicated in his book *The Sacred Science* (describing it in detail) that man's diet is (logically) similar to that of frugivorous animals and explains the motivations in detail.

We had to learn to feed ourselves with what we had available (game, wheat, milk) in order to survive. Today perhaps we could all, or at least a large part of us, feed on what was originally available in the Garden of Eden. Unfortunately, gluttony, but also bigotry, prevents us from renouncing to what is in excess[45] (this theme will be explored in another volume). I also want to anticipate the issues that I would like to elaborate later since they lend themselves to being examined logically. Chapter V of the Old Testament indicates

---

[45] Some Ayurvedic texts suggest having a meal a day (the best would be to assume it in the central hours of the day). Unfortunately, we have lost satiety perception and we eat as social customs prescribe (breakfast, lunch, and dinner) even not feeling the necessity.

the exact age of Adam's descent. According to the scriptures they lived all over several hundred years: Adam 970, Enos 912, Kenan 905, etc.

Now, we say that the Old Testament is an allegorical tale, that we must interpret what is written, etc. etc. But why should falsehoods be written in the Bible and, above all, why should things be said outside any human logic? That is, that some men lived over nine hundred years? So, it seems clear to me that either the years were counted differently from today or that, simply, we lived much more, and if we lived longer, for what reason? Is it possible because we only ate fruit? I will look into it in the next volumes.

So, God has ordained that we *shall have* (you shall have them for food), and not that we *might have*, fruit and plant but we think, perhaps, He may have been wrong. In fact, experts say that we need to eat meat, and other *illogical* foods causing a major environmental catastrophe and allowing inhumane exploitation and the unnecessary death of millions of animals. It is obvious that if there were not enough fruits and seeds we could nourish ourselves with other foods. Even Jesus Christ fed himself with the food of men. However, if there was the possibility of eating according to Nature, as happens today in many countries, then prohibited foods should be, at least, strongly limited. Beware I am just preaching well, though I am vegetarian, I eat very limited diary and grains, but I recognize that it is not our proper food.

It is, however, obvious that we can eat everything, but is it healthy and right? The Eskimos eat essentially only fish and live about half of what we live in Western countries. This could be due to the diet but, also, and above all, to the fact that they do not get enough sun. My question is: if we only ate fruit what would be our life expectancy? Probably the same as the current one or a little more, but, who knows? I am sure that some people decide not to become fruitarian because they think they could not live on fruit alone. Is it really like that?

Ehret has handed down, in his writings, the possibility of living ethically and biologically in full autonomy with only ten fruit trees for a family of four. I am sure that many will smile at this statement, but I would be ready to try it immediately, without fear of incurring a nutritional deficiency or fanciful theories developed by nutrition scientists. He saved his life and experienced virtually every variant by introducing, in a fruitarian diet, carbohydrates, dairy products, and meat, thus verifying the deleterious effects on a *divinely healthy body*.

Moreover, the experiments carried out by Ehret are much more than logic. In fact, he says, for having personally experienced it, that man is born frugivorous and this is his natural nourishment, the one that, together with fasting, saved his life and can save it to anyone who adopts it.

However, an omnivore that becomes fruitarian will probably go into a major detoxification crisis, as happened to Ehret. This condition appears, often, as a real illness conditions, at least until the body is completely clean. This condition of uncertainty often determines the failure of many who are demoralized by not immediately seeing obvious signs of improvement, as they are apparently obtaining the opposite effect. If not known in advance, one might not understand that it is the beginning of healing. It is important to research before making any major changes as the *side effects* might lead you to abandon your therapy.

The fruitarians say, logically, that we have the intestines proportionate to those of the apes, in contrast to the herbivores (much longer) and the carnivores (much shorter), and another long series of logific evidences. But whatever the various theories are on the enigmatic nutrition of man, we have a bold and enlightened character of history (Ehret) who has practically experienced the effects of such nutrition on himself. After being omnivorous and having risked his life because of Bright's disease, he decided to fast (perhaps thinking of shortening his suffering), while improving miraculously. Investigating the known naturopathy until then, he fed himself only with fruit and some vegetables (called by him later mucusless diet). After several fasts and pure food feeding, he completely recovered, finding what he calls *the perfect health*. Not yet satisfied and wanting to do good for his neighbor, he experimented by reincorporating the forbidden foods (starches, diary, and meat) into his diet and describing carefully the deleterious effects on the human body.

I hope you will not misinterpret my words; I do not want to preach and I do not want to tell you how to feed yourself. I'm just doing some reasoning. Ehret experimented with different types of nutrition. He has, in practice, tested the effects on his sick body and has therefore deduced, practically and logically, that the ideal nutrition of man is the frugivorous one. I repeat that although I'm not fruitarian, I recognize its validity and I fully support it, since I recognize it as our ideal diet. I do not even allow myself to tell you that carnivores (hunters) are criminals like many vegans or vegetarians do. In fact, I have respect for those who are able to kill animals and eat meat but not for those who eat them not being able to do it. I do not even tell you not to use furs (it's a problem of your own conscience). It is not by coincidence that free will exists.

Everyone is responsible for his/her own actions and even if we are endowed with good will and honesty, we can make mistakes. However, it must be strongly reiterated that we are determining a *bad life* for man with oil pollution and intensive farming. Yet, do what you believe is best for you and nourish as you please, but limiting animal products should be an environmental matter before being a consciousness matter. I certainly cannot lecture you, I'm not even vegan (although strongly restricting dairy products).

Today, we start producing mucus from when we are small kids with the wrong nutrients (sweets, sweetened drinks, starches, meat, and very few fruits and vegetables) and we normally carry it to the grave. We impede our sick children who have the natural instinct of fasting (as well as animals) to do so. We believe in doing the right thing by going against Nature, slowing down and preventing natural healing. Then we stuff them, and ourselves, with drugs because, rightly, we are worried and we make matters worse. I remember that my pediatrician, when I was a child, recommended to my mother not to give the antibiotic ever before the third day, who knows if it is still so? However, antibiotics, according to my personal opinion, should be used according to this rule and possibly after the fifth day of illness (if unavoidable). In this way, the body starts fighting by itself and when it gets a little help it maximizes it by using it as necessary. Remember, however, that there is colloidal silver, the Zapper, and a hoard of other remedies to combat diseases caused by pathogens.

Obviously, the argument between carnivores and vegans/fruitarians might go on for ages. To settle this doubt that we have been having for thousands of years, it would be enough to rely on the theory of liver cleansing that was rediscovered by Hulda Regehr Clark and that could help to unveil the arcane. It would be enough to analyze the gall bladder of the apes, or that of a fruitarian human being from birth, and verify if it contains gallstones, which could be present in most of the human population. In fact, gallstones are nothing more than accumulations of substances such as cholesterol, bacteria, and other decomposed parasites as well as other waste materials that would probably not be present if we adopted our original diet, the fruitarian one.

I already know that I will remain only one voice out of the chorus, but I believe that certain truths must be shouted to try to save as many people as possible. I keep on repeating to doubtful, not seriously ill cancer patients that the Breuss therapy lasts only 42 days and it would be rather improbable to lose one's life in such a short time if you are not a terminal patient.

In confirmation of the goodness of my reasoning, even Descartes helps me. In fact, he indicates in doubt, which arises from the experience of error, the instrument for arriving at the truth. In the case of Big Mafia there are no doubts, only deceptions. Though, perhaps, among the members of Pharmacine there could be some doubts. For this reason, Orthodox doctors should absolutely doubt in the Cartesian way and test empirically what have been affirming their eminent colleagues, past and present. Descartes says, essentially, that to be able to get to the truth, one must doubt when there is a slight semblance of doubt. In this case, not only is there doubt, but there is also the certainty of deception. However, should not the doctors do that, make sure you, passionately, do it yourself. *Be Doubtful! Inform yourself! Experience!*

It is therefore evident that man can certainly live well and in full health using only these nutritional elements. In the same way, to imagine man feeding only with meat or fish without other vegetable nutrients would, instead, be unnatural. It would also, very likely, cause important nutritional deficits, considerably shortening life expectancy. In my opinion, therefore, it is logical and absolutely irrefutable that man needs only nutrients similar to those of apes, but then allowing us small exceptions of taste, according to palate, that our evolution has made available to us. So, if we do not encounter major health problems we can moderately use the *prohibited foods*, but at the first symptom of illness we should go back to our primordial diet following the method developed by brilliant past personalities, such Gerson, Breuss, Kousmine, etc.

Obviously, man has a divine nature (it is written in the Bible that God created mankind in his own image), so we could adapt for the survival of the race and the divine nature. We were, then, able to broaden the intake of food becoming, in substance, omnivorous, though we did not have the right organs. The first hunters introduced the meat, the peasants brought forth the grains and the products of the earth and, lastly, the shepherds brought the dairy products. However, these nutrients were introduced into our diet only for survival and expansion reasons and it is absolutely illogical that they have now become indispensable for our good health.

Furthermore, the use of cooked food, which has allowed man to progress and survive, has nevertheless led to a loss of vitamin supplies. It is shown that the lack of fresh vegetables and fruit causes serious, and sometimes lethal, diseases such as the scurvy.

It is not equally true, however, that the lack of meat does the same; indeed the opposite is proven. Meat damages the organism, especially if it is in excess. It is obvious that in the modern era we must also consider taste issues and sociability. Nonetheless we must not hide behind a lie: man is an omnivorous animal. We could also eat *forbidden foods*, but let's do it with wisdom. If we eat mostly *forbidden foods*, how can we imagine not getting sick or having perfect health?

I therefore consider it absolutely clear that the main illnesses of the modern age, or at least those of the Western world, can be traced back to these imbalances, but also to the quantity, and not only to the type, of the ingested nutrients, as well as often to the complete absence of exercise, psyche, pollution, etc. However, Gerson has demonstrated that any condition can be reverted with *live* food. In the last century, man's lifestyle has radically changed from mass agriculture (which saw a large part of the population employed in the fields) to the advancement of industrial agriculture, where few machines do the work of thousands of men.

The tertiary sector has had an immense development, occupying most of the jobs of contemporary society. This means that the consumption of calories has drastically fallen. Sedentary jobs, in fact, do not allow us to consume what we ingest and the advent of widespread prosperity in modern society makes us witness the worrying phenomena of obesity and diseases related to this lifestyle.

The reduction of calories required in the modern world could be achieved by consuming only vegetables with few weekly or even monthly exceptions. Moreover, this type of diet would bring only benefits. Therefore, even if you eat large quantities of fruitarian or vegan foods, you cannot have particularly negative developments, since nuts and seeds, even if rich in fats, have, however, important nutrients that contribute to the regular functioning of our body's metabolites. They also take part (especially nuts) in the regulation of the sense of satiety.

In the last century, quality has also become overwhelmingly important. There has been, on the one hand, a tremendous acceleration in food preservation, with the advent of refrigeration, canning, and packaging. On the other hand, a compromise in the quality of food due to the chemicals used in production and conservation (present in the same foods) and transport, often intercontinental.

In fact, today's vitamin deficiencies are certainly also attributable to these factors. Vegetables are known to lose vitamins and other nutrients quickly. More and more rarely happens that the simple salad goes from the orchard to the plate and often it takes days, if not a whole week, before it is consumed. Moreover, we often cook vegetables, losing part of their nutrients.

It should also be considered the worst of evils: the use of chemicals in agriculture that, in addition to poisoning plants (all in all a minor evil), also causes an impoverishment of nutrients due to the depletion of agricultural land.

In other times, in the rare periods in which the products were available, they were picked and eaten at the same time. In the worst case, our ancestors went to the market in the morning and then cooked for lunch or in the evening and only organic fertilizers were used in the fields.

Furthermore, the advent of chemistry has meant that, in practice, pristine foods are increasingly rare. Even products labeled as organic suffer inevitable contamination. The seeds are often selected by large multinationals, which only look after profits and they are just as often contaminated with GMOs.

Organic products are subject, in part, to chemical treatments either deriving from non-biological neighbors or from polluted water or from the land itself previously cultivated with chemicals. More rarely are, likely, marketed by dishonest farmers. Furthermore, non-organic foods, as already mentioned, have fewer nutritional benefits since chemical fertilizers use only three organic components instead of over fifty present in natural fertilizers.

Basically, they are empty boxes that have poor nutritional properties. Obviously, the shortcomings of nutrients accumulated over a lifetime can contribute to the advent of many diseases. The theory of Pauling and Rath on the chronic deficiency of vitamin C and other vitamins and minerals appears, therefore, absolutely logical. It would be then logifically proven (since the scientific term is prerogative of Pharmacine) and the proliferation of many diseases could be the confirmation. We do not nourish ourselves according to Nature, so to compensate for these deficiencies we must integrate them artificially, with synthetic products that are nevertheless the least of the evils.

To overcome these problems related to organic contamination, perhaps it would be enough to identify a wide geographic areas where it would be possible to conduct only natural agriculture with seeds that are not contaminated with GMOs and without chemical poisons.

For obvious reasons of evolution and expansion, man has adapted to conditions other than those of apes. His body has evolved to digest and metabolize other foods. Therefore, the various tribes who have alternated over the millennia (hunters, farmers, and shepherds) have helped to make the man omnivorous. Unfortunately, pets have suffered the same fate of man. Dogs and cats do not eat anymore their original food (I have seen dogs eating pasta, fruit, and ice creams as human do).

However, it would appear that while human primordial foods generally do not cause any disturbance, even if ingested in excessive quantities, those introduced after it can alter, even significantly (especially in sedentary subjects), the state of health. In fact, dairy products, some kinds of cereals (especially refined) and meat can certainly have an important, if not exclusive, impact in the diseases and discomforts of our times. Furthermore, additives like salt and sugar (especially refined) would prove to be an important element in the onset of various diseases.

As evidence of what I have just mentioned, those who have blood values different from the norm and want to experiment would notice that only after a few weeks of a vegetable and fruit diet, many values (especially triglycerides and cholesterol) miraculously will fall within the limits, without taking drugs to keep them under control.

A fresh extract of organic vegetables and fruit a day, if ingested for decades, is tantamount to a medicine that is continuously taken. Therefore, good habits over time, as well as the bad ones, then determine what will be our state of health or illness. An organic juice a day is certainly a sustainable effort and would guarantee a minimum of those vitamins we need and which we no longer take because of the problems already exposed, related to the environment but, above all, to the greed and selfishness of man.

Unfortunately, it is difficult to renounce the *vice* of food, as it is difficult to renounce all vices. However, I think it should be highlighted how bad the vice of food can become. Eminent figures such as Hippocrates, Ehret, Gerson, Shelton, and others have clearly demonstrated and emphasized that the cure is the food.

Essentially, the human being is already equipped with a perfect machine, like the one of animals, which is able not to get sick and self-heal naturally. In fact, if it is in the condition to do so, not poisoned by other drugs and improper food, can heal from any type of disease. Of course, we can help this healing with other natural remedies, as the one partially mentioned in this book, but this is something more that, generally, is not useful because man is equipped with the ability to self-heal without any other artificial help beyond nature. Animals have abilities that we have lost as the one to recognize medicinal herbs and fast.

To sum up, I would like to say that it is perhaps not wise to renounce millennia of adaptation and evolution, but we should probably reconsider our eating habits, relegating the food of hunters, farmers, and shepherds to a marginal place in our diet (for example, Sundays, holidays, or for parties) and avoid as much as possible any refined food, such as salt, flour, sugar, etc.

I believe, however, that a basically vegan diet (even with some exceptions) can be easily pursued and can extend our life, provided we do not overdo the starches. However, we should get rid of toxins and mucus accumulated in a lifetime, starting from childhood, through long fasts and/or Gerson-like therapy to pursue the goal of perfect health, not easy at all.

It must also be said, to be fair, that there are cases of centenarians who do not adopt any kind of precaution not particularly caring about food, if not, sometimes, moderation and living genuinely. However, one thing is certain: if you get sick the cure is the vegetable and fruit one, adding herbs, vitamins, and supplements, fasting and baths of sun, light, and air.

For those who do not have ethical feelings related to food, the intake of food of animal origin may not have important repercussions on health, as far as moderation and physical activity are considered. Unfortunately, often in today's society, neither one nor the other is found; the first is abused and the latter is omitted.

I take solace in the fact that the writings of a man who has really experienced all this (Ehret) confirm these logical considerations. However, even Ehret had to get away from his loved ones to be able to experience his theories because those around us might be too influential on us.

There is still a strong diatribe about what foods are good for man, but the answer is simple: it is good for man all that is alive, natural and that is part of his original diet. Man does not need any other food, as wisely commanded in the Bible.

The preserved, artificial, highly processed, cooked, and stewed foods (except vegetables, possibly at low temperature and ingesting cooking liquids) are not good for humans. However, man, as a perfect machine, is able to tolerate them even for long periods, but we have made exception the norm. This would even be fine if we were at least able to go back once ill.

When we deviate too much from Nature we often encounter health problems, which are not very relevant if we do not *exceed the excess*, but when it becomes daily life we might face inevitable discomfort. If we then add the psychosomatic aspects, we can face serious problems that perhaps would not emerge with a good diet.

Meat is currently produced in quantities superior to our hypothetical real needs, creating enormous imbalances in the world.

For every kilogram of meat produced, it takes five to twenty times the amount of water used in the production of vegetables and ten kilograms of cereals. Consider also that the production of greenhouse gases in intensive livestock [46] production has even exceeded the emissions from the transport sector (18%). By now the vegetarian question is no longer an ethical problem but an environmental issue. Meat consumption needs to be reduced, as well as consumption of hydrocarbons.

Unfortunately, technological progress has made it possible to influence many functions of the human organism with chemistry and with drugs. What we do not want to understand is that man is already a perfect machine and that only conditions of extreme and inattentive use are necessary to spoil a perfect machine. If only we stopped to do a regular *service*, perhaps, we would avoid many illnesses of our century.

Fasting, enemas, and phlebotomies are now obsolete, also because they require time and effort (as well as being ridiculed by Pharmacine) and now there is no more time in the frenetic modern society. We only stop for a sudden failure of our *vehicle* (tumors, cardiopathy, or anything else).

Unfortunately, people do not want to give up until there is a *breakdown* or until they have serious problems. In fact, a few days of feeding only with juices, at regular intervals during the year, could be enough to keep healthy (or healthier) by resting the body and then making a *mini-service*. The average person, however, is not minimally

---

[46] https://knoema.com/infographics/maodxhb/global-greenhouse-gas-emissions-from-livestock

willing to sacrifice, we are not able to make a few days of only juices, let alone a fast-like period, even a short one.

Fasting has practically disappeared from the Catholic and social tradition. In the Catholic tradition, it was replaced by the Friday where, today, no meat is eaten, allowing, however, the fish. Yet originally it was not so, fasting was absolute, but obviously man tries to fix things he/she does not like. Some dogmas are softened and transformed according to his/her needs. That is also why, the absolutely logific theory of reincarnation might have disappeared from the Catholic tradition.

The Emperor Constantine has done nothing but do what modern politicians do by *adjusting imperfect laws*. He simply might have ignored some small details by approving the Christian religion (is it not a logifical theory?). But this too will be part of another volume.

It is, therefore, certain that fasting in the ancient Catholic tradition was a pillar, because, to raise the spirit, a clean body could prove to be an indispensable condition. In fact, all religions provide hygienic-food practices for this purpose. This is demonstrated by the numerous writings of Saint Hildegard who provides enlightening hygiene and food councils and affirms the importance of fasting (even long) to temper body and spirit.

Ehret also testified that with fasting the spiritual state varies greatly. Of course, modern experts can even question this direct line of Hildegard with God. I no longer wonder at all, but above all I no longer believe what I see, or what they want me to see.

It is obvious that asking to renounce sociality in the modern world is something unthinkable. However, moderate eating on the days when you can and, perhaps, transgress only occasionally, would

    Food, fasting and illness

allow us to go to the restaurant and eat what we want while maintaining an acceptable average of quality and *live* foods.

Once, during a short fast, a dear friend wanted to join and I remember, with sympathy, that he could not get to dinner time having to stop this very short fast very soon. Maybe a gradual adaptation to this practice, by first skipping one meal, then two and then all day, could help to get used to this practice. On the contrary, I find the Breuss method much easier as it allows you to avoid or reduce the most common side effects of fast (headache, weakness, sleep, etc.) giving you the possibility to restore your body quickly.

Another dear friend has only recently discovered fasting as a therapeutic form and has suddenly decided to try it. Well, he immediately undertook three days of fasting, reporting only a slight headache on the first day. Afterwards he undertook another one of a whole week without having any major problem. Despite being overweight, drinking numerous coffees, and not paying particular attention to the diet, he proved to be a subject, obviously, not very toxic.

This is to demonstrate the importance of the psyche that can turn into a poison or an antidote for our body. In fact, since he is a cheerful and positive character, it is very likely that in his case, the affirmation *a laugh a day keeps the doctor away* may apply. My father used to say: *laughs that the pain goes away*, without, perhaps, imagining how much he could be right. However, despite having happiness and positivity, certain scientific values, without the right food is certainly less effective.

As regards fasting, we have already said that it is inherent in primordial man and in most of the animals, the certainty of periods of fasting (total or partial) more or less prolonged. It is, therefore, certain, as shown by eminent physicians, that one can live without food for several days, keeping all the functions of the organism fully active.

Ehret and Shelton have documented many cases of therapeutic fasting, demonstrating that ordinary humans can survive without food forty to ninety days based on their physical constitution and body weight. The two scholars have undertaken long fasts (49-day Ehret) having only benefits from these (in Ehret they also saved their lives). Then, the extraordinary man, as Jasmuheen teaches us, can survive even without nourishment, or rather, nourishing oneself with Primordial Energy (Prana) or light, as she states in her book (but this does not concern this volume).

Shelton says in his book *Fasting can save your life*: "Among the first colds of childhood and death for cancer in middle age, there is a whole range of symptoms and intermediate complexes: colds, coughs, sore throat, constipation, diarrhea, headache, fatigue, irritability, apprehension, agitation, insomnia, bad breath, tongue, and many other symptoms and so-called acute illnesses, all of which are toxemic crises. The non-toxemic person will never develop the symptoms of a cold." The loss of energy is also a false myth as only toxemic people manifest it. I remember to have read in his book about a sprint he made after several weeks of fasting trying to catch the bus and Ehret was cycling for days while fasting feeling full of energy.

Between the late nineteenth and twentieth century, we witnessed the flourishing of the theories and experiences of a splendid handful of heroes of medicine, composed by Tilden (1851-1940), probably the first theorist of toxemia as the cause of the onset of the disease, Ehret (1866-1922), founder of *Ehrethism*, the mucusless diet and great fast adept, Shelton (1895-1985), also a scholar of therapeutic fasting, Gerson (1881-1959), Kousmine (1904-1992) and other doctors. Most of them have theorized, often converging into opinions, that toxemia and wrong foods are the cause of the onset of the disease. All their theories were based, in fact, on the body's ability to heal itself if given the opportunity.

It is also true that today the average age is very high but this is mainly due to improved hygiene conditions, prevention, antibiotics, and the evolution of diagnostics. Likewise, the quality of life has not evolved as much. In fact, beyond middle age, many individuals begin to develop disorders and become slaves of drugs.

Unfortunately, with the advent of Pharmacine, after that enlightened period, we no longer had characters of this moral fiber even though Pauling (second half of the twentieth century) and Rath (today's pioneer of vitamins) have contributed greatly, with the studies on vitamins, to the true medicine.

I believe that the writings and teachings that Ehret, Gerson, and Breuss have handed down to us are more and more current as those of Hippocrates, yet they are constantly ignored because they would cause great damage to Pharmacine.

These are really compelling readings that make it clear how the writers really understood the nature of things and the human body. If you have a minimum attraction to Nature and naturopathy, these writings will involve you. Ehret's texts are readings that I recommend passionately because they show the experience coming from the heart. This demonstrate as human beings cannot recognize anymore what is good or bad for them and what is the right food, as all other animals (apart from pets) can do.

For over two millennia, we have been told that food is our cure but we do not want to understand. People prefer to remain ill and die (doctors included) rather than to cure themselves in the only way possible, that is, by themselves, following the Nature and the teachings of the great personalities of history.

Professor Ehret[47] said: "The main difficulty with the average individual of modern civilization is that he/she refuses to think. He/she prefers the thought of the mass and, since everyone does it, it must be right! The reality of the facts shows the opposite." Who knows if he met Le Bon?

An absolutely logical theory hypothesizes that Ehret, having died prematurely, could be one of the first cases of *food-drug accident* related to the interests of the industries that produced drugs, meat and dairy.

Unfortunately, even today, nothing has changed and who knows if it will ever change. The masses keep on having their own way of reasoning, as asserted by Le Bon and demonstrated by the main dictators and politicians, which does not allow them to be rational.

Gerson, therefore, developing his therapy (due to his excruciating headaches that no doctor could heal), may have taken into account the works of his illustrious predecessors (Tilden, Ehret, and of course Hippocrates and others). This handful of true disciples of Hippocrates has given prestige to the doctors who were

---

[47] Ehret was closed for 49 days in a cage while fasting. Everybody could watch him while fasting and the thing that bothered him most was that the people were noisy (even during the night) and not the lack of food.

severely criticized by the aforementioned doctors and whose present behavior leaves, sometimes, astonished. This *handful of heroes*, between the second half of the nineteenth century and the beginning of the reign of Pharmacine (end of first half of the twentieth century), has given light to theories and methods of care that will remain (albeit contrasted) in the history of medicine ... the true one.

Toxemia would occur, however, not only from abuses, wrong foods, polluted environment, drugs and so on, but also from psychosomatic causes that vary the physiological processes related to the body's chemistry. Gerson's studies show that coffee enemas effectively detoxify bile products and have been used to replace painkillers which, being of a chemical nature, intoxicate the body.

From personal experience, I can tell you that total fasting, even if it is a formidable therapy, is also a challenging practice, not suitable for everyone, especially when one is toxemic, cannot interrupt the work and does not have enough time to rest. In fact, although there is normally no contraindication, it can cause some physical discomforts, even important ones based on the grade of toxemia. For this reason, I suggest the Breuss therapy, which obtains better results without most of the *side effects*. I have undertaken half a period of the Bruess fast-like therapy without having major problems and not being hungry at all.

I'll omit talking further of pure fasting as there is no need (if not for spiritual purposes). As I have just said, the Breuss system is even more effective and not upsetting at all. Toxins are expelled also through the tongue on which a white patina is formed (which is advisable to remove) with bad breath especially the firsts three days.

With a fast-like method, like the Breuss one, the discomfort inherent the psychological sphere are much less evident.

For those who have the strength to achieve complete detoxification, which normally takes place between the fifth and the sixth week (the 42 days of Breuss), you could witness an important regeneration of the body and, maybe, of the spirit.

As a demonstration of this detoxification process, I remember having undergone a three-day fasting (with only maple and lemon juice added to water) during which I felt pulsing, light headaches in the cervical area and drowsiness. I then repeated this fast with the same modalities, this time after about two weeks of Gerson therapy, and I have not felt the drowsiness that normally comes from fasting in toxemic subjects. This demonstrates the power that fasting can have, but especially that of Gerson therapy and its coffee enemas. For these reasons I recommend to those wishing to undertake therapeutic fasts to detoxify coarsely first with Gerson therapy and then begin with short fasts, as recommended by Ehret. Remember to ingest only foods recommended by the Gerson therapy or Ehret's mucuseless foods until obtaining the desired detoxification. The Breuss therapy should not give any unpleasant effects, especially if not particularly toxemic.

I can guarantee, from my personal experience, that Gerson therapy is very powerful, and can treat also extremely serious patients not curable with Breuss therapy and fast.[48] The Gerson

---

[48] I reckon fast may not be so effective in seriously ill patients, because there is not sufficient time to recover. An alternance between Breuss therapy (adding ESSIAC or Hoxsey herbs) and Gerson therapy might shorten the healing period dramatically.

therapy gives unexpected energies that one has never tried before or thought he could not feel. However, a thing is certain, ours is a *perfect machine*, used to every kind of abuse, but it absolutely needs *care and maintenance* and, above all, to *run with the right fuel*.

The coffee enemas, part of the Gerson therapy, seem to me, therefore, absolutely logical, as well as necessary and tremendously effective, even more than the hydro colon therapy practiced in the modern era. In fact, Gerson discovered, by chance, as it happens to most of the great discoveries, that coffee enema has an important detoxifying power, managing to free toxins that a traditional enema could not free.[49]

Unfortunately, Pharmacine's great experts judge and scorn the therapies they do not share without even knowing what they are talking about. They have been educated (in Pharmacine's academy) for doing so and for this reason they are paid. From Gerson's studies it would seem that coffee enema, for a serious ill patient, is absolutely essential as it dramatically improves the course of his illness. Even though I was not seriously ill, I had evidently accumulated enough toxins to cause an annoying pain in the area of the colon that disappeared completely with the enema. I can only imagine what relief it can be for a cancer patient.

Unfortunately, this practice, although relatively simple, is not often easy and many people live it as an avoidable torture, instead of seeing it as a necessary and sometimes life-saving practice. However, when the benefits are experienced, appreciation comes by itself. As

---

[49] https://draxe.com/coffee-enema/

for bloodletting, now there is no more chance to get them in public facilities, if not in the East, maybe. I have never experienced this type of practice that I believe being absolutely logical and straightforward. However, it still exists and is regularly practiced, especially in the East, the so-called cupping: cups of glass, plastic or other material that, applied on the patient's back, allow an accumulation of blood in the area, thus simulating bloodletting.

Cupping is indicated for the treatment of various painful, gastrointestinal syndromes, pulmonary diseases, coughs, asthma, and also for depressive and anxious syndromes, as well as for headaches, migraine, lumbago, and detoxifying the body. This practice would seem to have been experimented also by Michael Phelps in the last Olympics and by some other athletes. An old therapy of more than 3,000 years that proves more effective than modern drugs. Moreover, it can easily be done at home with the help of a family member or even alone, knowing what to do.

I have always wondered if the practice of bloodletting, in association with other holistic care, could still make sense. I think so, even though I have not personally experienced it. It is necessary, however, to highlight how the disease, in itself, is not a bad thing. It is essentially an alert of the body that tells us that it is no longer functioning well, according to Nature, and that we should change our behavior and habits so as not to incur in worse illnesses. The body warns us, first with the acute illness, then with the chronic one, telling us I cannot stand it anymore. What do we do instead? We fill it with toxic drugs, which further weaken the condition, and food, not allowing it to recover. After each pharmaceutical poisoning, a detoxification period should be taken.

As soon as an acute illness arises, it should be naturally healed, before it becomes chronic. We should do it with a fast-like diet or a few weeks of Gerson therapy, detoxifying enemas, and, last but not least, liver cleansing.

In juvenile subjects, fasting has a similar effect to when a plant is pruned and then, in the following season, will be more luxuriant. In older people these effects could sometimes be different.

The so-called *experts* make a certainly meticulous (however cruel) work of misdirection, misinformation and confusion in general. But as Ehret and Shelton have demonstrated and documented, fasting in young subjects (but not only) could be the fastest and less painful healing practice. As I stated before it is documented that Shelton fasting does not work optimally in the fight against cancer, but that is probably only because there is not enough time for recovery. In fact, the healing process sometimes could take well over forty days. Breuss therapy, as an alternative, has apparently overcome this problem introducing a tiny portion of highly nutritious juice and detoxifying herbal remedies that work very well and can treat even non-advanced types of tumors.

Fasting can last up to six to seven weeks without incurring in even lethal consequences while, to completely rehabilitate a body suffering from cancer pathologies it could take longer. On the other hand, an estimated interval between one and two years is required following the Gerson therapy. For this reason, therefore, the practices of Ehret (alternating fasts and mucusless diet) and Breuss (fast-like highly detox diet) are absolutely interesting. In fact, they might shorten the healing times of the already very effective Gerson therapy, but not healing some of the illnesses treated with the Gerson cure. In particular, the method developed by Breuss would seem to be absolutely effective against many cancer diseases and most of the minor illnesses in just 42 days.

For those illnesses that cannot be cured by Breuss therapy in 42 days, my opinion is to introduce then the Gerson diet until complete recovery. The Breuss method is developed in the intake of ¼ liter of the juice of a cocktail of selected vegetables on beetroot base and some purifying decoctions with results certainly worthy of note. In some desperate cases abandoned by orthodox medicine has given amazing results documented by some true jurors of Hippocrates.[50] Breuss claimed to have treated approximately 45,000 patients with his therapy. As I said, however, in extreme situations, the 42-day cure might still be too short. Therefore, in cases of terminally ill patients, other therapies should be considered, including the Gerson therapy.

Thus it is evident that the confusion, perpetrated by Pharmacine, is too important to be overcome autonomously by ordinary subjects. In fact, people must be disoriented and then counsel with the Pharmacine's expert who, of course, will advise him/her according to conscience, or even without conscience. Only the poor sick people will be the loser in this dispute, while Big Mafia enjoys the incomes deriving from people's disease.

I would suggest the following detoxifying therapeutic plan for a minimal detoxification of a person considered in good health by orthodox medicine:

---

[50] http://www.cam-cancer.org/Media/Files/CAM-Summaries/Biologically-based-practices/Breuss-Cancer-Cure

1. Fast for one or two days to check the degree of intoxication: if on the second day of fasting you do not have side effects, drowsiness, headache, body aches, etc. then, probably, you are not a particularly toxemic subjects and you can, if you wish, continue the fast.

2. If you encounter contraindications in the days of fasting, then take Gerson therapy with at least three daily juices (six to nine juices are recommended) for at least two weeks with at least one coffee enema a day. After two weeks of therapy, fast again as described above and if you do not experience the same side effects, continue with the following steps, otherwise repeat the two weeks of Gerson therapy until you have no evident side effects with your fast.

3. As soon as you fast without undesirable effects, you can adopt this procedure: two days of fasting by taking water, as necessary, with the addition of a tablespoon of maple and lemon juice or I adopt Kefir water (1 liter of water, 3 tablespoons of Kefir granules, 2 tablespoons of brown sugar (Panela or Muscovado), two figs or prunes or a handful of raisins and half a lemon organic which is squeezed into the water at the end of 24 o 48 hours); one day of only Gerson-type juices with coffee enema; four days of Gerson food regime, using the permitted foods (essentially fruit and vegetables), with at least three daily juices and a coffee enema.

4. Repeat this procedure until the desired results are achieved in terms of ideal weight, detoxification and possible regression of chronic diseases.

Consider, however, that the undesirable effects of fasting are common as long as the body is not completely detoxified. Much of the past evils that the body is trying to cure could appear in many forms. However, I will never stress enough that the 30- or 42-day Breuss therapy is certainly an amazing and rapid cure.

As Ehret brilliantly describes in his book *Teachings on fasting*, the body must get rid of decades of accumulation of decomposed and putrefied harmful substances present and enveloped in our bodies by the unnatural mucus that we produce with improper foods. Therefore, when it detoxifies, it brings with it the poisons accumulated over the years and this can cause various kinds of illness-like symptoms (which cause uncertainty and worry), until the organism has completely purified itself.

Consider that, in the average person, there are three to five kilograms of feces not evacuated. In severely obese subjects, it can even reach twenty kilos. So, fasting and enemas and other remedies help you to *get rid of evil*. Following this detoxification, we should be aware of the accumulation of other poisons with the nutrition and psychological conditions that lead us to somatize in specific illnesses, but above all we must be able to get rid of it immediately.

However, as Dr. J. H. Tilden (1851-1940) in his book *Toxemia explained: the true interpretation of the cause of disease*, fasting contributes greatly to the eradication of diseases because it has a powerful detoxifying effect. In fact, he claims that the disease always comes after a generalized toxemia, and the toxemia comes always after an energy weakening caused by a wrong lifestyle with intake of toxic foods (animal proteins), wrong food combinations and an unregulated life.

If the origin of the disease derives from a general weakening, it is logical that physical rest (with fasting or Gerson therapy), besides the psychological one, is fundamental. He also says that:

  Food, fasting and illness

"The cold is the proximal symptom of a complex whose distal symptom is cancer or tuberculosis or any fatal degenerative disease."

Imagine the savings for the state coffers if we would treat ourselves with these types of treatments. A therapeutic fasting cycle or a full Breuss therapy could, approximately, last a couple of months, considering an average fast 6 weeks and a few weeks for recovery. With this therapy, one could recover from so many important pathologies, but above all it would avoid incurring in unpleasant diseases and would be healthy for the public coffers too. In fact, one would not recover from an illness but from all illnesses and it would prevent the onset of new health problems.

When we come across an acute disease, we need to carry out a generalized detoxification treatment to avoid the worst to happen. It must be said that this type of therapy may not be suitable for everyone, because there are important psychological aspects to consider, but, nevertheless, those able to tolerate these constraints could have a quick benefit. For the others it would always remain the Gerson method, certainly longer, but very effective and not so food restrictive. Furthermore, we could recover from many other previous illnesses that we have accumulated over the course of our lives and, probably, we would learn the way not to get sick again.

As for the salt (, at first I thought it was all in all not very influential, or at least not so dangerous, until writing this volume. I have now realized the damage that salt (especially refined) added artificially to the human body can make. It would unbalance, in fact, the equilibrium of the 4 blood electrolytes (calcium, sodium, potassium, and magnesium), but above all the sodium/potassium one. So I find the *Gersonian* theory very much logifical, which explains how the cells are dangerously unbalanced with the addition of sodium (mostly refined and artificially added to processed food) in addition to that naturally contained in food. As a result, salt drains the potassium from the cells to compensate the excess of sodium (theory brilliantly explained in Jesse's video).

Sodium, therefore, in addition to being the major, and probably only, cause of hypertension, could have great influence even on an endless string of diseases, including cancer. In fact, the use of salt for a lifetime could unbalance many equilibriums, even unknown, in the human organism.

Good and bad habits can concretely change the state of health of man causing its healing or illness. Think about it; we use salt every day, but we cannot drink every day only one or two fruit and vegetable juices that, in all probability, would keep us away from so many ailments.

If you cannot completely eliminate the salt, however, it is good to limit it by replacing the common kitchen salts (which are not completely natural and have a sodium content of about 99%) with natural integral salts (Atlantic, rock salt, Himalayas, Cervia, common integral, etc.) that do not contain additives, have a lower sodium content (about 80%) and the presence of magnesium and potassium.

The damage caused by the excess of salt released into the body would also occur for magnesium, calcium, or potassium if also taken unnaturally and daily for a lifetime. The unnaturally unbalanced cells could change precisely because of this imbalance. According to Gerson theory, with the supplement of potassium (through juices and additives) they would find their equilibrium. This is proven by the facts and also ignored by Pharmacine as her interest is to keep as ill. Also Pantellini's cure is based on that, and it worked in many cases.

Of course, even Pantellini may have been subjected to the pharmacinical treatment of Pharmacine or at least to a complete disinterest. His successors, today, work in silence with the Pantellini foundation and they must have clear in mind that against Pharmacine one cannot even try to fight. They do, therefore, maintain a low and discreet profile. Only those who long to wake up and be lucky enough to run into their news can take advantage of their expertise.

After all, think about the possible spread of the news that cancer is being treated with potassium ascorbate! Pharmainquisition would probably not be enough and we would witness the gallows… and not the media one!

This would also explain the fury against Simoncini and its baking soda. I appeal to all cancer patients, but especially to those who pay medical care and who cannot afford them. Why not try, trivially, to take two or three doses of potassium ascorbate a day? What could happen worse? Exaggerate as well with the vit. C, possibly natural, or with ascorbic acid, up to 18 grams (as recommended by Pauling), or more. Of course, that would work more on less serious cancer patients, but it is worth the try.

I cannot explain how it is possible that so many people are still blind before this havoc and continue to trust the pharmacinical institutions. It resembles the time of Hitler no one believed, or wanted to believe, that the Jews ended the way they did. Just look at the videos of Charlotte Gerson present on YouTube to understand that there is something rotten that stinks from afar.

The business of Pharmacine is too big not to try anything to stop natural cures. And they put so much effort on it because they know that they work very well. But we, in this, are co-responsible because we continue to trust without experimenting and often only those who are at the last resort undertake natural cures, which also, not infrequently, work in hopeless people.

I believe that those who suffer with cancer and are prone to natural therapies should first eliminate the proteins (by eating only fruit and vegetables, possibly organic) and consult with well-trained natural therapists. However, when in doubt, immediately take potassium ascorbate three times a day and a tablespoon of vinegar in a glass of water 10 minutes before the main meals and then evaluate everything else.

Imagine if this was enough to heal many cancer patients! After all, Pantellini's experience is self-explanatory: a guy drinks daily a lemonade with bicarbonate of potassium for a year and heals from stomach cancer. Of course, maybe this remedy could only apply to stomach tumors, but who knows ... I'll never stop saying it: *do not trust anybody! Experiment!* The urgency of treatment is often not so pressing, especially if the illness is at an early stage. If it were, instead, at the final stages it would be useless. As I have previously stated, with the therapy introduced by Breuss (250 ml of juice and decoctions) in just 42 days you could recover from not too advanced and metastasized tumors. If you are suffering from serious diseases with metastases you could still undergo this therapy and then switch to Gerson therapy if it is not enough. Please do not make the following kind of objection: but so far nobody has thought about it? Or: why the 45,000 patients healed by Breuss do not scream at the world? It would mean that my message did not come to you at all. It is an association (Pharmacine) aimed at protecting its interests and hiding those of Medicine and ready to commit any kind of offense against man.

Instead, most unaware doctors of Pharmacine press on the need for immediate cure. For heaven's sake, it is right, but you can also take action by adopting a natural therapy that blocks or slow the tumor pathology and then see if with the same regresses. I realize that fear does not make us lucid, but when we get sick of cancer, perhaps we should stop and reflect a few moments, breathe deeply and consciously decide to change our lives. I am sure that 42 days will not cause much worsening, if they cause it at all, in non-advanced cancer patients.

Of course, if we were to die trying to heal in the natural way, the information organs and perhaps even the magistracy would be able to persecute us even in the underworld! We should also hope that we would not leave other people involved (parents, relatives, friends, doctors, etc.). Forgive the humor, but is it not this way?

I am often asked: what would you do if you had cancer or to prevent it? Obviously, I would immediately feel an important psychological discomfort, but later I would work to recover my life by adopting, in order of importance, some of these simple measures:

1) I would abstain from consulting with orthodox doctors because, according to my hypothesis, they would be deceived and therefore polluted by the great lie and would therefore see with blinders;

2) I would immediately cease to swallow both animal and vegetable proteins, eating only fruit and vegetables. I would drink only raw and organic fruit and vegetable extracts (but also Hippocrates and other steamed or raw vegetables, and without salt). I would also evaluate my physical condition to perform the very effective

liver wash rediscovered by Hulda Regehr Clark. In any case, I would try the Breuss therapy lasting 42 days, immediately after the protein breakdown, because it is the shortest, easiest and most effective way of getting rid of cancer. If what just mentioned did not work, I would start Gerson therapy as soon as possible;

3) I would assume daily potassium ascorbate, composed of 300 mg of potassium bicarbonate (about a plastic teaspoon), 150 mg of ascorbic acid (vitamin C, about half) and, if possible, 30 mg of ribose dissolved in 20 ml of water and mixed without metal tools (a potassium solution is also present in Gerson therapy). In addition, I would also take light carbonate of magnesium and calcium carbonate with vitamin C and other supplements recommended by dr. Rath. I would also consider the intake of vitamin C directly in vein, as many studies and doctors (*unofficially*) support;

4) I would use the ESSIAC by René Caisse, the herbs of Hoxsey or COD Tea or even the Swedish bitter (the latter much cheaper) and, last but not least, the aloe of Father Zago, and obviously I would dedicate a lot of time to my health;

5) I would eat the bitter seeds of the fruits (except citrus fruits) which contain amygdalin (vitamin B17), notoriously an adjuvant in the treatment of cancer. Bitter almonds, peaches, and apricots are the ones that contain more. I would consult with the doctor or document myself thoroughly before taking them, because they can cause intoxication and even death if taken in large quantities (especially bitter almonds). A simple rule is eating the seeds together with fruits we usually eat (apricots, peaches, apples, pears, etc.);

6) I would buy the book and the CD of Louise Hay; I would follow the advice and evaluate, if it were the case, the psychological therapy;

7) I would take organic apple vinegar (a spoon in a glass of water) 10 minutes before the main meals;

8) I would equip myself to produce colloidal silver at home and I would take it several times a day (even intravenously, if the case) and in association with DMSO (which is an excellent transporter of the healing principles of other remedies);

9) If it were melanoma I would use, in association with the other remedies and with the Breuss and/or Gerson therapy (exceptional for this pathology), cannabis oil (see Rick Simpson) and/or iodine tincture (Simoncini), brushing the parties involved up to 20 times a day, or, even, Swedish bitter poultices (even if they did not work these simple remedies would still not cost anything). There may be some problems in finding cannabis oil, but in case of need we can get involved: in Spain and in other countries there are clubs that also provide products for medical purposes;

10) I would carefully evaluate the possible procurement and use of the *real* Bradstreet GcMAF;

11) I would control the vitamin D in the blood and, if less than 30 ng/ml, I would take important doses (50.000 IU once a week for 8 weeks) until at least 50 ng/ml is reached in the blood, not exceeding 100 ng/ml and taking care to monitor calcium levels in the blood and urine;

12) I would ask the good Lord to have a few extra hours a day and a personal secretary (of course I'm joking!). However, some prayers never hurts!

13) Last, but not least, I would not involve in my choices any doctor, relative, or friend because, should end badly, they could be persecuted by *Pharmainquisition*. I would also leave something written, where it is highlighted that the choices made are attributable only to myself.

As a prevention, I would use some or all the following points: 2, 3, 4, 5, 6, 8, and 11 and possibly also point 7 with the addition of juices, fresh extracts of carrots, carrots and apples, and green vegetables according to the Gerson method. I would do at least one coffee enema a week, if it was not possible every day, taking care, possibly, to take at least three fresh juices in the day of enema. Of course, the day would not be enough to follow all these points, but the loved reader can organize himself/herself with only some of the remedies proposed, keeping always in mind that the Gerson therapy stands over all for effectiveness and the Breuss one would be the easiest and shortest.

I must say that, unfortunately, man's selfish soul is always ready to take advantage and when some non-pharmaceutical remedies work, they are treated almost like pharmaceuticals ones, with prices far beyond what is morally justifiable. The craving for wealth also affects those who propose so-called alternative or natural remedies, and we see flourishing important diets based on special foods where one would sell to the unfortunate person anything to make money. So we are assisting in the marketing of herbal teas, supplements, nutrient bars, or miraculous preparations that certainly make *healthier* those who offer them.

In many cases, one goes from the frying pan to the fire, although natural remedies cannot do too much harm, but they can do to the pocket if uncontrolled.

 Food, fasting and illness

For a period, Dr. Dukan's diet was pretty popular. He proposed eating protein foods for long periods. Here, this diet, in my opinion, if protracted over time, is certainly the best way to get cancer, exactly the opposite of what Gerson says! Moreover, it is obvious that a diet mainly based on protein make you lose weight because to digest proteins the body consumes a lot. It should, however, be stated not to extend it for a long time and in any case I strongly discourage its use. You may rather assume only biological extracts even for long periods.

Gerson even paid the train ticket for his patients who could not afford it. I wonder if modern doctors would do the same!

I would like to tell you: rely only on the basic theory of Gerson (which already includes a potassium solution) with the addition of apple vinegar but, above all, maintain a healthy lifestyle, by exercising and eating without too much excess. All people need to do regular exercise (this aspect has also been upset by modern man). In fact, most people do not even make a short walk every day. It would be enough, as often indicated by many, even just thirty minutes of daily walk to ensure a minimum muscle tone and a correct heart function. Yet, our frantic life often prevents us from doing so. However, although what has just been said is certainly important, it is not as important as a healthy diet.

One could also eat anything, if one's healthy, but should not overdo the starches, meat, and dairy products and limit the salt (if one cannot eliminate it) replacing it with integral ones, natural and uncontaminated, but above all, remember that *you are doctors of yourselves.*

Many characters and many books have had a significant impact over the centuries on human nutrition and have insistently repeated the importance of a mainly vegetable-based diet, but methodically all have been ignored and/or forgotten.

I fully realize that my statements, although might appear to be original, are not at all. Hippocrates was the first natural therapist. I hope, that this denunciation is not going to be hidden. Unfortunately, I also realize that before me an endless string of great men and women said, repeated and reiterated these concepts starting with Hippocrates, to continue with Paracelsus, Tilden, Ehret, Breuss, Gerson, Kousmine, Colin and Thomas Campbell (with their The China study) and many others. But those are mainly unheard voices.

In the end, the basic theory is the logific one that I confirm and repeat: our ideal diet is *logically* the primordial one of the apes, which is also the one assigned to us by the Creator (fruit and herbs). We must therefore be aware of this in order to better manage our health. We should then use improper foods only occasionally and, especially if we fall ill, return exclusively to our *assigned* diet.

I'm not telling you should forget our history and go back to being fruitarian and forget about taste and sociability. I just want to warn you that these habits could result in most of our ills and that the secret lies in understanding it, first detoxing from poisons accumulated in a lifetime of inadequate nutrition, perhaps blandly following Gerson therapy. Then, once this detoxification is achieved, care should be taken not to accumulate new toxins by regular depuration.

From what has been said above derives my recommendations of basing our nutrition on primordial foods and granting rare exceptions of natural and comprehensible *taste*. But if we make the exception the rule, then we must necessarily fill ourselves with drugs to eliminate the symptoms of diseases that will return, however, more and more arrogant and different shaped, if not, even with the risk of running into extreme troubles. However, I believe that the extreme modern problems can derive in large part from the massive use of drugs (especially vaccines) and more rarely from pollution and lacking or inadequate diet and/or from psychosomatic aspects.

Generally, in Nature, animals do not get sick, unless they are domestic animals or bred, or there are conditions of pollution induced by man or epidemics. So, *logically*, for what unknown rule of nature would this not apply to man? Do not you think there is something anomalous in the *animal man*? Heart attacks, gastritis, tumors, and endless kinds of illnesses. Are these normal?

Today, we have access to everything we need (fruit and vegetables) but, unlike animals, we have also been able to feed on food not created for us to enable us to survive, expand and multiply. In fact, the animals normally either eat the food assigned to them (meat, fruit or grass, ignoring the case of the vegetarian lion mentioned earlier, and of domesticated dogs and cats) or die. It is, then, absolutely logical that there is something wrong with our diet that leads to illness, which would otherwise be non-existent or, at least, marginal. It follows that the practical experiments made by Ehret and the statements of Hippocrates, Paracelsus, Gerson, and many others before and after them have obvious logifical implications. It appears, therefore, clear that man has become addicted to the diets imposed by reasons related to his own survival and expansion and that, now that he could, he cannot go back. Man now justifies his omnivorous diet with the imaginative theory of the need for proteins, carbohydrates, etc., and there are hordes of *experts* ready to swear, with absolute certainty, and against any logic, that it is this way.

I do not want you all to become fruitarians (otherwise I should also do the same), but I have the intellectual honesty to recognize that Ehret is certainly right when he says, empirically and logically, that our natural diet it is the fruitarian one. I consciously renounce to perfect health, accepting tasty and social compromises (also not to distort the family balance), but I do not allow myself to criticize Ehret or Gerson who have experimented and scientifically documented their medical successes. Of course, those who aspire to uncommon spiritual qualities should unquestionably adopt sobriety and natural nourishment, but this is another matter.

It is true that some subjects that do not care particularly about their nutrition come to age well beyond the threshold of one hundred years. However, these subjects often have one thing in common: they spend their whole life with a good balance between body, soul, and spirit which is the basis of our well-being. For all the others who manifest illnesses, there is no other cure than food as it has been repeated for thousands of years, starting with Hippocrates.

Medical Evidence

I will never tire of repeating that what does not hurt an individual may not be suitable for another. As an example, all the *vehicles* have a *motor* (heart), *a control unit* (brain) and *accessories* (organs, limbs, etc.), but each *machine* responds in a different way. Some *vehicles*, even if they do not replace the oil for a long time, continue to work perfectly, others have major defects and sometimes break the engine.

I remember, still in awe, that some acquaintances who suffered from debilitating migraines were treated by me (only an aspiring naturopath) with patches containing a silver alloy. They were applied to the fingers using the relatively new discipline of Korean acupuncture (Koryo Sooji-chim, created by dr. Tae Woo Yoo around the 1970s) with results that were amazing and almost unbelievable by the same subjects treated.

In fact, often, the same patients said they had consulted a horde of specialists but none had managed to understand the causes, similarly to what happened to Gerson. In particular, a lady who had suffered from intense migraine headaches at short and regular intervals, after a single treatment, no longer manifested this disorder until I then lost sight of her (at least for a year).

Korean acupuncture (Sooji-chim) does nothing but eliminate or reduce obstructions to the circulation of our vital energy either through needles or through patches containing silver or gold metal alloy or through moxa[51] applied on the palm and fingers of the hand, similarly to what does the Chinese one all over the body. I suppose, then, that I did nothing but remove the trunks that blocked the flow of water (vital energy) allowing the flow of energy, which apparently allopathic medicine cannot do.

Tell me, then, if the criticism of Dr. Tilden, of the prof. Ehret, and other doctors towards their own medical class is not shareable! The writer puts a patch on migraine sufferers for years after consulting an endless string of physicians and paying lots of money, and the miraculous patient heals (for free) and immediately. And these superfluous illustrious professors, as defined by their memorable colleagues, they do not even have the ability to understand the reason for the headache.

So, in your opinion, is it not better to go to an Indian shaman than to rely on certain doctors belonging to Pharmacine? A tempered suggestion: do it yourself, document, consult, and above all exchange experiences, because these are the foundation of true care. Do the opposite of what the deceived doctors tell you (often in absolute good faith), if what they say does not convince you. Rely on the internet and socialize in groups of experimenters, just as the opposite of what you are told. Hippocrates already indicated the cure for all diseases more than two millennia ago: food. Above all, however, remember that there can be no cure outside of Nature so

---

[51] Moxibustion or Moxa is a traditional Chinese medicine technique that involves burning an herb called Mugwort, to promote healing. It follows similar principles of acupuncture to stimulate the flow of qi and blood and maintain general health.

if you hope to heal with chemicals, you lose all hope. Of course, you will suppress the symptom, but it will change its appearance and return in the form of a new illness with more domineering symptom than before, until it becomes a chronic illness or worse.

As Saint Hildegard says: "Illness is neither a burden nor a fright, but the possibility of changing life, of freeing oneself from vices and becoming a new man." Likewise, she also identifies in the psyche a large part of man's illnesses, which can be solved with fasting, diet and proper action.

I remember once, on the occasion of a move, one of the movers asked me about my strange and unknown bottles of mineral water. When I told him that it was useful in many pathologies, including constipation, his eyes brightened because his daughter was suffering from this disorder and had consulted all the paid-for professors of Pharmacine, without success. I gave him a case of this highly mineralized water (Donat water, I only advertise for free because it can help many) and, surprisingly, I received his call after a week: he thanked me for resolving, with a chat, and without cost, the old malaise of the daughter, that no orthodox doctor had ever managed to eradicate (evidently there is no effective drug against constipation). And you continue to spend money on the top professors who, being deceived too, not only do not solve your problem.

I myself, trusting anyone no more, but believing the good faith of many honest doctors, I have experienced what all doctors (those deceived by Pharmacine at least) advise against, that is, not to stop taking the pill against hypertension. In fact, I recently read in the book by Charlotte Gerson and Beata Bishop *Healing the Gerson Way* that hypertension is not classifiable as a disease, but, rather, as a food habit (I would call it a mental condition, a papillary dependency and a vice). In fact, according to the authors, eliminating salt from the diet would eliminate the onset of the disease in 100% of cases, as certified by Gerson. I then began his diet for about 45 days, halving the dose of drugs after the third day and interrupting after the seventh day: to my astonishment the pressure values continued to fall reaching an incredible 120/70 that I did not even have in my youth.

Unfortunately, having always had the habit of salt, which permeates our everyday lives, after the reintroduction of normal, *social, food*, while limiting salt (with obvious familiar discomfort), the pressure is back to rise. I was then forced to resort again to drugs that I integrate with a mild Gerson-like therapy, with potassium ascorbate, calcium carbonate, and light magnesium carbonate in addition to the supplements recommended by Dr. Rath (vitamin C and E, proline, lysine, arginine, coenzyme Q10, and B vitamins, especially B12) for obvious fears of worse harms. I hope, however, that with the necessary time, one day I will be able to manage it without drugs even while consuming salt moderately. In fact, lack of vitamins and toxemia would make the blood thicker, carrying in it all the waste substances to get rid of. So, years of accumulation (leaving aside the salt) would contribute to this disorder.

It is certainly not easy to shake off a whole life of conditioning. Forgive me, then, if I sometimes *talk the talk and don't walk the walk*, at least in terms of moderation and exercise (remember that there is always a good preacher inside of us ready to do the opposite of what is preached). However, when life is at risk, we should forget all vices and conditioning and put it before everything. In fact, if we still have vital energy we can regret our mistakes (I am pretty sure that everybody would make sacrifices if life is at risk). But, if we shorten our life in advance, then, we will not be able to correct ourselves. I remember that when I decided to become a vegetarian, I failed on the first try and then tried again a few months later with greater determination and the right choice of timing, which is fundamental for the success of our projects. I waited to do the Breuss therapy (only 20 days, scheduled in advance) when I was certain that I could do it without being disturbed. Finding the right timing is half of the work.

I believe that those with at least one hypertensive parent should use these supplements from middle age and earlier, and in any case from the first hint of hypertension. Ascorbic acid (synthetic vitamin C) should never be lacking in a home as we do not get enough with our customs. In fact, many of Pharmacine's hypertensive drugs play with the values of minerals and with the substances present in the human body. Who knows if one cannot find a mineral balance that can effectively counteracts the salt. It would seem that potassium does it but also calcium and magnesium would have important contrasting functions. Indeed, it is evident that all the salt accumulated in a life time can influence important aspects of our health, starting from hypertension.

There are some testimonies of patients of Dr. Rath that his method works for all cardiovascular diseases, including hypertension, and I can partially confirm it after following it for a few months, although it is not minimally comparable to the Gerson therapy.

Rath says, essentially, that all cardiovascular diseases regress, normally, within a year of therapy, with the intake of vitamin C and other supplements.

I therefore find it logical to integrate vitamins and other minerals (potassium, magnesium and calcium) to compensate the salt introduced, if we do not want or cannot follow the Gerson therapy. Consider that modern food, also due to chemical agriculture, greatly limits the intake of these supplements. However, salt consumption should be avoided or drastically reduced because it is really difficult to compensate the huge quantities we take daily in every form. If not, we should at least use natural integral salts.

If some brave person wanted to verify my information, I'm sure they could not receive different feedback. In fact, during the 45 days of Gerson therapy I noticed a powerful diuretic effect that, in my opinion, is not found with other treatments (even with the most powerful drugs). It was as if the *dams* had suddenly opened up, and this is not only due to the fact that the food is purely liquid, but to a real thaw effect of water retention. If you are hypertensive and you are willing to eliminate salt, I am sure you will not be able to have a different response and say goodbye to the Pharmacine pill. You might get a similar effect also with the Breuss therapy and other natural cures but I am pretty sure that it will not be the same. It would also be interesting to listen to the experiences of others, but, of course, these could be misrepresented by the puppeteers who move the threads.

On the basis of my brief but significant experience (which comes from the heart and which is supported by logic) the body, as I have already mentioned with the *engine metaphor*, has its own resistance and *range* of wear.

According to this theory, a young body, under normal conditions, is able to withstand most of the work and works under stress without major problems. However, when the mind (the control unit) provides wrong information, it is possible to begin to manifest the first generalized maladies or even important (engine) *failures*. These *failures* can even culminate in a generalized and chronic inefficiency of the *human machine*. To such inefficiencies, due to the psychosomatic sphere, can be added bad eating habits (inadequate fuel, poor or dirty), unsuitable lifestyles (zero maintenance and engine cleaning, not careful driving) and the inevitable accidents that happen in the path of life.

So, contrary to what the experts and consultants of Pharmacine say, the diseases are also cured by taking care of the psychological aspect of the patient, which is then what, in most cases, allows (or at least contributes) to the disease itself to establish in a given subject (see Hamer experience).

Some Indian holy men ingest poison without dying, this shows that our psyche has strong influences in one sense and another. Ehret made numerous experiments after long fasts and fruit-feeding, pointing out that self-inflicted wounds healed in just three days and they were hardly bleeding. In the same way, he experimented that, with a carnivorous diet, the wounds bleed profusely and took over a week to heal. You will now be struck by the following affirmation (try to believe!). He has shown in practice that women who enjoy what he calls *perfect health* (some of his disciples) do not have menstruation which is, therefore, to be regarded as an anomaly of those who follow an improper diet. I realize that this statement can be strong but, as for many subjects, just try to believe. In his book *Mucusless Diet Healing System* he states that:

"If the FEMALE BODY is PERFECTLY CLEANED with this diet, THE MESTRUAL CYCLE SHOULD DISAPPEAR. Each of my FEMALE PATIENTS has reported that her menstruation diminished more and more - with intervals of two, three and four months, and finally disappeared completely, and this last condition was experienced by those who had done a PERFECT ELIMINATION PROCESS with this DIET.

Migraines, toothache, vomiting and all other so-called "pregnancy disorders" vanish. The painless deliveries, with abundant and very sweet milk, and children who never cry, children who are cleansed differently from others, are wonderful facts that I learned from a woman who became a mother after living with this diet ."

Also in this case, the Pharmacine's scientists (but also the average reader) will never be able to believe that a woman can become pregnant without a menstrual cycle and will be ready to spit sentences on the veracity of Ehret's empirical statements. He himself took note of an unknown condition that arose in his female patients solely following the completion of his diet.

However, it is very simple to verify it, just follow its dictates (it is not excluded that I will undergo his diet to prove its veracity). But do not publicize it otherwise the tamed media, will be ready to show up outside your home to submit you to the *food inquisition*.

As Louise Hay[52] teaches with her experience, it would be really interesting to check if her theories are only perverse fantasies of psychologically proven people or of a *desperate charlatan* (as some *witch hunter* has apostrophized her) or if they contain, in fact, important foundations of truth. If death occurred in cancer patients following the psychological Hamer method, as happened in a clinic of Pharmacine, they would have been charged only to have tried to cure an *incurable case*. But as they have been treated with *alien* methods, is unleashed the *tamed dog* (the media) of the masters of the world.

Because some people died with Dr. Hamer method, he is now a non-aligned person, as Pharmacine has perpetrated the most atrocious crimes against him, but his paradigm of care is absolutely logical: cancer can be establish in people who have suffered significant psychological trauma. Innocently, however, Pharmacine leaves out that his method was followed by many cancer healed people who got completely recovered, but that is an irrelevant news. He himself got healed without chemo, was it a miracle?

The human story of Dr. Hamer and his wife is absolutely explanatory of how the psyche can influence the organism. From the moment in which his family tragedy took place, he began to

---

[52] The life itself of Louise Hay is a beautiful metaphor of the teachings that she transmits through her books and training seminars. She was raped at the age of five and had a life full of adversity. After divorcing her husband, she discovers the Church of the Religious Sciences that teaches her the transformation of thought and studies the works of Hernest Holmes and the teachings of Maharishi Mahesh Yogi. In 1977 or 1978 she discovered that she had cervical cancer and came to the conclusion that it was due to resentment for the abuses suffered in her childhood. In 1976, Hay wrote his first book *Heal Your Body*, then expanded into his book *You Can Heal Your Life*, published in 1984.

investigate his illness reporting its onset to causes related to psychological trauma.

Since Dr. Hamer decided to dissociate himself from Pharmacine, against the advice of his colleagues and superiors, and pursue his cause, his life (until then exemplary) has suddenly turned into a nightmare undergoing a terrible Pharmainquisition with the following witch hunt who imprisoned him more than once. These are the Pharmacine's strong powers and, if you do not bend, like dr. Hamer did, then the punishment will be exemplary. But what else did he have to lose after a son and his wife[53]?

However, on how to deal with psychological discomfort one can certainly argue and not everyone is able to overcome in the same way. Plato said: "You should never try to cure the body without the soul," and I would also like to add that you should never try to cure the soul without the body.

Who knows why media do not talk about the thousands of deaths due to malpractice related to the numerous failures of chemotherapy treatments and other scandals! About eight million deaths in the world pass almost unnoticed every year. Instead, a single case (certainly noteworthy, like so many other people who died in the structures of Pharmacine), rises strongly to the headlines like the case of the century. Tell me if this is not pure Pharmainquisition.

I myself was mourning a distant relative in my family. He was a young boy affected by leukemia, treated with chemotherapy

---

[53] See the *forbidden cures* chapter.

who died after only three days. No one has ever been scandalized and indignant and the newspapers, miraculously, have remained silent. There were no newspaper titles of the type: "killed by chemo in three days." Think about it if this kind of propaganda would appear in the headlines would it be still the same? Would be the battle still one-sided?

After all, it is normal for cancer patients, treated in the structures of Pharmacine, to die (and thousands die every day) but, obviously, it is not normal that cancer patients can die, if not treated by Pharmacine. If that happened the media will let you believe it is the end of the world. Afterwards *Pharmacine adepts* are clever enough to send people die to their own homes and not in their facilities. When they realize they cannot succeed they get rid of the poor fellow and, maybe, the statistics will not mention it.

In the same way, today, it happens that the dozens of thousands of cases of vaccine damage, detected and non-detected, including many deaths, are not minimally considered, nor mentioned, by the media. Whereas some harmless case of measles seems to have caused terrible national epidemic. Do you still really believe in a free press? Tell me if this does not appear like news dictated by the bosses that the servants (journalists) cannot refuse to make public.

I still cannot explain the fury of the press and medical institutions in the absence of that of the families involved, indeed, in stark contrast to that of the families of origin of these *victims of life* treated differently from the *chemodeath*.

I wonder, logically, why in so many cases it is not the family who denounce but are the media fomented by Pharmacine? Everyone must logically find their answer, but it is suspicious that important television broadcasts are so blind and tame. I do not justify, nor support, nor do I approve the psychological treatment as the only cure. I say that I do not exclude that it can have a therapeutic value. Indeed, I am convinced of this cure, as demonstrated empirically by Louise Hay and Hamer himself and some other characters. However, I must admit that I would never treat myself solely with psychotherapy but would combine it with other proven natural remedies (Gerson, Breuss, René Caisse, Hoxsey, colloidal silver, DMSO, potassium ascorbate and others already mentioned). This does not mean that psychotherapy is the devil and chemotherapy or other treatments are the holy water, the opposite is more likely. Psychotherapy should then *always* sensibly supported by the other just mentioned therapies.

As I have repeated endlessly, cures for almost all diseases already exist, so if they tell you that *you must die, do not believe it!* And above all, *do not trust! Experience! Do not lose hope!*

An encouraging hope, as I said earlier, comes from the University Clinic de *La Charité* in Berlin, which experiments with great caution the coexistence between devil and holy water (i.e., chemotherapy and natural therapies similar to fast-like and/or Gerson-like). I wonder: why not try a proven and tested method like Gerson therapy without chemo?

As I said in the course of this *fantastic* story, I am convinced that cancer is established in physically and/or mentally weakened subjects, and/or with important karmic loads, who do not cure the various aspects of life (psyche, nutrition, physical activity, often all together) and/or exceed in pharmacological treatments that go however to overload the excretory organs of poisonous toxins. These toxins, often not eliminated, could contribute, over the years, to the onset of diseases and, last but not least, to cancer. The secret could be hidden in regularizing our digestive-assimilative-evacuative system with a Gerson-like diet, continuing an adequate *maintenance* of our *perfect machine*.

Unfortunately, healthy habits such as fasting, enemas, and bloodletting that contribute greatly to the expulsion of toxins have gone into disuse, and much more often physicians do not even know their potential but are rather pointed out as bizarre and antiquated practices, sometimes object of derision. Furthermore, the necessary attention is not paid to the treatment of intestinal problems, which often reveal themselves as the origin of the worst evils and the powerful practice of the liver cleansing is practically unknown to the most.

I realize that many people prefer to continue poisoning themselves with chemical toxins rather than abandon harmful eating habits and embark on a natural and rebalancing course of care. The average person prefers a *magic pill* that takes away all his/her illnesses. When one risks one's life, however, the flexibility and propensity to sacrifice of people is greatly increased.

Colloidal Silver

Despite being one of my first passions, I will not elaborate too much on the description of colloidal silver. There are many sites about it on the internet, often repetitive, and we can easily get an accurate idea. After all, the notion is very simple: silver is certainly the most powerful killer of bacteria, fungi, and viruses. From it derives colloidal silver and many other pharmaceutical topical products. In fact, pharmaceutical industries produces some creams and ointments strictly for topical use, since it can make them pay properly. In the United States, the production and commercialization of colloidal silver in liquid form is allowed only if clearly highlighted that the same must be used only topically because, according to Pharmacine, there is no scientific evidence. Well the evidence and scientific evidence is almost a century old but they do not care.

The antibacterial properties of silver have been known since ancient times. The Egyptians already knew its virtues and it was not by chance that the nobles, who could have used gold dishes, used instead silver ones. In fact, they had already noticed that those who used them rarely got sick.

The Persians used silver containers to carry water, and the Romans put silver coins in the water amphorae to sterilize it. History teaches us that all great peoples have used silver in a variety of ways to prevent infections. Precisely because of this daily use derives the term *blue blood* as a characteristic of silver, ingested coarsely, was to give a bluish blood coloring. In exchange, on the other hand, immunized kings and queens from the most common diseases of the past.

Colloidal silver owes its birth to the Italian chemist Francesco Selmi and the Englishman Thomas Graham who discovered colloid chemistry. Starting from their discovery it was used by the medical class as the main remedy against the most various diseases (including typhus), until the marketing of antibiotics after the Second World War took place.

The collapse of Medicine is mainly imputable to Big Mafia's control over the first universities started in the early 1930s as a consequence of the Great Depression. At that time, the first pharmaceutical products were already marketed but the universities were still independent. It was only after the war that the first antibiotics mass production started. As a consequence, colloidal silver (which was still accepted and widely used because there were no antibiotics) was gradually isolated and boycotted.

However, the desirable awakening of humanity is causing many more people, like the writer, to open their eyes and find alternative solutions to the use of the structures of Pharmacine. Gerson therapy, but also fasting and fast-like therapies, are certainly the panacea for all illnesses. Those who want can safely produce the colloidal silver (in the ionic variation) at home in complete safety to treat bacterial, fungal and viral diseases effectively, even more than antibiotics.

Colloidal silver is used against almost all known bacterial strains. Before 1938, it was used to fight the following long list of diseases: acne, arthritis, burns, blood poisoning, cancer, candida albicans, cholera, conjunctivitis, cystitis, diphtheria, diabetes, dysentery, eczema, fibrosis, gastritis, herpes, shingles (Shingles), impetigo, intestinal problems, leprosy, leucorrhoea, lupus, malaria, meningitis, Lyme's disease (borelliosis), pertussis, athlete's foot, pneumonia, pleurisy, rheumatism, rhinitis, salmonellosis, scarlet fever, seborrhea, septicemia, skin tumors, warts, syphilis, tuberculosis, toxemia, tonsillitis, trachoma and ulcers, inflammation of the gall bladder. In addition, it treated the following infections: yeast infections, ophthalmic, ear, prostate, streptococci, flu.

It would also appear to be effective against the most dreadful bacteria that Pharmacine struggles to fight, such as the antibiotic resistant strains of Pseudomonas, MRSA, Methicillin-Resistant Staphylococcus Aureus, and Escherichia Coli. [54] It is unbelievable the way Pharmacine works: rather than letting one use a non pharmacinical therapy they would let one dye.

Out of curiosity, try to ask an orthodox doctor what colloidal silver is. Most of them do not even know its existence, demonstrating the brainwashing that Big Mafia operates in its universities managed in conjunction with Pharmacine. They simply

---

[54] https://www.ncbi.nlm.nih.gov/pubmed/19726047
https://sites.google.com/site/argentocolloidale10ppm528hz/12---argento-colloidale-ionico-e-le-infezioni-da-pseudomonas

ignore it, and such remedies (which can save lives) do not seem to exist. However, orthodox doctors insist on not prescribing it because they do not know (and must not know) the existence of colloidal silver. So, they do not even know what it is and they are wary of a harmless, watery solution that is very powerful in counteracting bacterial diseases because they were taught this way.

They are not, however, equally suspicious about their poisons, which are the fourth cause of death after heart attacks, tumors and strokes.[55] Coincidentally, they are wary of some water with silver ions dissolved in it that it cannot cause anything but a simple excess of detoxification. How can you still believe them? *Do not trust!* Orthodox doctors are simple, willing, unaware and deceived officers under the orders of Big Mafia and Pharmacine. They cannot even realize what is outside their world, for many of them there is only chemistry and only one master. *Do not trust! Experience!*

I myself produced at home ionic colloidal silver which has been of great use to my family and friends. I gave ionic colloidal silver to a relative of mine who had been suffering from a cold for over a month and who could not get rid of it. Well, after only few hours from the intake of colloidal silver, the cold had miraculously disappeared. It is also excellent for problems with prostate and vaginal infections.

---

[55] https://www.collective-evolution.com/2013/11/20/how-pharmaceuticals-came-to-be-the-4th-leading-cause-of-death-in-america/
https://health.usnews.com/health-news/patient-advice/articles/2016-09-27/the-danger-in-taking-prescribed-medications

Even for cystitis (tested on an acquaintance who had recurrent infections treated with drugs that then punctually returned) gave positive results after a few days and the annoying malaise has not returned again. This suggests that it would work well (even better than antibiotics) for all bacterial diseases in general, as well as viruses and fungi, as non pharmacinical scientific experiments show. If injected directly in the vein (as they used to do in the 1930s), then it could work wonders, especially with new products created with modern technology. Moreover, if you can use directly on the infected part, then it really turns into a formidable killer (the tests done in vitro are a proof). Unfortunately, colloidal silver needs a minimum of accumulation before becoming exponentially effective, so if you ingest sufficient quantities of colloidal silver during the year you will guarantee a fairly effective protection against most of fungi, viruses and bacteria.

Imagine, all this mentioned so far obtained with homemade ionic silver in a traditional way, even though with care, but without the tools that could have specialized companies or equipped hospitals. But then where would the antibiotic business go? I should also quantify it as well, but I do not want to, forgive me ... So, as Max Gerson brilliantly demonstrated, and as his daughter, Charlotte [56] says, there are no incurable diseases, not even autoimmune diseases (for which Pharmacine does not attempt even a cure). It is equally true that: "The pharmaceutical industry market is your body, but until it is sick," as brilliantly stated by Dr. Matthias

---

[56] https://www.youtube.com/watch?v=UL5qSegu2ds;
https://www.youtube.com/watch?v=GoM78CO3gdo

Rath in his book *Why Animals Do Not Get Heart Attacks ... But People Do!*

If we want to simplify as much as possible, we can say that there are two types of colloidal silver: one that is normally called ionic colloidal silver (ICS) or ionic silver (IS) and the other that is called colloidal silver (CS), even if it is generically referred to as colloidal silver. The difference between the two is essentially in the composition of the particles, in the type of silver dissolved in water and in the production methodology. The first one is made by electrolysis (two electrified silver slats or bars immersed in distilled water) and has a minimum quantity of silver colloids (nanoparticles), around 20%, and many parts of silver in ionic form. The other contains instead around 80% of nanoparticles (colloids) and is produced in a different way, industrial and more laborious.

From studies, nano colloidal silver would appear to be much more effective than ionic silver since the former interacts in a lesser way with the salts present in the organism and is made up of smaller and more effective particles. The principle is the smaller the parts, the higher the efficacy. However, I can personally testify that even ionic silver is absolutely decisive, as it was already in the early 1900s, to even cure typhus. In fact, an injection of 50 ml a day for three days was already used at the time, and if patients were treated within 48 hours of the onset of the disease, they had about 80%[57] chance of survival.

---

[57] Gabriele Graziani e Luciano Graziani, *L'argento colloidale: un potente rimedio naturale*, (colloidal silver: a powerful natural remedy) Macro Edizioni.

The evolution of technology means that now we speak of colloidal silver in nanoparticles that are more and more evolved, smaller and more effective. I am convinced that this type of therapy could be used effectively in all hospitals as an antibiotic treatment, administered by drip to increase its effectiveness with more efficacy then antibiotics and without side effects. I have seen a close relative affected by pericarditis die in Pharmacine's hospital, knowing that more could be tried. Unfortunately, I did not dare to confront myself with the Pharmacine primaries knowing that they must follow the strict protocols imposed by Big Mafia.

I do not want to go further on this subject because it is enough to know that it exists. Those who are interested in it should know that with a few hundred dollars you can produce an excellent homemade ionic silver, absolutely effective for many diseases, especially the most difficult, and that is absolutely safe even intravenous as shown by the administrations in the 1930s of the last century. I have recently learnt that there might be an easy procedure to turn ICS in CS, but I cannot testify its efficacy.

I can only imagine how effective the new products in nanoparticles would be for infections that, today, claim many lives, such as bacterial pericarditis and endocarditis, which antibiotics, often, cannot defeat. Obviously, the Pharmainquisition prohibits even talking about these hypotheses. Who is affected by these diseases either takes care of himself or dies, as unfortunately, sometimes happens, with the certainty of not having been treated according to the Hippocratic oath.

Think about it, diseases such as hepatitis C, which treatment can cost up to one hundred thousand dollars, could be treated with few dozen dollars with Gerson therapy or colloidal silver or, even, more simply, with Hulda Regehr Clark's Zapper, but nobody does it because of the business there is behind this.

In the Western world, doctors no longer think in terms of treatment but in terms of protocols that are clearly imposed by pharmaceutical companies. In fact, doctors now act following a manual (of course, written by Pharmacine).

DMSO and MSM

The art of healing comes from nature, not from the physician. Therefore the physician must start from nature, with an open mind.

PARACELSUS

DMSO (dimethyl sulfoxide) is a by-product of paper processing. It is frequently used as a solvent in organic chemistry. Its therapeutic properties were discovered thanks to the studies of dr. Stanley Jacob, also in this case by chance. In fact, during industrial processes, utilizing DMSO, it was noticed that the workers who were in contact dipping their hands in it, did not suffer from joint pains. From here began the study of Dr. Jacob who pointed out its effectiveness for a long string of diseases, including tumors.

Another unique feature of DMSO is to be a natural carrier of the active ingredients present in other medicines that reach the affected organs without too many obstacles. For this reason, it is also used, in association with colloidal silver, in the treatment of cancer and other diseases and can be taken in combination with aloe and other therapeutic preparations.

DMSO is effective for an endless list of physical problems: amyloidosis, Alzheimer's and dementia, athletic injuries, burns, cirrhosis, diabetes, digestive problems, eye problems, fibromyalgia, carpal tunnel, otorhinolaryngology, fungal infections, scalp problems (baldness), infections and inflammations, migraines, lupus, mental illness and retardation, pain therapy, multiple sclerosis, respiratory problems, radiation protection, mouth and gums, etc.

It can be used both orally and topically by diluting it, in both cases, from 50 to 90% with distilled water or with aloe vera juice.

Unfortunately, especially when taken orally, it causes an annoying smell similar to garlic, due to the presence of sulfur in its composition. For patients not suffering from serious illness, therefore, it becomes very difficult to use, especially for those having a social life. However, when administered by the dermal route the undesirable effect does not occur with the same speed as when taken orally. Obviously, for serious pathologies, the discomfort of the garlic-like smell becomes understandable, tolerable, and even welcome.

From Jacob's studies, it would seem to be a formidable remedy for joint problems. The DMSO can be bought either pure or diluted (ready to use).

As for DMSO, MSM (methylsulfonylmethane) is also a sulfur-containing remedy that (like, and more, of garlic and onion contains sulfur) has exceptional characteristics against many diseases. It is essentially the younger brother of the DMSO.

As I said before, the remedies are similar, even if, perhaps, the MSM is not as effective as the DMSO. However, the ductility and ease of use increase its potential exponentially. It is, in fact, used in many supplements for sports and other types of supplements such as those for hair loss and to improve hair appearance. The MSM powder can be easily purchased. Also in this case, there are experiments to fight cancer.

Obviously, this chapter only serves to bring the public's attention the existence of these remedies and does not serve as a therapeutic guide. It will be possible to deepen the subject with internet readings and books present on the market.

In view of the fact that all sulfur-containing remedies are very effective in the treatment of human diseases, it is really advisable to make a periodic visit to the spas to restore the body.

Bacteriophages or Phages

*At the base of the enormous profits of the
pharmaceutical industries there is not the ability
to fight diseases, but the patents of new synthetic
molecules, unknown to the human body.*

Dr. MATTHIAS RATH

The phage[58] therapy is essentially a biological therapy that makes a natural selection between bacteria, a bit like it happens in organic agriculture where the presence of some parasites it is countered through its natural antagonists.

Phages are, essentially, microorganisms that attack bacteria and do not harm human cells by behaving similarly to how a virus behaves. Once the bacterium is colonized, they use their own apparatus to reproduce and multiply repeating this process until the colonization and destruction of that particular bacterium are complete. In fact, phage therapy can only provide the contrast to a single type of bacterium or a small cocktail of bacteria from the same strain.

The phages, which are virtually unknown, could prove, together with colloidal silver, the future of antibiotics, since the latter are always more depleted. In fact, pharmaceutical companies are ending the so-called refueling pipelines and do not want to

---

[58] https://www.ncbi.nlm.nih.gov/pmc/articles/PMC3109452/

experiment with new products because research is no longer convenient. Thus, an alternative to antibiotics is finally conceivable. Unfortunately, Pharmacine is also destroying antibiotics, an important pharmacological resource (perhaps the only one), making it a reckless use.

The phages owe their birth to Felix d'Herelle, a Frenchman who then moved to Georgia. Their diffusion is, in fact, concentrated almost exclusively in the former USSR. Phages were studied and used more there because the pharmaceutical research was not as developed as in the West. Moreover, with the advent of antibiotics, they have suffered the same fate of colloidal silver, despite being a formidable resource.

Obviously, even this remedy is not scientific (because it cannot be patented) and is not accepted by Pharmacine, although, in this case, the infamous double-blind tale could be applied. Unfortunately this eventuality will not occur, at least as long as antibiotics exist. This demonstrate that those of Pharmacine are only lies and deception.

Have not you figured out who we are dealing with yet? If you need to cure yourself from deadly bacterial diseases that Pharmacine cannot fight anymore, you should easily fill in colloidal silver or use phages at will if you really want to recover. I am ready, at the first symptom of serious illness, to insert a needle into my vein and feed it with colloidal silver self-produced. I am sure that it will be more effective and less dangerous than Pharmacine's poisons. Or I will recover the phages in a former USSR country.

Moreover, from the ethical and safety point of view, the phages would appear absolutely safe. In fact, once the bacteria that attacks the human organism are killed, the phages follow the same fate, disappearing completely from the organism.

Phages and bacteria then undertake a struggle until a balance is reached which then allows the body to fight the infection by its own means. The phages can also modify themselves similarly to what happens for the bacteria.

So, why are not we using the phages? Let's see if you have understood! This time I will not give you the answer.

Phage therapy has been used for the following infections: genitourinary infections (including chronic prostatitis), osteomyelitis, purulent meningitis, acne, purulent otitis, diabetic foot and purulent wounds, gastrointestinal, orthopedic and respiratory infections. Practically a phage remedy could be developed for any type of infection it is enough just to find the right phage by taking it from nature or from a bacterial culture where there is that type of bacterium.

In the former USSR countries, there are phage banks, continuously updated, from which to draw if necessary and which can defeat bacteria for which antibiotics have become ineffective. In practice, this type of therapy has no limits; if a bacterium exists, its antagonist will exists too, so it can be fought effectively.

Unfortunately, this formidable remedy, which is still completely distant to most of the public, will be countered in a proportionally increasing manner compared to its knowledge and dissemination. Also in this case those who have experience of biology can do themselves quite easily. Be sure that phages can not hurt us in any way, certainly no more than Pharmacine does.

Obviously as this treatment is not of interest to Big Mafia (it cannot generate the expected revenue, as not patentable), in all likelihood will never be allowed in the realm of Pharmacine. We only need to hope that they will survive at least in the former Soviet Union countries.

It should be said, to be fair, that the best care is to stay healthy and avoid getting sick with regular fasts and with a Gerson-like diet (including enemas) or following, at regular basis, Ehret's mucusless diet.

Vitamins

*Of all the flowers, the human flower
is the one most in need of sun.*

JULES
MICHELET

I have decided to devote an entire chapter of this book to vitamins because the logical process to these human nutrients can be applied extensively. In fact, everything that goes around vitamins (particularly D and C) could turn out to be the tip of the iceberg of modern medicine (as a consequence of what I have stated on the chapter related to nutrition about our original frugivorous human diet).

The opinion that the vitamin D is a very important propaedeutic element to human well-being is now a given fact. It is, as well, given for granted the fact that its deficiency can lead to an endless string of diseases, including cancer and degenerative bone syndromes, heart illnesses and other types of diseases, including autoimmune diseases (Alzheimer's, Parkinson's, SLA, etc.), though for the latter I would point the finger more on vaccines as I logically state on my other book about vaccines.

However, it should also be said, in advance, that Gerson does not use this vitamin in his therapy and his patients are in magnificent shape. Perhaps the vegetables could somehow compensate for this vitamin, not surprisingly the Gerson therapy is very well suited for osteoarticular problems. Ehret also insists on the importance of sunlight and open air by recommending baths of sun and air, as Breuss does.

With the same logic concerning the nutrition of man we can discuss the question of vitamin D. In fact, incomprehensibly and naively, in the past I had never stopped to think, logically, on the problem of vitamin D, at least until some doctors raised the logical problem.

It is only necessary to check how much is the shortage of this hormone (classified only after studies following its discovery as a steroid hormone) called in the initial stages as vitamin D and which has then maintained this name.

The deficiencies of vitamin D in humans have been highlighted in many historical periods, in which, among other things, it could not be treated because there were no available tools. However, the contemporary age is, perhaps, the one that sees the worst conjunction of events that cause a worrying and endemic shortage of this hormone. In fact, the questionable habits of the social *animal man*, however understandable, greatly influences this, still only marginally perceived, lack.

Man in the modern and contemporary age covers himself more and more integrally, he lives in closed spaces even in summer and when, those few days a year, he exposes himself to the sun's rays he does so with protections that do not allow the acquisition of UVB rays, responsible for the production of vitamin D. As a matter of fact the medical category is one of the most affected by this problem because they seldom stay open air and uncovered.

The question of vitamin D does not fully interests Big Mafia, as it is not yet measured the severity of this health deficiency. However if, as believed, it can really help in an endless series of illnesses, then Big Mafia would have a strong economic interest in maintaining this deficiency in modern man. As a matter of fact they do not encourage the use of vitamin C and D (may be they are scared to lose some income from drugs).I would then suggest, let alone the supplements and ingest plenty of organic fruit and vegetable and spend some time under the sun uncovering large parts of your body, without sunscreens and being careful not to get sun burnt.

The monkeys, the animals most similar to humans, do not cover their skin, probably they seek shelter from intense sunrays, but this is normal in many animals. Since it would seem that only ten or twenty minutes of intense sun are sufficient to accumulate high quantities of vitamin D, the people that do not cover too much have the possibility to acquire the quantities they need. If taken according to seasonality, then, gradually the organism takes what it needs. It is a perfect mechanism, as well as everything that comes from Nature.

It is absolutely logical, therefore, that the man, having distorted his/her animal habits, has also modified the intake of this natural hormone. It is therefore evident how the habits of modern man can influence his health. Modesty in man ensures that we do not uncover our body when we should, contributing to our discomfort.

Vitamin D, in other words the sun, seems to be essential, according to recent medical studies, to maintain good health. It is believed, in fact, that it can affect depression, osteoporosis, diabetes, rickets, multiple sclerosis, influenza, cancer, chronic pain, asthma, autoimmune diseases, senile dementia and much more.

The sun is therefore an essential element at least until we mature a genetic change (if ever possible) that makes us feel good even without sun. Therefore, moderate exposure should be encouraged, rather than, as is often the case, demonized.

In fact, it is obvious that exposure must be moderate. As the pioneering physicians of the subject indicate, you should expose yourself up to a maximum of half the time needed to flush. So, if you get an erythema in half an hour of zenith summer sun exposure, then you will have to expose yourself for a maximum of fifteen minutes. If it takes an hour, you have to expose yourself for a maximum of half an hour, and so on. However, the basic rule is that one should not flush under the sun's rays.

According to Nature, man (as any other animal) should not wear cloths. We were used to wear a loincloth, and in the winter months some animal skin to protect ourselves from the cold. From the beginning of spring, therefore, we would be naturally struck by sunrays which would pigment the skin gradually and without the burns that occur in modern man because, in most cases, it only expose his/her body in July or August for many hours all of a sudden.

Only man (apart cold-blooded animals) lie for several hours to brown in the intense sun, often without even having prepared the skin before. Normally man is covered with clothing, until he/she goes to the beach for the first time and take a sun overdose that, in this way, can certainly be harmful. No other living being behaves this way.

It is obvious that if we go to the seaside for the first time in mid-August and only at that time expose ourselves (maybe in the wrong hours) we can suffer unpleasant consequences. It is equally true that using solar shields containing chemicals such as octyl-methoxycinnamate[59] such risks can even increase.

Perhaps man should take simple precautions, using covering clothes or sunscreens that do not contain harmful substances, after taking our *sun dose* without protection.

The gradual increase in pigmentation would, therefore, be natural and probably the regulation of this hormone within the body would be correct. Logically, in nature, we would get a feast of vitamin D in the firsts solar expositions in spring months decreasing later as melanin is produced and the skin darkens.

At the same time, with the coming of summer, the intensity of UVB rays increases with a consequent increase in vitamin D production. There will also follow a reduction of the absorption of vitamin by the human body, due to the pigmentation of the skin, which would however allow a continuous accumulation of vitamin due to the increased intensity of sunlight. It is a perfect mechanism that only Nature can create.

If we followed the natural way, we would really need little. We would not need sunscreens, even with holes in the ozone layer. In my opinion we should not demonize the intake of small doses of sun, even intense, but encourage it, paying the utmost attention.

---

[59]Charlotte Gerson, in her book, highlights its toxicity that doubles when exposed to the sun. Yet, about 90% of sunscreens contain this substance, not caring about people who should be protected.

Unfortunately we are very far away from that path and therefore we have to make changes to our social behaviors, to what we eat, to our physical exercise, etc.

As far as I am concerned, in modern man, the wise words *In medio stat virtus* (virtue stands in the middle) are applicable to many, if not all, fields of our life and human society and this saying also applies to the right balance between natural and artificial. So, if there is a real need to take antibiotics (because you have neglected mind or/and body) or undergo surgery to make sure you save your life, you should not hesitate too much. But you should also take good care of yourself by avoiding illnesses that can be prevented by eating healthy, *live* natural food and with a little of *natural life* (physical and mind exercise and open air and sun exposition).

Having said that, I would suggest to expose to the sun a part as large as possible of our body during the summer and take small amounts of sun (even 10-20-30 minutes, according to skin type) front and back. In fact, the wider the area of exposure, the greater the intake is especially in the central hours of the day, since they are those where the UVB rays are more intense.

This exposure, in fact, would appear to offer a considerable amount of vitamin D that would probably keep us away from unpleasant illnesses, also due to its deficiency. At the same time I believe that only a short period of summer sun cannot be the cause of extreme evils. In fact, this short exposure (without protection) would seem to provide important amounts of vitamin D that are, parsimoniously, accumulated by the organism (perfect machine) without giving any kind of anomaly, contrary to what could happen with the synthetic vitamins if taken in huge quantity.

It would appear that a light (not tanned) skin type, can receive well over 50,000 IU (International Units) in a very short period under the midday summer sun. So we should learn to have a certain relationship with the sun. Protect ourselves, but intelligently, not criminalizing sunshine, as often happens.

As stated by the highest authority in the field of vitamin D, Dr. Michael Holick: "The American Academy of Dermatology and the solar protection industry have carried out a thirty-year brainwashing of the world population with the pressing message that people should never expose to direct sunlight because it can cause skin cancer and lead to death." By mere coincidence in the last three decades melanoma cases have tripled. Another mere coincidence is that autoimmune diseases were unknown before the first vaccine was introduced[60]. No comment!

On the contrary, it would appear that the ratio between the cases of cancer imputable to the sun exposure and those attributable to its deficiency are 1 in 50. So, doctors who recommend total and complete protection from the sun should maybe reconsider their indications.

When you are at the seaside, maybe, it would be enough to apply the sunscreens only after 15-30-60 minutes of exposure without filters or even, after this period, wear opaque clothing. This, however, would not be the case for dark skin. In fact, the more intense the color of the skin, the more sun is needed to get the same amount of vitamin D.

---

[60] See my book about vaccines.

The studies state that very dark skin requires from 6 to 8 times the exposure times necessary for a light skin to get the same amount of vitamin D. So, a Negroid[61] should stay about three or four hours under the scorching sun to get the same amount of vitamin D that an Europoid would take in just thirty minutes. In the middle of this range would be the mongoloids and the Australoid.

Therefore, it is absolutely recommended for a Negroid, or even just an Australoid, to take important quantities of synthetic vitamin D, since from the original places (that, evidently, allowed a proper supply of vitamin D) many have moved, often, over the 35th Parallel (the minimum threshold indicated for the acquisition of vitamin D in the cooler months – November-March).

This geographical migration has meant that in Negroid individuals, who live in the North of America or in Europe, there is an important vitamin D deficiency which, according to statistical studies, could be the cause of a greater number of cases of vitamin D related diseases (including tumors) in nigger[62] subjects compared to subjects of other races in North America.

---

[61] The world population can be generally divided into 4 major races, namely *Europoid* (white, Caucasian) *Mongoloid* (Asian), *Negroid* (Black) and *Australoid* (aborigines, indigenous people to Southeast Asia, South Asia, Australia, Melanesia and parts of East Asia). This is based on a racial classification made by Carleton S. Coon in 1962. There is no universally accepted classification for *race*, however, and its use has been under fire over the last few decades.

[62] I refuse to give a connotation of racism to the word nigger. Black, colored, *opposite of white*, or whatever, can be as racist as the term nigger, because racism is in the attitude of people and not in the terms used. White, *light, pale* might have the same connotation if intended in a discriminatory way. Whatever is the origin of this word (Spanish, Latin or from a misspell of *Nigeria*) all the obloquy and contempt and rejection about this term was given by white *Europoid.*

Since there have been continental and latitudinal mixtures of human races, even the various types of skin have undergone upheavals. For example, blacks living in the north or south no longer receive the necessary amounts of sun, both in latitude and in the lifestyle they lead. So, what Nature had planned for them was upset by man. This also happens for other breeds, but while it is easy for a Europoid to obtain the right amounts of vitamin D, even living in a different latitude (Africa or Asia), it is not the same for a Negroid living in Europe or in North America. In the worst case scenario, the white European will have to protect themselves from the sun, but the Negroid will not get enough, which is, in my opinion, far too worse.

I highly recommend, therefore, to everyone, but especially to those who have black skin or in any case olive complexion (Australoid), to perform a vitamin D analysis annually and to integrate with modern supplements, albeit synthetic, if sun is unavailable. I believe that, as recommended in many books, 2,000 IU of vitamin D daily are the minimum recommended in winter months (many medical experts advise either 50,000 IU a week for 8 weeks or 10,000 a day for 8 weeks). Personally I have taken 50,000 IU of vitamin D for about ten weeks reaching 70 ng/ml, starting from 25 ng/ml.

Vitamin D intoxication, according to current data, can occur only above 150 ng/ml, although it is recommended not to exceed 100 ng/ml present in the blood. I challenge any common sense person to obtain these toxic values if not taking daily disproportionate quantities (well above the average of 10,000 IU daily) for very long periods. On the contrary, there is, apparently, the opposite problem (i.e. for fear of improbable vitamin D intoxication people do not take enough).

Unfortunately, as many scholars of the topic state, we went from one excess to another. In fact, in some northern European countries and in North America, in the 80s, vitamin D supplement was added to many processed foods. This determined that a daily consumption and accumulation of such foods could cause a vitamin D intoxication. For example, if you had milk, fruit juices, cereals, snacks reinforced with vitamin D, perhaps all together and every day, could, in some cases, determine vitamin D excess.

Although I am not a supporter of synthetic supplements (since I believe that man cannot imitate what Nature has created) I still find myself having to support the use of synthetic vitamin D supplements as our nature and social life is different from the one of animals. There are, in fact, only two ways of assuming it: either from *supplementation of sun*, taken sparingly and intelligently; or through supplements. Nature cannot be mimed and knows exactly what to do. However, our acquired customs over the centuries, has apparently changed, even substantially, what was originally established by Nature. Any effective corrective measures, such as synthetic supplements, therefore, can only be welcome if they do not cause damage and if they are really effective.

As far as supplements are concerned, while still considering them useful (especially some of them), I believe that the alchemy of Nature cannot be reproduced (at least not yet) artificially. In particular, it is not known how a certain food is alchemized in the organism and what are the interactions with other foods, etc. So, how can you think that the supplement is the panacea? Certainly it can be useful, but when we ingest spinach or a lemon we do not ingest, for example, only vitamin C, but an important series of nutrients (vitamins, minerals, enzymes, etc.) and we probably do not even know all of them yet.

It would be interesting, on the other hand, to reproduce synthetically what is present in a fruit, for example, or in a vegetable. We should then hope that it would behave, interacting with our organism, like the fruit or the vegetable itself.

However, although I believe that supplements are not as effective as nature, they may still represent a useful tool to improve our health, balancing the damage we do with modern life and nutrition. As I have already said, while considering vitamin D as an important supplement, I noticed that it was not used by Gerson with his patients (probably because it was a relatively new discovery, similarly to vitamin C). It follows, therefore, that the natural way overcomes every obstacle.

As for vitamin C, the studies of Prof. Linus Pauling, in relation to the benefits of this vitamin, are certainly to be held more than in due consideration, and should be used as a cornerstone of modern medicine, especially since the vitamin C has no side effects and can be taken, in the form of ascorbic acid, daily at different doses, even quite high (Pauling recommends the use of 6 to 18 grams daily but from more recent studies it would appear that can be reached amounts of 50 to 100 grams and administered even in vein).

This would then confirm Ehret's empirical studies and my logical considerations, that is: we are frugivorous creatures! And deviating from that diet can cause discomfort. In fact, had we eaten only fruit and vegetables (organic) we would have all the necessary vitamin C. As a matter of fact, being ascorbic acid an artificial derivative is not as effective as natural vitamin C and it is hypothesized that the organism can assimilate a much lower quantity. Therefore, it is advisable to use natural supplements containing acerola, camu camu or kakadu plums[63], if they are accessible and economically reasonable, since they would be more effective. Then, if you can, plant an acerola or a kakadu plum tree in the garden, do it.

I believe, however, that the general practitioner should prescribe vitamin C in the form of ascorbic acid or freshly extracted vegetable juices, acerola extract, or whatever else regardless of diseases and health conditions. This would be particularly true especially if you are close to the middle age, as deficiencies accumulated in previous decades could be highlighted.

Vitamin C (in the form of ascorbic acid) does not, in practice, have side effects (if not some mild stomach movement) even at high dosage, and only for the first few days of ingestion. In these cases it is sufficient to take it on a full stomach and regulate the quantity considering that the organism gradually gets used to larger quantities. Many people take Pauling's advice by increasing their intake gradually until they reach 10/18 grams a day.

On the contrary, the benefits can be enormous, but even in this case, everything that works or that can work to improve human health goes against the coffers of Big Mafia. It follows, therefore, that the whole machine of Pharmacine is set in motion to defend Big Mafia's products. Consider that there is even someone who dared to question Pauling's studies (the only Nobel Prize winner who has received two awards not shared with others) just to point out how anything that is not pharmaceutical is useless. Hearing such

---

[63] Acerola and Camu Camu are fruits originating from South and Central America while kakadu plums are originated from Australia.

statements, the Hungarian Albert Szent-Györgyi (discoverer of vitamin C) would turn in his grave.

Rath in his book *Why Animals Do not Get Heart Attacks ... But People Do!* unequivocally highlights its importance in the prevention and treatment of heart problems, together with other elements such as magnesium, lysine, proline and coenzyme Q10, etc. Therefore, ascorbic acid should never be lacking in daily use and should, if anything, replace salt. If we learned to take even just three grams a day (a teaspoon), perhaps with a freshly made juice, we would certainly have some important benefits.

Other important vitamins are certainly those of group B and in particular Niacin and Cyanocobalamine (B3 and B12), also used by Gerson in his therapy.

Unfortunately, the depletion of our vitamin heritage means that the integrators are being overwhelmingly detecting as a necessary source of support for what we are no longer able to assume naturally, mainly due to chemistry, pharmaceuticals and agriculture.

As already mentioned before, poisons and chemical fertilizers used in agriculture considerably deplete the vitamins from the vegetable that arrive in our tables. We twist the soil with all poison and barbarism while (as calculated by that charming and brilliant character that was Ehret) ten fruit trees would be enough to allow a family of four to live in good health and without further contributions. I realize, however, that this would still be an utopia.

CONCLUSIONS

It is absolutely evident how vocations can be biased. All religions should tend to the salvation of the soul, by obtaining the truth, and there should be no friction between them, but rather, exchanges to better reach the one and last truth.

In the same way, politics should not have contrapositions between the different parties, if not indicating preferences for one subject or the other but should aspire to the good of the *res publica*[64], thus setting aside personal egoistic practices or political ideologies that are an end in themselves.

Today, those who are not inclined to lie can hardly do politics, since lying is used to keep the people good, similarly to

---

[64] *Res publica* is a Latin phrase, loosely meaning "public affair." It is the root of the word "republic," and the word "commonwealth" has traditionally been used as a synonym for it; however, translations vary widely according to the context. "Res" is a nominative singular Latin noun for a substantive or concrete thing – as opposed to "spes," which means something unreal or ethereal – and "publica" is an attributive adjective meaning "of and/or pertaining to the state or the public." Hence a literal translation is, "the public thing/affair." https://en.wikipedia.org/wiki/Res_publica

what adults do with children to keep them quiet. Politicians adopt similar stratagems to keep the masses quiet. Usually the people are told a lie or sweetened with a candy and calm down and then forget. Of course, there are also honest politicians, but they have no say in the matter, they stay on the sidelines observing what is happening around them, probably by stopping their noses and, perhaps, also closing their eyes.

Therefore, medicine should absolutely remove any bigotry, ideology, selfishness, personal gain, malice and deceptive business from what should be the cure to alleviate the physical ills of man.

The people mentioned in this book and their studies are an example of how the conduct of a real Hippocratic juror should be. Now, instead, the *magicians of drugs* and those of *cutting and stitching* are idolized, completely ignoring the human aspect of the person.

The French film "150 Milligrams" shows Big Mafia as a *drug cartel*. People are just numbers and the *murder* of millions of people through drugs appears irrelevant because it often happens slowly and obviously must not be related to drug. It appears not to weigh at all on the consciences of Big Mafia and Pharmacine[65] chiefs. They do not care, they just do not see the *extermination camps*. That is why natural therapies must be hidden and condemned, because they are the salvation and might be very dangerous for their business. In this film Pharmacine leaders have unusually dissociated from Big Mafia, withdrawing the drug in question from the market, because the

---

[65] Pharmacine chiefs might not necessarily be corrupted. But if they are not, then, are certainly guiltily blind.

evidence was too clear and because Irène Frachon (the main actor) would not let go. Furthermore, the French company Servier is certainly not a corporate behemoth. You can be sure these episodes are just exceptions. Usually they always win because the fight against Big Mafia is too much of a burden. Be sure that there are hundreds of drugs that kills but they stay on the market… not by chance drugs are the fourth cause of death.

As a general rule, I adopt just the opposite of what Big Mafia impose on us, i.e. that collateral effects must be proven. When you have a malaise and are taking a drug you can, logically, assume that depends on the drug itself, at least until it is proven the opposite. So the burden of proof should be on the drug and the pharmaceutical firm and not the other way around. Only the simple doubt about a drug should implement this path. Unfortunately, until people will not take the burden of healing on themselves not trusting anybody, this kind of episodes will be a daily occurrence and illness will not be defeated.

Today it happens that everything revolves around the despicable money, even the giant steps made in diagnostics (absolutely noticeable). Easy money generally corrupts everyone and everything, sacred and profane; biological and not; science and not science. For almost a century now (even if, in their times, Tilden and Ehret already complained about their malfeasance) it has been impossible to practice the real medicine, except in an occult way, because it is the exclusive prerogative of Pharmacine.

The image of Pharmacine coming out of this long examination is certainly debatable. In this organization there are naive doctors (who trust a not credible institution) and heroes of the medical profession who try to do the right thing according to the true principles of Hippocrates and paying their tolls.

The leaders of Pharmacine cannot accept the doubt that there might exist a non-pharmaceutical cure, so they must destroy the enemy (natural therapies) with every weapon available (Pharmainquisition, etc.) before it can prove right.

The conflict is clearly part of the game because often there are interposed interests. Unfortunately, in all vocational fields there are important factors of convenience relating to aspects of money, selfishness, hypocrites and lack of humility.

I believe that people's trust, however, is very slowly dwindling in all these disciplines. Politics is now despised and unpopular in most countries and the low percentage of voters in most nations is a demonstration.

Even religion is progressively following the same fate, beginning with the process of secularization, now consolidated, in the Catholic one. This process might also *infect* the other major religion, the Islamic one, leaving out the Eastern religions, somehow less dogmatic.

Finally, we come to the medicine that cannot be ignored because it is necessary for our physical well-being but that it is increasingly treated with diffidence since it is polluted with chemistry (the social tendency towards Nature and natural cures are a demonstration).

During the writing of this volume I asked myself repeatedly: will not I be a little too exaggerated to compare Pharmacine to Hitler? Then, going forward, I found more and more evidence that told me: no, there are no doubts, the evidence leads to these conclusions, so it must be so (it is like the anecdote of the Earth that seemed flat but was instead spherical). I wondered many times: perhaps you are too conditioned and do not see what reality is and what most of the people see. How can you think that someone can stain oneself of these heinous faults?

And yet, the comparison with Hitler now seems more and more fitting. The only differences would be in the methods of elimination of Hitler that were more bloody, but what about the Pharmacine one? Consider that the hypothetical Pharmacine extermination has been going on for dozens of years and might have claimed hundreds of millions of victims and not just tens of millions as Hitler caused in about five years of war.

Both Hitler and Big Mafia suffer from the same desire for conquest: Hitler wanted to conquer the world physically. He wanted to be the master and the absolute dictator, while Pharmacine would be content to conquer only the part that matters: the economic and political one and is succeeding in this plan. I am convinced that it will also take root in nations where it is not yet so present and will soon become the biggest economic superpower ever existed and unreachable by any other real country. We are close to the image of Charlie Chaplin holding  the globe with his hand in the film The Great Dictator. The main difference is that to support it, now, there is a handful of influential characters and not just one.

I keep telling myself that maybe I should not write these words because they could be damaging and offensive to honest professionals. However, my conscience tells me that these are the right words and that these logifical findings are not going to be denied over time. Indeed, perhaps, in another century, they will be confirmed, if this big lie, linked to cancer, but also to vaccines and all drugs in general, should eventually collapse. I hope, however, with all my heart, to be proven wrong. In fact, I would be very happy, as well as relieved, if this logific theory of mine should, for some illogical and incomprehensible reasons, turn out to be wrong.

If anyone who knows and has seen Pharmacine's extermination camps (the fraudulent organization behind chemotherapy and drug business) as, probably, the former FBI and FDA directors mentioned in previous chapters, could have spoken freely, perhaps the fight against these brutal mafia lobbies, it could have taken a bit further. After all, what is the Mafia if not a lobby of the crime? It is no by coincidence that Big Pharma has been addressed as Big Mafia and in the United States it would be even using physical elimination to achieve its goals.

Unfortunately, as long as the people will not be aware of being deceived and the previously mentioned chemotherapy extermination camps will not be visualized in the collective imaginary it will be difficult to defeat Pharmacine. The only way to do this is by not trusting, personally testing what the respective parties are saying. Let me repeat that chemotherapy poisoning is often irreversible and prevents other natural cures to be effective, while Breuss or Gerson therapy cannot do any further damage and one would later be able to undergo chemotherapy without further problems, should not it work. Listening to Pharmacine's propaganda it seems just the opposite.

On the results of Pharmacine, we have already gathered enough information, especially in the fight against cancer (almost non-existent, apart from the surgical results, which are sometimes more comforting). Indeed, it would appear that chemotherapy destroys even the little good that has remained in our body. Be assured that if you do not use surgery, chemo alone will not lead you to anything good. Yet, they continue to do it only because, at the moment (2014), it brings $7 trillion into the coffers of Big Mafia.

The results of *Medicine*, on the other hand, are ignored, boycotted, hidden, opposed and counterfeited by any means with significant media effort, through a network of affiliated subjects. So, until word of mouth about the effectiveness of natural therapies spreads, this struggle cannot come to an end. It is very hard for that to happen because the word of mouth spreading takes much, much longer than media and generations follows one another forgetting the memories of the previous one. But, as I said before, this new generation has internet on its side, which might speed up this process.

Since modern medicine considers only the pharmaceutical remedies, perhaps we should also subdivide the current medical faculties into two branches: *Pharmacine* and *Medicine*, where, after a common path that includes knowledge of the human body, one specializes on the one hand in *Pharmacine* and in allopathic and chemical medicine and, on the other hand, in holistic and natural medicine. In fact, if there were also the faculty of Medicine, and not just the one of *Pharmacine*, Gerson's teachings could be studied in depth, contrary to what happens today. Unfortunately, I think that this eventuality will never be feasible, because Big Mafia knows exactly how effective the natural therapies are and therefore will obstruct them with every possible mean. If they were really ineffective it would allow their use freely as their ineffective use would have strengthen the allopathic medicine.

Today we are close to the achievement of a century of *olicracies* following the defeat of man due to the world wars. Since then, in the main *olicracies* of the western world, there has been a continuous acceleration, amplified by the advent of the internet, which makes improbable to glimpse a very long period of this regime on the horizon. An upheaval could, therefore, be at the door, and probably it will not be necessary to wait for the Twenty-second century to see an important transformation of the actual forms of government. A probable transition from the so-called indirect democracy to direct democracy (with the adjustments it will cause) or to other forms of government is very likely to take place, and then other changes will occur in cascade.

I wonder: if you can operate your bank account from home, tell me for what strange reason people could not make their choices with their Smart phones from the comfort of their couch? Would democracy be at risk? But then, what democracy? The one that strong powers made us believe (credibly) we are living. The actual democracy is a safe harbor as long as those who really count on the world can still decide for us manipulating the people itself through the media. What we are leaving looks pretty much like real democracy... as long as you do not ask for genuine cheap cures, clean energy, proper politics, etc.

On the other hand, should it become everything clear (not yet probable), the careers of politicians who pull the threads of this evil game would be at risk. It is, nonetheless, true that the people are perhaps not yet mature for this eventuality because it might still be manipulated with the methods I described earlier. However, the people (conditioned through manipulated information), is comparable to a small child growing, that should have the possibility to make mistakes rather than be defrauded by the deceiving politicians. In this way we could be the architects of our destiny learning to contrast politically guided deception.

However, we (the peoples) should be the ones to decide, not our political representatives (who often represent only their needs). This kind of popular sharing would already be possible today (at least for important decisions) considering that *electronic* certified transactions are already possible since many years. But of course it is easier to manage the public (*Res publica*) in full autonomy, without the people being able to interfere. It must be said, as well, that the masses can still be easily influenced, and would be influenced, for personal advantage. In fact, it has become popular the recent figure of the social media *influencer*, that most of the time influences effectively people on demand.

History shows that at the end, every wall collapses. When political, economic, and social conditions are brought to exasperation maintaining inequality and even raising it furthermore, great upheavals could finally occur. As a matter of fact, so many disturbances in an era like ours have, perhaps, never been seen before. The 20th century brought an acceleration in the whole of society and also in the succession of events that are increasingly precipitous and always closer to each other.

In the last century, we have witnessed the consolidation of the industrial revolution; two world wars; the rise of totalitarian and communist regimes; a ruthless and terrible economic crisis; the collapse of most communist regimes; the presence of man in space, and the evolutions/revolutions continue. The last revolution is the advent of the internet that has *distorted* the sociality of the human being, but which has also changed his way of thinking and, above all, the access to information and its manipulation.

Today the monopoly of media manipulation with the advent of the Internet is no longer just in the hands of the world *bosses*. Though, of course, the latter would try to discredit the *inconvenient* news by labeling them as fake news or hoaxes.[66] Unfortunately, fake news are often produced and determined by the same information manipulators who, instead of protecting us, are the main deceivers. Their obvious intent is to assimilate the pranks (easily recognizable) to what they deliberately label as fake news (correlation between vaccine and autism, natural cancer therapies, etc.).

Thus, there might be a change of direction in the manipulation of the people where, the true and dark powers, are, maybe, late and where much of their survival is played within.

In the current period, we are witnessing a more marked rejection of politics and, above all, of old politics. Moreover, in the current millennium, we assisted to the Arab Spring; the rise of

---

[66] Just out of pure fantasy: Big Mafia would have all the interest, motivation technical skills and moral attitude, to hire fleets of fake social influencer to try to mitigate the effects of this wave of nature holistic wind that could lead to its ruin.

populist[67] movements like the Five Star Movement in Italy and of Podemos in Spain; the election of Donald Trump (which represents, however, a high degree of political dissociation for the US system). These events might show that there may be a latent ferment in the middle class that is not yet well addressed and whose future implications cannot yet be known. I am sure it would not surprise you if I state that: Politics is governed by characters who are more inclined to shameless lies and others who pronounce them more intelligently. However, lies are implicit in politics.

The United States has lost a historic opportunity, preferring, in the year 2000, George W. Bush in comparison with Al Gore. This matter could be the demonstration that lies are stronger than the truth, at least until they reach the extreme point of tolerance. On that occasion, in fact, the American people were deceived by a character who, after his election, gave ample evidence of the lies that he was able to put in place. Like all liars, he was able to deftly hide his wrongdoings by looking, perhaps, himself as the victim. Sooner or later most lies are revealed, in fact, his many lies have now become part of history. They could, anyway, be hidden long enough to allow him to take good care for his core business.

As I said earlier, lying is implicit in politics, so it is also implicit in the election of any political figure. With the current system it is absolutely likely that any President of the United States who comes to power owes something to someone and, necessarily,

---

[67] A person or a politician who is mainly interested in the problems and needs of ordinary people. (https://dictionary.cambridge.org/it/dizionario/inglese/populist)

has to pay his debt and in most so-called *democracies* the system is pretty similar.

In the end, I hope that the people will gradually realize how easily they can be deceived and manipulated with the same stratagems used by Hitler and many other rulers. I passionately hope that the world peoples will manage to shake off themselves the imposters and manipulators, finally realizing that they are very vulnerable. According to Le Bon and to the experience of the most recent statesman and/or dictators, it is enough to touch the right button with the perfect lie to bring home the desired consent and to continue to perpetrate their interests (and not ours, as they want us to believe). In fact, lies are said to pursue a goal. Those who have no personal goals to pursue are not interested in telling them. Hence, power interests related to politics and economical business (Pharmacine, Energy, armaments, chemistry, etc.) encourage politicians to tell lies and the bigger they are the more profitable and believed might be.

The story shows, however, that one cannot push one's luck forever and that, sooner or later, the game ends. So, unless unexpected and unlikely sudden changes in the political classes that govern at the time and/or serious adjustments in the social sphere, we will see a further, important, change or peaceful revolution, hopefully, that will significantly change our society. Capitalism, the way it is, cannot last much longer.

In many esoteric and sacred text it is, indeed, reported that between the end of the second millennium and the beginning of the third one begins an era of greater prosperity and knowledge for the human race. Sri Yukteswar (Priyanath Karar), a great and enlightened Indian saint, in his book *The Sacred Science* indicates in the second half of the second millennium (1700) the beginning of Dvàpara Yuga, a period of mental elevation. This era would be established completely in 1900 (considering 200 years of transition) following the Kali Yuga, a period in which man manifests only a quarter of his potential. Even the civilization of the Maya roughly considers the advent of this millennium as a period of prosperity. The precious words of the celestial powers channeled through Eugenio Siragusa[68] open an entirely new way of approaching the mysteries of creation disclosing realities that we could not realize on our own.

The *new age* movements that shyly look out in the social and cultural landscape of the various democratic (or so considered) peoples, bode well for a peaceful revolution that could bring better times and a real *new age* that will lighten up the world peoples. Of course, according to these sacred texts, which are reflected in many Earth cultures, we live close to the culmination of the end of an era (which certainly was not serene) and the beginning of a new era that should reveal peace, harmony and wisdom. When this era will be fully established we might see humanity fully rise, probably, as we can only imagine in science-fiction film. However, to savor this sensation we will have, perhaps, to wait a few centuries or even an entire millennium (the alternations of the various ages are beautifully explained by Sri Yukteswar in the aforementioned book).

---

[68] I have only recently discovered the work and life of Eugenio and I will deal with his disclosures, in the next volume.

The coefficient of acceleration that occurred in the last century suggests that if we do not destroy our Earth before, and as soon as the deception becomes clearer, the peoples will face a flourishing and serene evolution towards the glory that belongs to the divine being dwelling in us. Of course, much depends on the decision of the powerful (therefore of the rich). In fact, if they choose of sharing voluntarily (through a reasoned redistribution), the richness accumulated we could witness to a fairer sharing. In the end, everyone would benefit out of it, including the powerful ones, who could *rebalance the relationship between white balls and black balls* in their abacus of life.

Common sense leads me to say that, in the end, the consciences evolve and even the worst powerful character could take, finally, the road to rediscover its innate consciousness. If they will not do it voluntarily they will be forced by social... and conscience... evolutions. We have assisted to important recent examples of very rich people who, finally, spontaneously decide to renounce to part of their wealth (even if sometimes they do not do it in the most useful way).

Remember, as well, that *everyone is the best doctor of oneself*, as witnessed by many holistic doctors. In this regard, I recall all the accusations made by Pharmacine to doctors like Bradstreet, Wakefield, Nacci (and all the less recent ones) who are not certainly ladder climbers, megalomaniac and greedy as might be some members of Pharmacine. Indeed, Gerson did not even ask for the fees to people in need. Actually, to someone he even gave them the money to get the train back home. This is the true spirit that should inspire a doctor who truly believes in the Hippocratic oath.

As I said earlier, it is encouraging the fact that we are witnessing the birth of so many websites that promote natural treatments and often denounce Pharmacine misdeeds. Following this path, maybe, Pharmacine will not be able anymore to loot our body, though people will not have, however, support by medical institutions. Unfortunately, still too many profiteers and impostors hide behind natural cures to spread miraculous supplements for the cure of all ills. Beware of them! Those who really care about your health do not ask for stratospheric compensation for their literary and/or natural products

Though justice is not of this world we must, however, certainly resist to the advance of evil (either real Mafia, Big Mafia, the seven sisters or whatever), dissociating ourselves from the *metastases* that inevitably infest society and above all try not to become accomplices, victims and/or unconscious perpetrators of their misdeeds.

Until a few years ago, I did not believe that Pharmacine deception could be superior to that of *Petroline* (the seven sisters). To tell the truth, I did not even assume it. I thought it might have treated only of personal convictions and cultural bigotry. After this writing and the related further research, I must admit that I fear there are no comparisons. The relationship in terms of brutality, extensiveness and involvement could, in fact, not even be minimally comparable, making Petroline deception seem like something almost innocent and innocuous.

During this research I also realized that the hopes of dissolving the deception are gradually increasing. In fact, the information sites that oppose Pharmacine disinformation are considerably more numerous and of better quality, compared to the

 CONCLUSIONS

past. In addition, Pharmacine's opponents, especially in the US, where the bloodiest battles take place, do not remotely intend to surrender to Pharmacine, even if many holistic doctors' lives and careers are at stake.

This would seem to highlight that the *big lie* is gradually emerging and perhaps we are walking the path towards the unveiling of Pharmacine *extermination camps*. I hope that, if and when we will get there, the scenario that will open up in front of us will be less chilling than what the first men who have crossed the threshold of Hitler's death camps lived.

Allow me to say that had I taken an oath like the Hippocrates one I would feel the stringent and inalienable moral obligation, to verify that what was stated, experienced and documented by my medical colleagues would not be simple pranks or guilty lies, or worse, as sentenced by Pharmacine, acts of charlatanism.

I repeat that I have no connection or interests related to the natural world, so those who want to label me can do it by calling me a *naturalist bigot* or perhaps (using a term more suited to Pharmacine) a *naturalist charlatan*.

IPPOCRATIC OATH (Modern version)

I swear to fulfill, to the best of my ability and judgment, this covenant:

- I will respect the hard-won scientific gains of those physicians in whose steps I walk, and gladly share such knowledge as is mine with those who are to follow

- I will apply, for the benefit of the sick, all measures [that] are required, avoiding those twin traps of overtreatment and therapeutic nihilism.

- I will remember that there is art to medicine as well as science, and that warmth, sympathy, and understanding may outweigh the surgeon's knife or the chemist's drug.

- I will not be ashamed to say, "I know not," nor will I fail to call in my colleagues when the skills of another are needed for a patient's recovery.

- I will respect the privacy of my patients, for their problems are not disclosed to me that the world may know. Most especially must I tread with care in matters of life and death. If it is given me to save a life, all thanks. But it may also be within my power to take a life; this awesome responsibility must be faced with great humbleness and awareness of my own frailty. Above all, I must not play at God.

- I will remember that I do not treat a fever chart, a cancerous growth, but a sick human being, whose illness may affect the person's family and economic stability. My responsibility includes these related problems, if I am to care adequately for the sick.

- I will prevent disease whenever I can, for prevention is preferable to cure.

- I will remember that I remain a member of society, with special obligations to all my fellow human beings, those sound of mind and body as well as the infirm.

- If I do not violate this oath, may I enjoy life and art, respected while I live and remembered with affection thereafter. May I always act to preserve the finest traditions of my calling and may I long experience the joy of healing those who seek my help.

I am certainly not the first to report Pharmacine*'s* malfeasance but I could, perhaps, be the first to hypothesize the existence of *mass extermination camps* voluntarily created by Big Mafia with the help of Pharmacine. Chemotherapy might just be a killing drug, maybe not in the short term, but probably in the long term. Moreover, they would certainly have the chance to do whatever they wanted to. Consider that Big Mafia is placed in the international context as, and perhaps more, of a great world power at the levels of USA or China, with the difference that has ramifications (or, to stay on topic, metastasis) in much of the world and its foundations are right in the USA.

From the analysis made in this long path, it is therefore evident that there is a big lie that can be kept standing also through the incitement to bigotry, which plays in favor of the puppeteer who moves the threads (Big Mafia). They instigate and increase it with bigger and bigger lies because it is now certain that "the bigger the lie is, the more credible it is, especially if repeated often." Those who are willing to do any wickedness for personal gain are also willing to tell any kind of lie and will not even be touched by thousands of deaths (150 milligrams) or millions of deaths (chemotherapy).

As for the association between Nazism and *pharmacinism*, I noticed a certain similarity between the blind abnegation of many Nazi-era officers and the guilty and naive approval of some modern *officers* belonging to Pharmacine, which uniform their behavior, only sometimes unconsciously, to Big Mafia crimes.

Big Mafia, on the other hand, surrounds itself with loyal *senior officers* who would never betray the orders of their *Führer* facilitating their appointments to strategic offices. They do not even wonder whether it is right or wrong, as happened with Hitler's few loyal officers, after all the Führer could not be wrong.

The remainder of Pharmacine's actors, either doctors or not (*unsuspecting officers of the modern era*), do not dare to oppose the diktat of the supreme chiefs and meekly follow Pharmacine's orders (protocols). These few, high officers, of course, are not only physicians but they also range in all other areas where Pharmacine is involved.

Some other doctors (strive to go unnoticed, trying to do the right thing and to follow the oath they have sworn not disturbing Pharmacine's business. Their attitude must be pretty similar to the one of Schindler trying to save, with his list, as many human beings as possible from the clutches of Hitler.

Fortunately, the number of these modern heroes continues to rise and there are more and more examples of medical realities that deviate from Pharmacine trying to pursue what a real Medical Jury should do. Obviously, these bastions of Medicine, who know who they are dealing with, do not publicize their work. However, as soon as they become known, they fall under the attention of Pharmacine through the Pharmainquisition or worse practice. Those who ingenuously do not suspect the existence of Pharmacine, on the other hand, take a real *pharmainquisitor* and media beating that permanently annihilate them.

Following on what's been stated so far, let me say that, if it is true that religions are the opium of the masses, it is equally true that the ignorance and ingenuity of the people are the cocaine of the rich and the powerful. In fact, ignorance is the first weapon that the rich and the powerful have to tame the people to their will and ingenuity is the tool that the rulers have to cheat the masses.

Ignorance, then, would not only be cultural but also, and above all, *cognitive ignorance*[69], much more difficult to fight as it includes every social stratum and all cultural levels. There may exist, as they do, cultural but not cognitive ignorant and vice versa. For example, there might exist highly educated people who are absolutely cognitive ignorant. Indeed, it is likely that a higher percentage of cognitive ignorance lies in the more cultured social strata, perhaps because they think that authority cannot be unfaithful. In fact, sometimes, the cultural ignorant provided with logic is more likely to unveil the deception than those who are more cultured but lacking in logic.

For ease of comprehension, I would like to associate cognitive ignorance with the digital divide,[70] but not the physical one linked to communication networks (that could instead be assimilated to cultural ignorance) but the cognitive ignorance linked to the understanding of the digital process, to what happens inside and behind a screen and that often does not go hand in hand with culture.

---

[69] With this term, I want to underline the lack of logic that does not allow a person to understand a certain logical process or a series of related episodes.

[70] The term digital divide describes a gap in terms of access to and usage of information and communication technology. It was traditionally considered to be a question of having or not having access, but with a global mobile phone penetration of over 95%, it is becoming a relative inequality between those who have more and less bandwidth and more or fewer skills. Conceptualizations of the digital divide have been described as "who, with which characteristics, connects how to what." (www.wikipedia.org)

To demonstrate this theory, I remember seeing a television service, a couple of decades ago, about digitization and the access to it. The program consisted of showing what was happening in a small village in India where an anonymous column with an integrated computer and interactive touch screen was placed in the town square. No child had ever seen a PC, and from the hidden camera you could see how some kids had an innate familiarity with the foreign object while others did not even understand what it could be and how it could work.

Well, most of today's population could be equated to that child who does not even understand what that little column is and what can be done with it. The remaining part, including the few enlightened physicians supporting the only existing Medicine (which consequently hinders Pharmacine) that use logic, can be assimilated to those children who, in a moment, have understood that unknown machine, effectively interacting with it.

The balance of body and mind is essential for good health and imbalances are never good for the body. Unfortunately, man often seeks a cause that determines a single illness, as in religion he seeks only one creed to bring him where he has to go. We do not realize that we are the only cause of our unique disease: toxemia. Treatments are often complementary, despite the fact that many take sides for one or the other forgetting that frequently these intersect each other obtaining a single result.

I think of the Gerson therapy which, very simply, is a metabolic therapy based on detoxification and vitamin supra-nutrition. Furthermore, many of the therapies and theories mentioned in this book probably yield similar results (detoxify, eliminate mucus, kill pathogens, rebalance acid/alkaline ratio, etc.).

Essentially, these are therapies lead, in all likelihood, to similar results, which are absolutely not in opposition but could often be combined if awareness spreads. The only differences between natural therapies might be in terms of lengths and, sometimes, efficacy.

Psychological therapy aims to identify the conflict-shock-experience and heal body and mind. Consequently, therefore, we will learn to overcome our conflicts also nourishing ourselves of healthy food and avoiding harmful habits for our body. It appears true, now as then, what our ancient wise men have already said millennia ago: "...so neither ought you to attempt to cure the body without the soul" (Plato).

However, the first truth, and probably the only one, about the disease is that food is our cure. If we stuck to a fruitarian or possibly vegan diet (preferably without flour that produces mucus), or at least if we adopted it when we get sick, perhaps we would free ourselves from all diseases. Of course, illnesses might also appear in fruitarians subjects, were they exposed to a psychological trauma, but those would be just rare exceptions.

Unfortunately, man is too immersed in his *gluttony* and does everything to justify it (I'm not fruitarian but just a vegetarian tending on vegan... affected by gluttony). Nevertheless, I recognize, of course, that our right diet is the one written in the Bible, even though I cannot define myself as being religious, certainly not in the traditional meaning. Ehret's empirical experiments leave me no further doubts.

True physicians and real researchers, such as Hippocrates, Paracelsus, Gerson, Ehret, Tilden, Shelton, Hulda Regehr Clark,

Breuss, and others are only anxious for the patient's care, following an innate vocation and an instinctive curiosity for the cure. Do you see any of these qualities in many modern doctors? Those who still have them are easily recognizable because they are either being investigated by the Pharmainquisition or hiding from it to avoid being discovered, or else, they practice disciplines in which Pharmacine is not interested.

Today it is possible to counteract various types of pathogens effectively but, if you do not rebalance the body and do not detoxify it, then it will be useless, a new disease or a recurrence of the same one will occur again. I repeat that, in my opinion, the basis of any treatment should include a Gerson or Gerson-like treatment or fasting (Breuss-like), also integrating it with other findings to facilitate and speed up the healing process, taking into account the psychosomatic aspect of each disease and of every personality.

As Tilden has brilliantly highlighted in his book *Toxemia: the basic cause of disease*, the disease arises when the body jams, slows its excretory functions and is no longer able to expel toxins. Thus, the elimination or reduction of toxemia in the body, as indicated by the figures mentioned earlier, is certainly an important step in the healing process.

Instead, what usually happens? Pharmacine's doctors intoxicate the body further, causing increasing in toxemia and further illnesses. They treat a symptom for a short time, then the symptom returns accompanied by other diseases until it develops a chronic disorder or further diseases and/or cancer.

Here is another possible reason why we are witnessing a notable increase in cases of cancer: there is a high increase in the assumption of intoxicants[71] (especially drugs), and when someone shows visible side effects, we are surprised. But, remember, *there cannot be correlation between body pollutants and the increase in the number and importance of diseases*. Who knows if we can ever go back to the real medicine ...

As far as I am concerned, I have no doubt: Gerson was certainly, after Hippocrates, and perhaps Paracelsus, the greatest doctor of all time, albeit accompanied by great twentieth century luminaries (Ehret, Shelton, Hulda Clark, Breuss, etc.). In fact, if it is true that the discovery of penicillin has helped to fight bacterial diseases it is equally true that any disease cannot establish in a healthy body. Consequently, antibiotics or treatments would not be necessary.

To demonstrate this, here is a clear example: not everyone got sick and not all those who got sick died. This means that some organisms, with more active immune defenses, do not get sick regardless of what they eat. I imagine there may also be statistics concerning patients who have continued to use Gerson therapy over the years. It would be useful to check how often they got sick in their life, will ever somebody bother to check this data? Again, the film *150 milligrams* shows how nobody cares about the easily detectable statistical data. It is unbelievable how we trust the *untrustworthy*. In my other book about vaccines, with a relatively easy research, I found out that autoimmune diseases were practically

---

[71]Other reasons are: wrong food and excess, pollution, chemicals (used for producing and preserving food), mind implications and so on and so forth.

nonexistent before the advent of vaccines, but, still, nobody cares. Of course, the victim has to demonstrate the wrongdoing and not the perpetrator. *Do not trust! Experiment!* That is our only weapon.

It is incredible how, for a game of destiny, chance, or karma, Germany has been the mother of great geniuses of good (Gerson, Einstein, Ehret, Breuss,[72] etc.) and of evil (Hitler and associates), as if it were used to compensate all the evil done by Hitler. Unfortunately, the seeds of deception, and the studies done about its application by Hitler, are *wisely* used by the new modern *olicratic rulers*.

It is however true that there are also many unfair professionals who find the golden goose in the sale, at great cost, of miraculous books associated with imaginative natural products put together with herbs remedies and sold at high prices. These users exploit the favorable tendency moment to attract, with a decoy, the unaware subjects, easily influenced by blowing smoke through remedies that have existed for thousands of years. They pack a new herbal cocktail remedy, give a soundly name a disproportionate price and that's it. Behold, these are individuals ethically questionable and from which to stay away. Selling a book or a natural remedy at a high price gives me the chill. It would be different if one would draw a fair and equitable profit from literary work and natural therapies designed with care and love for others.

---

[72] Breuss was Austrian, so was Hitler.

Imagine, moreover, if it were enough to eat bitter almonds or a few apple, apricot, or peach seeds or simply take potassium ascorbate or one of the dozens of methods mentioned in this book to recover from cancer. You might say: but it is absurd! Neither did I think it was possible until recently, but not anymore. *Try to believe!*

The story I told you about the mineral water that treated the constipation or the one about my non-surgical operation to extract the gallstones or the cured headaches be sure may also apply to tumors. Of course, it would not be immediate, but if the body has still the energy to recover, it works wonders, just let it be done giving it the right tools: body and digestive rest, supplements, detox... and time

You might ask: "do you want to compare constipation with cancer?" Yes, because many Orthodox doctors are blind, unfortunately they are simple *Pharmacine's officers*, trained to have a narrow-minded tunnel vision. In all their life they were taught, in Pharmacine's schools how to treat patients. So, I would not be surprised at all if a pinch of bicarbonate a day or a bit of natural apple vinegar or even the apricot seeds or the lemon cure[73] were enough to get rid of tumors. I know people who have been given a few weeks of life that have survived for ten years. Unfortunately, they had not adopted any of the methods mentioned in this book, yet they lived for ten long years. Imagine if they had been aware of these remedies! So, do not you still believe that doing nothing is

---

[73] Described in Romolo Mantovani's book.

better than chemotherapy? If you really want to poison yourselves, you might use scorpion venom or bitter almonds, they are much cheaper... and above all, *natural poisons* (of course, beware! You can die!). Chemotherapy does good only to Big Mafia coffers!

If one day they will tell you: "I'm sorry you have no hope of survival", *do not believe it!* In addition to life, they also take away the real hopes of survive. Do as Ehret, Breuss or Gerson did, *experiment! Do not give up!*

Ehret was examined by many professors, they all said: "We are sorry but you have no hope of survival". In Gerson case, a long string of his renowned colleagues said: "There is no cure for your migraine", Breuss, was accused, by the many physicians who examined him, of being an imaginary patient and did many *surgery experiments* on him. In all these cases they all realized that the *luminary physicians* did not have a clue on how to treat them. That is why we know today these brilliant truths.

From these experiences derived the greatest medical evidence after those of Hippocrates. The truth has always been within everyone's reach from Hippocrates onwards: "Let food be thy medicine and medicine be thy food", or even the absence of food for a certain time, I would add.

I believe that only technical specialties such as orthopedics, trauma, diagnostics, emergency surgery, etc. would be necessary in modern medicine. Similar disciplines should coexist with this principle which should inspire a large medical faculty of holistic medicine. Surgeons have been imposed a strict tunnel vision; they see only body parts; they realize are compromised; then they skillfully have the techniques and ability to remove it. They do not care about cure, because they were taught this way! And those physicians who should cure do not have the means: free will and the Hippocrates teachings applied through the many methods displayed in this book (Gerson, Breuss, Ehret, etc.). Their job is removing and most of them do it very well, though, often, unnecessary.

Let me tell you in no uncertain terms: *we are lambs to the slaughter!* Would you avoid slaughtering the pig for the party? In the same way Big Mafia's members do it, often with the help of Pharmacine. If you have to feast you must slaughter the pig (ourselves) and you must not think, as everyone does, that such atrocious reality cannot happen, because Pharmacine knows well that: "If the lie is of hyperbolic proportions, people will not even think that it is possible to construct such a profound falsification of the truth," as Hitler said and as all the dictators knew and as nowadays powerful men must well know.

In my opinion, Le Bon's assertions are comparable to a physical law (if you drop an apple, it slams to the ground). In the same way, if those in power, and of which we often naively trust, tell a big lie, repeating it until the nausea, in the end the people will be convinced. It is a little trick that until it is unveiled it works and will always work and the people accept this truth because they cannot understand that they are a sacrificial victim to serve the interests of a few. *Do not trust!* Do not even trust me, *inquire and verify*. History repeats itself after all.

You will have noticed some concept often repeated in this volume: yes, if Hitler repeated up to twenty-six times the same sentence in half an hour of speech to imprint for evil and for personal gain his ideas, I would like to repeat a thousand times these concepts but for a good purpose. *Do not trust! Experience!* Give up chemo which is a historical false! (but take care of yourselves with what is described in this volume). If you refuse to undergo chemotherapy, you would see what ruckus would pop up. Try to take away the golden goose from their hands and the world will never be the same.

My repetitions are not aimed at useless redundancy but rather serve to impress concepts in your minds. My goal is that you will have well impressed the concepts and names of Ehret, Gerson, Breuss, Hulda Regehr Clark, etc.

Do not trust the institutions, do not trust the teachers, do not trust all those who tell you that there is no hope, that the only hope is chemotherapy. *Do not trust! Experience! Research!* I tell you these words because I feel sadness and so much pain in seeing so many souls distressed by health problems that can be solved in a less traumatic, more effective and completely natural way. Then it's up to you to experiment.

Not long before Steve Jobs died as a consequence of a pancreatic tumor,[74] orthodox doctors wanted to experiment on him though it is well known that pancreatic cancer is recognized as being incurable by Pharmacine. He succeeded to survive for eight long

---

[74] Being the brilliant man he was, he must have realized by himself what was the right cure for his disease as he started nourishing himself also on juices. I reckon he was an extraordinary person and one of the few people to have ever met Babaji. Probably his intuition helped him live longer as pancreatic cancer is usually very fast. Pharmacine's doctors wanted anyway to experiment on him as they did for Marchionne, but only with chemical products and not natural ones.

years not trusting the established medicine and following natural remedies. He had the right intuition but apparently did not know the Gerson therapy that can, according to Charlotte Gerson, treat successfully this kind of tumor. Of course, now Pharmacine's expert say they could have saved him, but they omit to mention the thousands of people that send home to die because their cures are unsuccessful. Marchionne, for example, lived only one year after was discovered his illness... certainly Pharmacine has a good justification also for that. These episodes demonstrate that even the powerful are deceived and those who, rightly, do not trust (like Steve Jobs) may not know the real alternatives because nobody teaches them at university.

He must have known about the juices but probably did not follow the strict Gerson therapy consisting in 13 juices, 4 coffee enemas, and other supplements daily. Thanks to his *natural healing knowledge,* he lived however longer than expected. Be sure that we would have lost him much earlier would not have thought about healing himself autonomously. Statistics[75] are very clear: only around 4% of people affected by this disease survives more than five years. Had he followed the Gerson therapy who knows what would have happened. I am more than certain that he lived more and better not being treated as a human guinea pig. I had thought of writing to him about the Gerson therapy, but at that time I did not know about his liking towards natural therapies. I regret that so much.

---

[75] https://pancreaticcanceraction.org/about-pancreatic-cancer/medical-professionals/stats-facts/prognosis-survival/

From the moment you discover that you are affected by cancer to the moment you start Pharmacine therapy or remove the evil with a surgery operation (if you think it is appropriate), you still have some time. So, why not immediately use some remedies among those listed in this book (potassium ascorbate, apple vinegar, bitter seeds, ESSIAC, Hoxsey herbs, Swedish bitter, Father Zago aloe, medicinal mushrooms and, above all, Gerson, Breuss, etc.) or at least you only feed on fruits and vegetables, if you really cannot follow the full Gerson therapy. If you decide not to rely on Pharmacine and realize that the tumor, while following these rules, increases instead of stabilizing or decreasing, do not hesitate to undergo surgery (if possible), which can certainly extend your life.

Let me repeat it to infinity, *do not trust!* Orthodox doctors are not criminals (Big Mafia is), they are just mere deceived officers, among other things without even knowing it. Doctors are not bad, they want to do, in absolute good faith, the best for you, according to what they have been taught, and they do not implement the real therapies that heal because they are also deceived and cannot betray their fathers (Pharmacine) that have raised them. They are the first victims and the day they will realize it will be terrible for them. The demonstration of this last concept is the evidence that also the majority of physicians die of cancer treating themselves with chemo.

In Western countries Pharmacine's leaders have established modern courts of Pharmainquisition where they practice their trials without appeal. Tell me if Simoncini, Hamer, Wakefield, Nacci, and the long list of known and unknown physicians, were entitled to a normal and regular process! No, they were tried and sentenced without being able to defend themselves just because they *practiced medicine in freedom and independence, avoiding any undue influence and pursuing the defense of life* as prescribed by their oath.

Nowadays, to decide the suspension or the radiation of a doctor is simply a pharmacinical man/woman put there by Pharmacine's leaders to do exclusively its own interests and not those of real medicine. So, we are witnessing doctors like Wakefield who are threatened with suspensions and radiation from the *pharmacinical board* or doubtful doctors on vaccines and chemotherapy who are radiated forthwith.

It is well known that the powers try in every way to protect their interests. They do this by producing weapons and selling them, thus fueling the wars, because if they were to produce weapons without selling them, it would not do much, but above all there would be no new requests.

In the same way, this small caste that dominates the world evidently has strong interests and thinks that, with money, everything can be bought. In fact, it has enough money and power to influence most of the public and private authorities of our world. It is no coincidence that the leaders of the modern Pharmainquisition courts (medical boards) are usually appointed by Pharmacine.

They will find themselves, however, also to face something unknown, not programmable and above all that cannot be bought. I am sure that these powerful people have never asked what happens after we have exhaled the last breath and they are certainly not equipped with the necessary logic to extrapolate the truth that is revealed to all logical people.

I fully understand that the detractors of this work could be irritated if this text would receive sufficient, though unlikely, media attention because of the attempt to unveil their plans. They will say that are only *hoaxes* and that is *partial, biased information, not scientifically proven, from unrecognized sources* (by Pharmacine). I repeat and continue to repeat: if the double-blind trial cannot be carried out (for the reasons previously described), then, why do not we do the experimentation in two hospitals? One holistic, treating patients with natural cures and the other of Pharmacine. We would then demonstrate what is the most effective method. I am sure there would be enough human guinea pigs willing to test the natural and real treatments.

As I have already mentioned, the natural hospital already exists, the Gerson hospital in Mexico, and it would be enough to introduce external observers (impartial) who honestly certify their therapies. But this will never be done until the big lie is revealed because that would mean the possible end of Pharmacine with the collapse of a 10 trillion-dollar colossus built on shaky foundations.

Do not believe that this deception is the result of chance or simply bigotry. The whole system is studied off the table. To prove it, there are several dictators and powerful men in history who used the same method with extreme effectiveness: a lie (the bigger, the more effective) repeated until the nausea and finally the people, even out of despair, accepts it and makes it its own truth.

Moreover, those who would not like to cure themselves with Pharmacine's methods and protocols, which other assisted care options would they have? None! In the US they have no chance of undergo other *unrecognized* treatments, in Europe, where public health is free, they should pay for everything by themselves and bear the burden, as well as not having any facilities (apart the minor Gerson clinic in Hungary).

I would also like to have the satisfaction of saying it by myself, before it can be said by those of Pharmacine: yes, I am a charlatan! And I'm proud, as they were/are (according to Pharmacine) Gerson, Hamer, Louise Hay, Hoxsey, Nacci, and most of the characters mentioned in the previous chapters and I'm sorry that they cannot suspend or radiate me like they did with many of them because this would be a source of pride rather than shame.

To the aware leaders of Big Mafia and Pharmacine, I say: may you be forgiven for the evil you have done, the one you do at present and the one you will do in the future.

To the members of Pharmacine, and especially to the doctors who unwittingly do so, I say wake up! Turn yourself into real doctors, because, remember, you swore! *The force* flows within you, you just have to rediscover it. You have sworn, and you must do everything to respect this bond. So, check personally and empirically that what your colleagues say it is not true. Also, you should not trust anyone, not even the highest institutions, and you should not be duped by Pharmacine's tales on *scientifically proven, double blind*, etc.: they are just fables created for the simple people.

To the doctors of medicine, I say resist. The wall will eventually collapse!

To the people, I say transform yourself! From *irrational and simple mass* to complex, rational and thinking mass and *do not trust!* The worst disasters of man are those made in good faith, believing that what you do is right. The people were burning at the stake, because they had been made to believe that witches really existed.

Today the people are deceived for money and power, but even in those days the reasons were similar and were manipulated through bigotry and ignorance (exactly like today), but also to divert attention from their miserable condition.

To biologists, I say: put a drop of colloidal silver in a bacterial culture and personally verify its effectiveness (and be phage and Zapper disseminators. To those who practice the medical profession and to the treating physicians, I say: do not be prejudiced and study and experience the work of other colleagues even if they are not approved by Pharmacine's universities.

To the people, I say: give up chemotherapy! As Gandhi fought the strong and corrupted powers, renunciation to chemo might help to unveil the great deception and allow to crumble Pharmacine's huge rubber wall and could help saving people, in some cases. Furthermore, I fully agree with the phrase on the Pantellini Foundation's institutional website: "We are deeply convinced that there is no official science and an alternative. In fact, science is either such or not a reality worthy of being taken into consideration." I therefore want to affirm, without major fears of being refuted, that Pharmacine's science is not at all a science but merely a great and profitable business on the skin of the unfortunates.

I have been told of putting too much pathos in this work and it is probably true. I feel exactly as if I were observing a massacre from the window while snipers lurking over the buildings throw poisoned darts on the unsuspecting passersby who mistake them for the pinch of an insect but cause death after some time without discovering their association. I shout to passersby vehemently but they do not listen to me and do not believe what I say because they cannot see the snipers. You would not do the same in a similar situation, would not you try to shout out to the crowd trying to save as many lives as possible? Unfortunately, the massacre can only be stopped by ourselves, through awareness.

Therefore, if you believe it, continue to trust blindly in Pharmacine. I feel only the weight of responsibility in having to state what I state in this book, wishing, however, to make a striking mistake.

Certainly, there is something suspicious about Pharmacine's arrogance and hatred towards these, often, harmless, innocent, natural cures. After all, what does it cost to take potassium ascorbate or apple vinegar three times a day? You could even do this while you are being chemically poisoned and maybe take the herbs of René Caisse or COD Tea at the same time. It would not really matter if merits would be given to chemotherapy and not natural remedies as long as you would be saved.

They are all remedies that should not interact in any way with the *poisons of Pharmacine*, if not making these natural cures less effective, but it is not the same the other way around. Surely, those who come out strongly influenced from the schools of Pharmacine will tell you: no! What is this nonsense? *Poison* is much better than a small amount of bicarbonate, because the conditioning is so deep that it is not even possible for them to realize it.

From the times of the holy inquisition to the present ones of the Pharmainquisition, nothing has changed. The people are always hostage of the strong powers and it is always the sacrificial victim and at the same time the executioner of beings of their own kind. Moreover, in modern times, the people has become the *ATMs* of the rich and the powerful providing the human matter on which *to withdraw*.

The hopes that we can wake up from this illusory torpor of *libertè*, *egalité* and *fraternité* are placed at the moment in the movement of people born in Italy with the Five Star Movement and that continues in other countries with similar movements like Podemos in Spain. These realities are still very unstable and it is not absolutely certain that they will ever be able to access the power, the real power, and above all, that they will be allowed to manage and administer it. The power of the modern inquisition is always strong and can still do so much because the people can still be too easily manipulated.

Please allow me to launch an appeal to good will people to marshal your strengths by gathering into groups doing social support. There is need of a free information through a real free people TV channel. Information today is manipulated and distorted at the source, so what we get is the final result they want us to learn. Investigative journalism is always less impactful and numbers as the ownership of news media (newspapers and TV) usually belongs to the powerful who have the interest in controlling the information as it is the source of power.

To be able to reach this real independence, the people should collect fund autonomously or, as I suggest, realities like 5 Star movement in Italy (that give up most of their parliamentary salary) should contribute to the birth of such reality. Even in this case information could be manipulated at the origin but there would be a more free and accessible analysis. It is necessary to reveal the deception and this can only be done using their own weapons.

This approach could also be used in the medical field by implementing, with raised funds, a holistic hospital. This would greatly help to reveal the deception. It would be finally possible to enter in the television schedule all the news that Big Mafia and its associates call, *deliberately*, fake news. In this effort, Big Mafia would be supported by Pharmacine itself, through a fully contrived script and a disinformation program pursued with every means to make it seem true, in pure *hitlerian* style, *the big lie*.

Unfortunately, the work of a great character in modern history, Gustave Le Bon, has simplified the already easy task of modern dictators, from Lenin to Mussolini, Hitler, Stalin, and I am convinced that his book, *The Crowd: a study of the popular mind*, does not lack in the libraries of the new *power men* or those who want to become.

To really live in freedom the evidence of Le Bon's work should be taught at school to allow the people to have at least the awareness that they could be manipulated, as "mass thinking differently from individuals." If the people were aware of the work of Le Bon, it would probably not be so easy to fool it so trivially.

The satirist Bernard de Mandeville (1670-1733) in his scripts provocatively argues: "If a horse knew as much as a man, I would not be his rider". This could be taken as an example of how the impression of freedom we get is just that: *an impression*. In fact, keeping the people in ignorance, and immersed in the great lie, it makes easier to administer and *tame* it for their own interests. If the people unveil the secret implications of the administration of power, then everything would be different, *the horse could indulge and revolt against his master*. It is important, therefore, that the horse does not know what man knows. For this reason every *media weapon* (television, newspapers, internet, physical suppression, modern inquisition, etc.) is used so that the *horse* will always remains a *horse*.

Continuing in the metaphor, often the *horse* does not want to know the truth because it would means that his master does not love him at all. Unfortunately, *truth is something that few want to believe.* The powerful have always taken advantage of the people and continue to do so. The people prefers to remain in ignorance because it would be too painful to recognize their gullibility. After all, *it is easier to believe to a lie than to the truth, because it makes us feel better,* and so we do not have to face the pain of betrayal.

It is, in fact, obvious that *a political figure, associated with Pharmacine, will rarely care about your interests because has to care about his/her own.* By now the vocation has been superseded by stronger powers that use improper weapons. In fact, *there is the politician driven by vocation and the politician driven by interest, but the motivations of the latter is far more powerful because it involves lying.* So if the people cannot recognize those who lie they will be condemned to always be *horses*.

In conclusion, let me say that it is obvious there cannot be evidence of what I affirm and there will never be as "there is none so blind as those who will not see." There is, however, logifical evidence, that is certainly more than a clue, that Pharmacine has something to hide. What I argue in this book may easily be traced back to allegations, as could have been the sphericity of the Earth a few centuries ago, or how it could be the affirmation that there is life in the universe. These are essentially allegations endowed with a disarming deductive *logical path* which therefore makes them logifical *proofs*. As a matter of fact, scientists have statistically, and in uncontroversial manner, demonstrated that life exists in the universe, besides being absolutely logific. We can therefore state that there is no evidence that we are witnessing a pharmacological slaughter, but it is absolutely logifical that it might exist.

However, one thing is certain: if you want to avoid getting sick but above all if you want to recover from sickness:

"Let food be thy medicine and thy medicine be the food."
Hippocrates

Acknowledgements

In the hope that the deaths of cancer ... and vaccinations will drastically drop, I want to express my gratitude to all those who contribute or have contributed to unveil *the great lie* but, above all, to those who have died for this reason and to those that, unfortunately, will die to show it. Caution! Holistic doctors, your knowledge is very dangerous!

Thank you prof. Ehret, thank you Dr. Gerson, thank you Dr. Bradstreet, thank you Dr. Nicholas Gonzalez, thank you Dr. Barone Holt, thank you Dr. Bruce Hendendal, thank you Theresa Sievers, thank you Patrick Fitzpatrick, thank you Dr. Ron Schwartz, thank you Dr. Abdul Karim, thank you Dr. Jeffrey Whiteside, thank you Mary Bovier, thank you Mitch Gaynor, thank you Dr. Marie Paas, thank you Jerome E. Block, thank you Dr. Jamie Zimmerman, thank you John Marshall, thank you Dr. Rod Floyd, thank you Prof. Alan Clarke, thank you Paige Adams, thank you Ceryl Deboer, thank you Dr. Armon Antony Bert, thank you Dr. Henry Han, thank you Dr. Harsch, thank you, Dr. Rose Polge, thank you Dr. Rasmussen, thank you Dr. Clogston, thank you Dr. Suutari, thank you Dr. Alex Shvartsman, thank you Dr. Mary Louise Yoder, thank you Dr. Tiejun Huang, thank you Dr. Jenny Shi, thank you Dr. Alfredo Bowman ... and thanks also to all the others who have abandoned this world without even suspect that their departure might have depended on *medical* reason, or better, *pharmacinical.*

DO NOT TRUST!

While anticipating that this book will not cause any concern to Big Mafia and Pharmacine, not reaching a worrying notoriety for them, and although my origin, with roots in Italy, guarantees me a partial immunity from accidental and inexplicable death, and suicide, let me, however, stipulate my personal life insurance with you, if my real identity should be accidentally revealed. I think it is better to say *who knows* instead of *if I had known*. Unfortunately, not being *pharmainquisible*, because I have basically nothing to lose (if not the family), such an eventuality is the only possible way to silence me.

I, the undersigned Gaia Straus, declare solemnly that: I would never commit acts aimed at harming my life or that of any animated being, even under evident stress and pressure. I am also a careful driver and it is highly unlikely that I could be subject to fatal accidents. I have no cases of heart attacks in my family and it is not conceivable that I could lose my life prematurely. In addition, I am well hydrated and I drink very adequate quantities of water and vegetable juices (I would not like to run into death due to dehydration). In short, if I die prematurely, it might be, logifically, a pharmacinical death.

Anyone wishing to write to the author to report cures or therapies not included in this volume or for any other reason can do so at the following e-mail address: gaiastraus@tutanota.com. A website with the following address has been implemented: www.gaiastraus.com, though it needs further development.

Similarly, those wishing to make a crowd-funding donation to attempt to build a better world can do so at the same e-mail address, via Paypal.

The objective of this initiative is to create a non-profit association aimed at facilitating those who want to take care of themselves naturally by supporting the patient through the specially created site and, possibly, (if the sums collected are adequate) with the creation of a special structure that can act as a counselor for those who need it. Unfortunately, it is useless to try to create a holistic hospital in the US and in most of the other western countries as the Gerson hospital (exiled to Mexico) and the Hoxsey's affair shows that is, probably, not yet possible. However, "never say never."

The donations will be documented item by item, through the website, where all the items of expenditure will be described.

I realize that in this *dirty world*, there is little to trust, but as my father wrote: "Hello Hope!" Sometimes, from the most bizarre ideas, significant realities can arise.

AFORISMS

The thing that bugs me is that the people think the FDA is protecting them - it isn't. What the FDA is doing and what the public thinks it's doing are as different as night and day.

Dr. HERBERT L. LEY, former FDA Commissioner

The individual is handicapped by coming face-to-face with a conspiracy so monstrous he cannot believe it exists (talking about communism).

J. EDGAR HOOVER, ex-director of the FBI.

The pharmaceutical industry is as big and powerful as the arms industry, with the difference that the war ends but not the disease, as long as there is someone who keeps it alive.

HANS RUESCH

If voting made any difference they wouldn't let us do it.

The problem does not come from things we do not know but from those that we believe are true and are not.

If you don't read the newspaper, you're uninformed. If you read the newspaper, you're mis-informed."

The only way to keep your health is to eat what you don't want, drink what you don't like, and do what you'd rather not.

MARK TWAIN

The pharmaceutical industry is an investment industry driven by the profits of its shareholders. Improving human health is not the driving force of this industry.

The marketplace for the pharmaceutical industry is the human body — but only for as long as the body hosts diseases. Thus, maintaining and expanding diseases is a precondition for the growth of the pharmaceutical industry.

Vitamins and other effective natural health therapies that optimize cellular metabolism threaten the pharmaceutical "business with disease" because they target the cellular cause of today's most common diseases — and these natural substances cannot be patented.

Dr. MATTHIAS RATH, (Excerpt from the book Why Animals Do not Get Heart Attacks, But People Do!)

Autism taught me more about medicine than the medical school I attended.

Dr. JAKE CROSBY

A foolish faith in authority is the worst enemy of truth.

ALBERT EINSTEIN

Beware of the half-truths. You might know the wrong half.

God helps those who help themselves.

In herbis salus. (health is in the herbs).

Digestion starts in the mouth.

Mens sana in corpore sano. (a healthy mind in a healthy body).

Everything in Nature follows a rhythm. Healing also has its own.

Trusting is good, but not trusting is better.

If you have nice thoughts about people, you will not sin; if you have bad thoughts you'll be right.

ANONYMOUS

The greatest obstacle to discovery is not ignorance but the illusion of knowledge.

DANIEL J. BOORSTIN

Doctors are responsible for the fourth cause of death, represented by their medications properly prescribed and taken.

BRIAN F. WALKER

The art of healing comes from nature, not from the physician. Therefore the physician must start from nature, with an open mind.

PARACELSUS

Let food be thy medicine and medicine be thy food.

Cancer is not cured with the surgeon's iron but with the vegetarian diet and the medical herbs. (that is exactly what Gerson, Breuss, Kousmine and many others have proved right).

The more you feed a sick person, the more you hurt him.

In Nature there is all that is needed to truly heal ourselves.

Nature in man is constituted in the image of Nature in the world.

IPPOCRATE

One should never try to treat the body without the soul.

Learn to teach and teach to learn.

PLATO

The air we breathe is more important than the food we eat.

GALENO

Of all the flowers, the human flower is the one most in need of sun.

MICHELET

Honest is he who changes his thought to accord it to the truth; dishonest is he who changes the truth to accord it to his own thought.

ARAB PROVERB

If you tell a big enough lie and tell it frequently enough, it will be believed.

If a lie is so colossal, no one would believe that someone could have the impudence to distort the truth so infamously.

Any lie, if repeated frequently, will gradually turn into truth.

The receptivity of the masses is very limited, their intelligence is small, but their power of forgetting is enormous. In consequence of these facts, all effective propaganda must be limited to a very few points and must harp on these in slogans until the last member of the public understands what you want him to understand by your slogan.

Through clever and constant application of propaganda, people can be made to see paradise as hell, and also the other way round, to consider the most wretched sort of life as paradise.

But the most brilliant propagandist technique will yield no success unless one fundamental principle is borne in mind constantly and with unflagging attention. It must confine itself to a few points and repeat them over and over. Here, as so often in this world, persistence is the first and most important requirement for success.

All great movements owe their origin to great speakers, not to great writers.

(Unfortunately, these truths are still valid today and the masses continue to trust the new Hitlers. Do you believe that a honest person could go to power without telling lies? Until the masses realize they are a mere instrument, no real transformation can take place. in modern societies.).

ADOLF HITLER, Mein Kampf (Mein Leben)

The great mass is always ready to roll towards the part where the weight of power is at the moment; I knew that the same voices shouting "Heil Schuschnigg!" today would have called "Heil Hitler!" tomorrow.

STEFAN ZWEIG

Democratic regimes can be defined as those in which, from time to time, the illusion of being sovereign is given to the people.

MUSSOLINI

The masses have never been thirsty for truth. Who can give them illusions easily becomes their commander; those who try to destroy their illusions are always their victims.

To excuse evil means to multiply it.

Thoughts without action are but a vain mirage, action without thought is a futile effort.

For many, freedom is the power to choose their own slavery.

The crowd is a flock that cannot do without a master.

By the mere fact of being part of a crowd, man descends the scale of civilization by several degrees. Isolated, he would perhaps be a cultured individual, in the crowd he is an instinctive, consequently, a barbarian.

People are more easily dominated by excitement of passions than by taking care of their interests.

In politics, as in life, success generally belongs to the convinced and rarely to the skeptics.

Peoples live above all with hope. Their revolutions aim to replace the old hopes that have lost their strength with a new hope.

In terms of feelings, illusion quickly creates certainty.

The multitude is always ready to listen to the strong man who knows how to impose himself on her. The men gathered in a crowd lose all the willpower and return to the person who possesses the quality that they lack.

Crowds rarely understand anything of the events they perform.

The need for certainty has always been stronger than the need for truth.

To dominate or be dominated, there is no other alternative for the female soul.

The crowds have never been thirsty for truth. Faced with the evidence that they dislike, they turn away, preferring to deify the error, if this seduces them. Who knows how to deceive them, can easily become their master, those who try to disillude them is always their victim.

What strikes us most about a psychological mass is that the individuals who compose it — regardless of the type of life, occupations, temperament or intelligence — acquire a sort of collective soul simply by becoming mass.

As soon as one possesses the strength, one ceases to invoke justice.

Men in society cannot live without tyranny, the most acceptable one is still the one of laws.

GUSTAV LE BON

… Do we not owe the Growth of Wine To the dry shabby crooked Which, while its Shoots neglected stood, Chok'd other Plants, and ran to Wood;But blest us with its noble Fruit, As soon as it was ty'd and cut: So Vice is beneficial found, When it's by Justice lopt and bound; Nay, where the People would be great, As necessary to the State, As Hunger is to make 'em eat. Bare Virtue can't make Nations live In Splendor; they, that would revive A Golden Age, must be as free, For Acorns, as for Honesty.

BERNARD DE MANDEVILLE – (The fairy tale of the bees)

Fanaticism is the only form of willpower to which the weak and irresolute can come.

NIETZSCHE

When I was a young student, iodine and iodine potassium were considered universal medicines. Nobody knew how they worked, but we knew that they worked exceptionally well.

A vitamin is a substance that makes you feel sick if you do not eat it.

ALBERT SZENT GYORGY - discoverer of vitamin C

Iodine is the best antibiotic, antiseptic and antiviral of all time.

Dr. DAVID DERRY – endocrinologist

He who does not bellow the truth when he knows the truth makes himself the accomplice of liars and forgers.

CHARLES P'EGUY

Dr. Gerson dedicated his life to the mastery of this scourge of cancer and all should honor his great work.

HONORABLE CLAUDE PEPPER - Member of the US Senate

Very often the simple truth is absolutely not credible.

You can heal from cancer but not from chemo.

Out of fifty cancer patients, who decide to treat themselves with chemo, only one of them will still be alive only five years after the first chemo.

(from Giuseppe Nacci's book *1000 plants to heal from cancer*).

...You are gods. (John 10:34)

...Know the Truth and the Truth will make you free. (John 8:32)

JESUS

The disease is never "an accident" but always the consequence of our mistakes.

Don't take the symptom for the cause.

Nature has given us life: only She can restore our health.

If you really want to heal you must always strive to improve.

Healing a disease is possible, but it is much more difficult to cure men from the "medicines" disease.

Be a man, know how to respect your body not getting it dirty by cluttering it with ignoble things. It is only through purity that one reaches health.

ROMOLO MANTOVANI

Nearly all men die of their medicines, not of their diseases.

MOLIÈRE

The cure of most chronic diseases must be preceded by fasting.

Dr. VICTOR PAUCHET

The study of Medicine must, sooner or later, become part of the education of man.

F.V. RASPAIL

To the pure, all things are pure, but to those who are corrupted and do not believe, nothing is pure. In fact, both their minds and consciences are corrupted.

SAN PAUL

The more you know, the more you love.

LEONARDO DA VINCI

Misfortune to the one who was silent because he believed he was speaking in the desert.

BALZAC

Truth is a common good, and he who possesses it must extend it to his brothers.

BOUSSET

Fasting is the first principle of medicine.

RUMI

Give man a mask and he'll tell you the truth.

There are people who know everything and that's all they know.

OSCAR WILDE

Truth is something that few are looking for.

It is easier to believe to a lie rather than to the truth, because it makes us feel better.

The politician will never do your best because he'd rather do his own.

There is the politician by vocation and the politician by interest, but the motivations of the latter are far more powerful because they imply lying for profit.

The Earth, which we are making suffering, will survive any outrage, while we will not.

If they were to condemn all the doctors belonging to Pharmacine who kill someone, there would probably be very few left.

Chemotherapy, and vaccines are essentially a justification for extorting money from the people and the states.

If it is true that religions are the opium of the peoples it is equally true that the ignorance of the people is the cocaine of the rich and the powerful.

GAIA STRAUS

BIBLIOGRAPHY

Baiss, Egidio	*Babaji Mahavatar*	Edizioni Mediterranee	1993
Breuss Rudolf	*Cancro Leucemia e altre malattie apparentemente incurabile sono guaribili con metodi naturali* (The Breuss Cancer Cure: Advice for the Prevention and Natural Treatment of Cancer, Leukemia and Other Seemingly Incurable Diseases)	Accademia nazionale di scienze igienistiche naturali "G. Galilei"	2017
Buchwald, Gerhard	*Vaccinazioni: il business della paura*	CIVIS	2000
Carey, Ken	*Starseed Transmissions, The*	Harperone	1991
Clark, Hulda Regehr	*La cura di tutte le malattie* (The cure of all diseases)	Biblioteca Del Benessere	2016
Del Negro, Piero | Nacci, Giuseppe	*Diventa medico di te stesso* (Become your own physician)	Editoriale Programma	2010
Erhet, Arnold	*Insegnamenti sul digiuno* (Teachings on fasting)	Juppiter Consulting Publishing	2004
Erhet, Arnold	*Digiuno razionale per il ringiovanimento fisico, mentale e spirituale* (Rational fast for physical, mental and spiritual rejuvenation)	Juppiter Consulting Publishing	2007
Erhet, Arnold	*Così parla lo stomaco* (This is how the stomach speaks)	Juppiter Consulting Publishing	2012
Erhet, Arnold	*Uomini Malati* (Sick men)	Juppiter Consulting Publishing	2012
Erhet, Arnold	*Il sistema di guarigione della dieta senza muco. Un corso completo per chi desidera imparare ad avere controllo della propria salute* (The mucusless diet)	Juppiter Consulting Publishing	2013
Gerson, Charlotte | Bishop, Beata | Pietrini, Daniele	*Guarire con il Metodo Gerson + DVD* (Healing the Gerson way)	Macro Edizioni	2009
Govindan, Marshall A.	*Babaji. Lo yogy immortale* (The immortal yogy)	Jackson Libri	1995

Author	Title	Publisher	Year
Graziani, Gabriele | Graziani, Luciano	*L'argento colloidale: un potente rimedio naturale* (Colloidal silver: a powerful natural remedy)	Macro Edizioni	2015
Gustave Le Bon | L. Morpurgo	*Psicologia delle folle* (the crowd)	Tea	2004
Jacob, Stanley W. | Zucker, Martin | Lawrence, Ronald M.	*Miracle of Msm The Natural Solution For Pain, The*	Putnam Adult	1999
Jasmuheen,	*Pranic Nourishment: Living on Light*	Self Empowerment Academy	1997
Khalsa, Soram	*I poteri curativi della vitamina D.* (Vitamin D devolution)	Biblioteca Del Benessere	2013
Krishnamurti, Jiddu | Krishnamurti, J.	*The Impossible Question*	Penguin Books	1999
Mantovani, Romolo	*Il Libro Delle Cure Naturali* (The Book of Natural Cures)	Edizioni Mediterranee	1981
Moritz Andreas	*Guarire il fegato con il lavaggio epatico* (The Amazing Liver and Gallbladder Flush)	Macro Edizioni	2009
Moritz Andreas	*Timeless secrets of health and rejuvenation*	Ener-Chi Wellness Press	2007
Padmasambhava, | Jinpa, Thumpten | Coleman, Graham | Lamparelli, Claudio	*Il Libro Tibetano Dei Morti* (The Tibetan Book of the Dead)	Mondadori	2007
Ramana, Maharshi	*Consigli Per La Pratica Spirituale* (The Spiritual Teaching of Ramana Maharshi)	Astrolabio Ubaldini	1999
Raphael,	*Tat Tvam Asi. Tu Sei Quello* (You are the one)	Ashram Vidya	1982
Raphael,	*Oltre L'illusione Dell'io. Sintesi Di Un Processo Realizzativo* (Beyond the illusion of the ego)	Asram Vidya	1995
Rath, Matthias	*Why Animals Don't Get Heart Attacks*	Health Now	1994
Romano, Bruno | Langella, Rigel	*Ayurveda: Longevità e Salute* (Ayurveda: Longevity and Health)	Gremese Editore	1996

Schiller, Reinhard	*Le Cure Miracolose Di Suor Ildegarda* (The Miraculous Cures of Sister Hildegard)	Piemme	1994
Scott, Archie H.	*DMSO, The Handbook for Doctors*	iUniverse	2013
Shelton, Herbert M.	*Digiunare per rinnovare la vita* (Fasting Can Save Your Life)	Edizioni Paoline	1986
Smith, Trevor	*Homeopathic Medicine: a Doctor's Guide to Remedies For Common Ailments*	Thorsons Pub	1983
Sui, Choa Kok | Sui, Chao Kok | Gantioque, Benny	*Advanced Pranic Healing*	Weiser Books	1995
Swami Sri Yukteswar	*La scienza sacra* (The holy science)	Astrolabio	1993
Tilden, J.H.	*La Tossiemia causa primaria di malattia* (Toxemia explained)	Manca	1986
Treben, Maria	*La Salute dalla Farmacia del Signore* (Health Through God's Pharmacy)	Ennsthaler	1982
Yogananda, Paramahansa	*Affermazioni Scientifiche Di Guarigione/scientific Healing Affirmations*	Self Realization Fellowship Pub	1998
Yogananda, Paramahansa | Evans-Wentz, W.Y. | evans-Wentz, M.y. | Yogananda, Swami Paramhansa | (Paramahansa.), Yogananda	*Autobiografia Di Uno Yogi* (Autobyography of a yogy)	Astrolabio-ubaldini	1978

Riferimenti On-Line

https://www.ncbi.nlm.nih.gov/pmc/articles/PMC3109452/

http://www.scienzaeconoscenza.it/articolo/cancro-dr-gerson-clisteri-caffe

http://www.cancerresearchuk.org/health-professional/cancer-statistics/worldwide-cancer#heading-One

http://www.nature.com/bjc/journal/v112/n5/full/bjc2014606a.html

http://www.pharmafile.com/news/498031/pharma-industry-worth-more-1-trillion-and-growing

https://www.youtube.com/watch?v=1RUrIO3Emws

http://www.faredelbene.net/public/news/articoli/6339/la-celiachia-non-esiste-il-vero-problema-il-roundup.html

http://www.mednat.org/cancro/MORGAN.PDF

http://www.consulentiolistici.it/cancro-statistiche-ufficiali-cure-alternative/

http://www.mednat.org/cancro/nacci_chemio_statistiche_uff.htm

https://www.youtube.com/watch?v=UL5qSegu2ds;

https://www.youtube.com/watch?v=GoM78CO3gdo

http://www.my-personaltrainer.it/integratori/metilsulfonil-metano-MSM.html

https://it.wikipedia.org/wiki/Terra_piatta

http://online.scuola.zanichelli.it/lanciotti-files/B01_Batteriofagi.pdf

https://www.ncbi.nlm.nih.gov/pmc/articles/PMC3170075/

https://www.youtube.com/watch?v=axi5drXcbfw

https://www.youtube.com/watch?v=89e0EdKZq9g

https://www.ncbi.nlm.nih.gov/pmc/articles/PMC3170075/

http://gcmaf.se/gcmaf-science/how-gcmaf-works/

https://it.wikipedia.org/wiki/Teoria_del_vaccino_orale_antipolio_sull%27origine_dell%27AIDS

http://vaccines.global-summit.com/america/2016

http://mondos-porco.blogspot.it/2015/10/piu-di-50-metodi-di-cure-alternative.html)

https://www.youtube.com/watch?v=axi5drXcbfw

http://www.alternative-cancer-care.com/god-vinegar-lemon-and-cancer.html

http://www.alternative-cancer-care.com/gerson-therapy-cancer-diet.html

http://www.alternative-cancer-care.com

http://www.nationalgeographic.it/scienza/medicina/2014/10/27/news/la_storia_delle_e
pidemie_ebola-2350296/?refresh_ce

http://www.associazionelatorre.com/2014/02/il-mappamondo-del-cancro

http://www.healthnutnews.com/recap-on-my-unintended-series-the-holistic-doctor-
deaths

http://www.anagen.net/sodio.htm

http://www.maurizioblondet.it/ma-quale-celiachia-chiamatela-roundup/

http://www.rethinkingcancer.org/resources/magazine-articles/2_1-2/cancer-cures-more-
deadly-than-disease.php

http://www.greenreport.it/news/scienze-e-ricerca/contro-resistenza-agli-antibiotici-si-
recupera-terapia-sovietica-dei-fagi/

https://healthimpactnews.com/2015/is-the-u-s-medical-mafia-murdering-alternative-
health-doctors-who-have-real-cures-not-approved-by-the-fda

http://www.bbc.com/news/health-34326801

http://www.healthnutnews.com/breaking-4th-doctor-an-md-found-dead-gunshot-wound-
to-head/

http://www.cure-naturali.it/medicina-tradizionale-cinese/964/coppettazione/1090/a

http://www.siommms.it/supplementazione-di-vitamina-d-anche-per-dosi-elevate-il-
rischio-di-tossicita-e-molto-raro/

http://cronologia.leonardo.it/lebon/indice.htm

http://www.frasicelebri.it/frasi-di/gustave-le-bon/

http://www.corriere.it/datablog/i-numeri-che-mangiamo/carne/scheda-
8.shtml?refresh_ce-cp

http://le-citazioni.it/autori/bernard-de-mandeville/?q=182269

http://www.biotechland.it/appunti_farmacologia_1.html

https://www.youtube.com/watch?v=5WyEsN9DzSo&list=PLdfMmaU0DR8DbtrpHEFe
5A8oxs3h-z0sg

http://alternativa-za-vas.com/en/index.php/clanak/article/lugols-solution

https://sites.google.com/site/argentocolloidale10ppm528hz/12---argento-colloidale-
ionico-e-le-infezioni-da-pseudomonas

http://www.quotidianosanita.it/scienza-e-farmaci/articolo.php?articolo_id=4679

http://www.corriere.it/salute/14_marzo_31/con-fagi-torna-moda-vecchia-arma-contro-
batteri-c26edaea-b8ac-11e3-917e-4c908e083af6.shtml

http://www.usl7.toscana.it/index.php/servizi/infoticket/esenzione-dal-pagamento-del-ticket

https://www.disinformazione.it/ricercatori%20eretici.htm

http://www.mednat.org/cancro/ricercatori_osteggiati.htm

http://www.aifa.gov.it/sites/default/files/Rapporto_OsMed_2015_AIFA-acc.pdf

http://stopalcancro.blogspot.it/2011/10/il-potere-della-natura.html

http://blog.ilgiornale.it/locati/2014/12/09/le-mie-metastasi-sparite-con-la-dieta/

http://www.unric.org/it/attualita/26636-un-nuovo-rapporto-fao-analizza-le-emissioni-di-gas-serra-del-settore-caseario

https://www.ncbi.nlm.nih.gov/pubmed/15630849

http://www.autism-society.org/what-is/facts-and-statistics/

http://www.cure-naturali.it/maitake/4115

https://www.greenme.it/mangiare/alimentazione-a-salute/18564-proprieta-funghi-medicinali

http://www.mednat.org/vaccini/primo_caso_autismo.htm

http://www.mednat.org/cancro/chemio_nonrisolve.htm

http://www.comilva.org/si-dissolvono-le-illusioni-sul-vaccino-anti-morbillo/

http://www.registri-tumori.it/PDF/AIOM2016/I_numeri_del_cancro_2016.pdf

https://en.wikipedia.org/wiki/SV40

https://www.ncbi.nlm.nih.gov/pmc/articles/PMC1200696/

http://www.nhs.uk/Conditions/vaccinations/Pages/the-history-of-vaccination.aspx

http://www.nationalmssociety.org/NationalMSSociety/media/MSNationalFiles/Brochures/Brochure-History-of-Multiple-Sclerosis.pdf

https://en.wikipedia.org/wiki/Amyotrophic_lateral_sclerosis

http://www.fibrocenter.com/fibromyalgia-disease

https://en.wikipedia.org/wiki/Muscular_dystrophy

https://socioecohistory.files.wordpress.com/2009/08/little_effect_of_vaccines.jpg

https://www.istat.it/it/archivio/109861

https://www.ncemch.org/suid-sids/statistics/

https://www.cdc.gov/plague/maps/index.html

http://www.express.co.uk/news/world/602618/Plague-outbreaks-countries-with-cases-of-plague

https://www.dionidream.com/lavaggio-epatico/

http://www.naturpedia.it/index.php?title=Manuale_pratico_di_medicina_naturale/La_cur
a_Breuss

https://seer.cancer.gov/cgi-in/csr/1975_2014/results.pl?pagenumbers=87

https://en.wikipedia.org/wiki/History_of_cancer_chemotherapy

https://www.cancer.net/cancer-types/melanoma/statistics

http://www.gerson.hu/all-about-gerson---videos#.W03jSC5uaUl

https://en.wikipedia.org/wiki/Haidakhan_Babaji

https://pancreaticcanceraction.org/about-pancreatic-cancer/medical-professionals/stats-
facts/prognosis-survival/

https://www.dr-rath-foundation.org/2017/08/the-laws-of-the-pharmaceutical-industry/

https://responsibletechnology.org/category/glyphosate/

https://www.researchgate.net/figure/A-world-map-of-cancer-incidence-displaying-
geographic-distribution-of-core-collection-of_fig2_257884786

https://knoema.com/infographics/maodxhb/global-greenhouse-gas-emissions-from-
livestock

https://draxe.com/coffee-enema/

http://www.cam-cancer.org/Media/Files/CAM-Summaries/Biologically-based-
practices/Breuss-Cancer-Cure

https://www.ncbi.nlm.nih.gov/pubmed/19726047